Pills for the Poorest

An Exploration of TRIPS and Access to Medication in Sub-Saharan Africa

Palgrave Macmillan Socio-Legal Studies

Series Editor

David Cowan, Professor of Law and Policy, University of Bristol, UK

Editorial Board

Dame Hazel Genn, Professor of Socio-Legal Studies, University College London, UK
Fiona Haines, Associate Professor, School of Social and Political Science, University of Melbourne, Australia
Herbert Kritzer, Professor of Law and Public Policy, University of Minnesota, USA
Linda Mulcahy, Professor of Law, London School of Economics and Political Science, UK
Carl Stychin, Dean and Professor, The City Law School, City University London, UK
Mariana Valverde, Professor of Criminology, University of Toronto, Canada
Sally Wheeler, Professor of Law, Queen's University Belfast, UK

Pills for the Poorest

An Exploration of TRIPS and Access to Medication in Sub-Saharan Africa

Emilie Cloatre
Kent Law School, University of Kent, UK

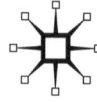

© Emilie Cloatre 2013

All rights reserved. No reproduction, copy or transmission of this publication may be made without written permission.

No portion of this publication may be reproduced, copied or transmitted save with written permission or in accordance with the provisions of the Copyright, Designs and Patents Act 1988, or under the terms of any licence permitting limited copying issued by the Copyright Licensing Agency, Saffron House, 6–10 Kirby Street, London EC1N 8TS.

Any person who does any unauthorized act in relation to this publication may be liable to criminal prosecution and civil claims for damages.

The author has asserted her right to be identified as the author of this work in accordance with the Copyright, Designs and Patents Act 1988.

First published 2013 by
PALGRAVE MACMILLAN

Palgrave Macmillan in the UK is an imprint of Macmillan Publishers Limited, registered in England, company number 785998, of Houndmills, Basingstoke, Hampshire RG21 6XS.

Palgrave Macmillan in the US is a division of St Martin's Press LLC, 175 Fifth Avenue, New York, NY 10010.

Palgrave Macmillan is the global academic imprint of the above companies and has companies and representatives throughout the world.

Palgrave® and Macmillan® are registered trademarks in the United States, the United Kingdom, Europe and other countries

ISBN: 978–0–230–28284–1 hardback

This book is printed on paper suitable for recycling and made from fully managed and sustained forest sources. Logging, pulping and manufacturing processes are expected to conform to the environmental regulations of the country of origin.

A catalogue record for this book is available from the British Library.

A catalog record for this book is available from the Library of Congress.

À Rémi

Contents

Preface	ix
Introduction: Global IP and Pills for the Poorest	1
Questioning TRIPS, IP and access to health	2
Ghana and Djibouti	4
Exploring local networks	6
Overview	9
1 TRIPS as Assemblage	11
Material societies and the fluidity of the 'legal'	11
Unpacking TRIPS	29
Conclusion	44
2 From Global Scripts to Local Translation	45
Translating TRIPS in Djibouti	46
TRIPS and Ghanaian IP	52
Expertise and IP in Djibouti and Ghana	55
Questioning the 'TRIPS project'	61
Conclusion	63
3 From IP to Public Health in Djibouti and Ghana	65
The travels of patents and TRIPS as regulatory scripts in Djibouti and Ghana	66
Circulating in Djibouti	69
From books to action: enrolling patents in the public health networks of Ghana	78
Registering drugs in Ghana	79
Licensing, registration and the translation of projected networks into daily practices	83
Where do those discontinued networks leave patents?	87
Conclusion	88
4 Pharmaceutical Patents as Silent Regulatory Tools: Escaping Branded Drugs in Djibouti	91
Accessing healthcare in Djibouti	92
Silent regulations and materials	95
Making connections: how patents travel to Djibouti	100
The emergence of new networks of generics	110
Conclusion	113

5 Ghana, Pharmaceutical Patents and the Ambivalence of Generic Medicines	**116**
Networks of healthcare and the challenges of enrolling patients	117
Enrolling generics in the healthcare system	124
Fluid labels and the shifts of generic medicines	131
Conclusion	150
6 Global Movements, Changing Markets and the Reshaping of Health and Disease	**152**
Dislocated effects of TRIPS and the reordering of health networks	153
Stories of AIDS	160
Conclusion	176
Conclusion: Pharmaceuticals and Socio-Legal Ambivalence	**177**
From texts to social orderings	177
Law, regulations and the day-to-day	178
TRIPS and the transformations of global/local health governance	179
Legal movements and boundaries	181
Bibliography	183
Index	197

Preface

This book has two primary concerns: first, it interrogates medicines, and how those may or may not make their way to poor people. Second, it explores legal objects, and the ways in which what we have come to label as law works in contexts that had little bearing on its creation. The starting points of this inquiry are the so-called 'margins'. The places I explore matter for and by themselves, not only for those who inhabit them, but also as specific, maybe less-explored, corners of the world. They also matter for what they can teach about the constitutive reality of phenomena, and 'things' we take for granted – the nature of 'medicines', but also the nature and modes of action of the law. It proposes a particular approach to looking at law, in terms of standpoints and in terms of methodology, that I hope is of interest for socio-legal scholars quite broadly, without a necessary interest in the subject matter of intellectual property (IP). The core themes that animated me in the process leading to this research are not inherently, in fact, linked to IP. The cross-cutting issues of inequalities, dependency, persistent dissymmetry in opportunities and possibilities that underlie most of the themes I discuss here are not specific to IP, nor to the pharmaceutical field, but illustrative of much broader questions. The ways in which law gets transformed and adopts meaning that makes it unpredictable, sometimes ineffective, sometimes overly effective, sometimes acting in new ways, are not specific to IP. By visiting them in this particular context, I hope to invite others to reattribute this complexity to the deployment of the legal in other contexts and to feed into the questions that socio-legal scholars have asked about the law for several decades.

I started the research that led to this book in 2002, in the context of a PhD at the University of Nottingham, jointly with the School of Law and the Institute for Science and Society, and therefore, in terms of academic discipline, borrowed from law and science and technology studies (STS). Like many people at the time, I was interested in exploring what global IP meant for access to medicines for the poor. Like many first-year PhD students, I started by reading very broadly the literature on the topic – already wide at the time. I had envisaged that this PhD would have an empirical dimension and be based around a selection of case studies – one of which was going to be Djibouti, as I thought it would be useful to look at those questions in the context of a least-developed state. Within a year of the PhD, I had done a first trip to Djibouti, which provided me with the opportunity to carry out a short pilot study. The few interviews I carried out at the time were in such fascinating opposition to everything I had read so far that I soon decided, with my supervisors, that this example warranted in-depth attention, and the focus of my thesis shifted to be entirely about this particular context. At the very core of this redesigned project was a desire to question assumptions (my own, but also those of the literature I had familiarized myself with), and to re-evaluate what 'mattered', how and why. The methodological tools I chose to employ enabled me to move away from anything I assumed or knew about the law, which was essential if wanting to start research afresh in new contexts, without creating set expectations about what I might find, and I explore this in further depth in the introduction and throughout this book. The questions opened up in Djibouti led me to want to revisit IP and healthcare in other new contexts, to explore further the layered complexity of this relationship, but also to carry out the methodological exploration of the law and of legal tools that the Djibouti case study had opened up. I explain in greater detail the rationale for both case studies and for studying them alongside each other in my introduction. Here, I wish mainly to draw attention to the broader curiosity that generated this project and to the aspects of it that made it a most interesting journey for me, as a researcher: by using particular standpoints, and a specific methodological toolbox, I hope to have opened up questions about the nature of law, and about how we can, could or should go about studying it. In one of my very first interviews, a French co-operant in Djibouti told me that the case study I chose was 'not any good', because Djibouti was different, because 'nothing worked', and therefore it was a 'bad example'. With this book, my starting point is in radical opposition to this: namely, there is inherent value about studying 'difference', non-representative examples, exceptions and places where things 'don't work'. Those places matter because failures, transformations and things 'falling apart' teach us a lot about expectations, assumptions and norms, as ethnomethodologists, for example, have aptly demonstrated.

I have many people to thank for this book and for the opportunity to research on something that still fascinates me. As is often the case, personal history has largely influenced the direction that this research took. I spent a substantial part of my childhood in several former African colonies in which France has kept hospitals where my father worked as doctor. My parents' own critical eyes and open-mindedness enabled me to view both some of the successes and some of the failures (and most importantly, some of the complexity) of the health networks we encountered, and I am most grateful to them for this. This research was initiated in the course of my PhD and would never have been possible without the generous support of my supervisors, Robert Dingwall and Tamara Hervey. I still feel extremely grateful that they not only welcomed, but actively encouraged me to undertake a PhD based on a case study in Djibouti – and I am still not sure that the suggestion would have been received with such enthusiasm by a different supervisory team. I could not have hoped for better support and I am vastly indebted to them for the help they provided me with during my PhD and ever since. I am also grateful to Robert Dingwall for his comments on a previous version of this manuscript.

Part of the research leading to this book was supported by the Economic and Social Research Council and I am grateful for its sponsorship.

This project was also shaped by the many enriching discussions I had with colleagues over the years. Versions of this work have been presented at the University of Bristol Law School, the School of Law, Birkbeck, the Ghana Institute for Management and Public Administration, the Institut de Recherche Interdisciplinaire sur les Enjeux Sociaux and various conferences, and the very helpful feedback I received from colleagues on those occasions has greatly helped me reshape my thoughts and arguments. The project benefited from much thinking and refining during visits at the Centre for the Study of Law and Society, UC Berkeley, and the ESRC Genomics and Policy Research Forum, University of Edinburgh. I am indebted to the colleagues who over the years engaged with this research, pointed me in new directions, read drafts, provided feedback and offered me the friendly support that is much needed in any such project. I was privileged to start this project with an exciting group of colleagues (and fellow PhD students) at the University of Nottingham and to finish this book in a similarly stimulating environment at Kent Law School. There are a few I wish to thank by name: Ilke Turkmendag, Murray Goulden, Michael Morrison, Cecily Palmer, Paul Martin, Irit Mevorach, Sujatha Raman, Richard Tutton, Nick Wright, Yin-Ling Lin, Paolo Vargiu, with whom much of this project started; Donatella Alessandrini, Kate Bedford, Helen Carr, Vicky Conway, Maria Drakopoulou, Emily Grabham, Francesco Messineo, Nick Piska, Sally Sheldon, who followed closely the end of this process and provided much needed support. I feel very lucky to work with such bright, thoughtful and generous colleagues. Without Mairead Enright's support, and our many writing sessions, I am not sure this book would have been finished; I feel privileged to be working with such a wonderful friend and colleague, with whom exchanging thoughts and ideas is always so enriching. A special thank you as well to Martyn Pickersgill: collaborating with him over the past two years has greatly helped me refine my thoughts on law and STS, and helped me remember that research can be exciting and rewarding when it felt hard and frustrating. My exploration of actor-network theory and STS has also been enriched by supervising truly wonderful PhD students – Catriona Rooke, Matt Howard, Will Mbioh and Gearoid O'Cuinn. I am very grateful to Dave Cowan, for his support over the years, for inviting me to publish this book, for his patience in this rather long process, and for his enthusiasm for the project as a whole. Thanks also to Rob Gibson, and to the team at Palgrave Macmillan, for the support given to this project, and their kind help throughout, to the anonymous reviewers for their helpful and constructive comments, and to Marie Selwood, a wonderful editor, for her careful handling of my text and the many improvements she brought to it.

This book would not have been possible without the help of Jemima Agyare in collecting the data in Ghana, and the 'we' I use in this context refers to our collaboration. I am most grateful to her for helping me, but also for her friendship over the years, and for welcoming me so warmly in Accra.

At a more personal level, I am grateful for the support and understanding of my close friends and family, and for the patience of my little boy, Rémi. I am particularly indebted to Julie Godefroy for her long-lasting friendship, and for being so supportive over the many years of this project.

Finally, and most importantly, I am indebted to all those who took some of their time to speak to me over the course of this research. The generosity of many of the informants with their time, with the information they provided and with their welcoming attitude made this project possible, enjoyable and an enriching personal experience. I have done my best to faithfully reflect the many stories that they told me and to do justice to the complexity of their experiences.

Introduction: Global IP and Pills for the Poorest

The desperate need for a vast part of the global population to access better medicines in more reliable ways is a persistent social concern. Since the mid-1990s, it has also evolved into one of the most cynical and disheartening aspects of international politics, as we have seen the interests of a few conflict with the needs of the many. The conflicts between the rise of global intellectual property (IP) rights and the deployment of cheap medication for the poor have been extensively discussed since shortly after the adoption of the Trade Related Aspects of Intellectual Property Rights (TRIPS) agreement in 1995. A plethora of academic writings on the topic has been produced and the media have extensively commented (sometimes accurately, sometimes less so) on a subject that has now become familiar to many. However, since starting the research leading to this book in 2002, I have remained convinced that there are too many dimensions of the debate that have been left unexplored. Whilst this book does not claim by any means to provide an exhaustive story of TRIPS, it aims to unpack some of these unexplored aspects, but also to bring together bodies of analyses and questions that have not been confronted with each other in this context. I do this by bringing together qualitative data collected in two states of sub-Saharan Africa (Djibouti and Ghana) and the conceptual insights of actor-network theory (ANT) to propose a socio-legal exploration of the links between IP and access to medicines. I explore TRIPS as a multiple actor, flowing along networks that bring it from the World Trade Organization (WTO) to Djibouti and Ghana, through offices, into drugs, encountering AIDS, malaria, patients and activists on its way. I explore pharmaceutical patents as part of TRIPS, but also as part of materials, including medicines, and as part of the daily lives and practices of many other human and non-human actors, and question the co-constitutional roles of diseases and regulatory politics in the context of IP. I am primarily interested in the 'small' and in localized connections, while understanding those as always entangled in events and linkages happening elsewhere. In this process, ANT provides a useful toolbox to analyse the multidimensional interactions between the wide range of actors that is relevant to TRIPS. I have chosen to use ANT in an open and flexible way, and hope not to have betrayed any of its fundamental claims in doing so. Instead, I hope that this book provides an opportunity to question the possibilities and limitations of engaging with ANT in socio-legal studies, and in the study of global legal instruments. Reciprocally, using ANT to explore a particular set of legal tools enables me to question the processes of ordering and production that surround their deployment into new networks, offering an analysis of the law that opens questions beyond these particular case studies.

Questioning TRIPS, IP and access to health

Since the adoption of TRIPS, the relationship between IP and access to medicines for the poor has been at the core of intense controversies. With pharmaceutical patents being one of the most criticized aspects of TRIPS, the new IP standards galvanized networks of opposition, challenge and resistance across the globe (Sell, 2002a; 2003). They have also become symbolic of the conflicts of interest in a field in which research and innovation, and their financial rewards, often clash with the immediate needs of the poorest in states with limited resources to support them. In spite of the vast amount of academic comments on TRIPS, certain facets of these complex issues have remained underexplored.

The initial controversies over TRIPS and pharmaceutical patents have been richly explored in the literature, but in ways that sometimes struggled to move away from some key dichotomies. Patents have, on the one hand, been portrayed as a significant obstacle to access to health. Based on the idea that stronger patents would have a negative effect on the availability of generic drugs, and therefore on the cost of medical treatment worldwide, this position explained how strengthening patents would make modern drugs unaffordable for people already in a critical health situation (e.g. Bass, 2002; Barton, 2004; Mercurio, 2004). On the other hand, those supporting the TRIPS agreement and defending the strengthening of IP that it generates insisted on the importance of patents to maintain a thriving research industry in the pharmaceutical field, and linked this argument to the right to property, rejecting the idea that patents limited access to drugs (e.g. Attaran and Gillepsie-White, 2001; Dimasi et al., 2003). Similarly, the links between IP and the emerging pharmaceutical industry were predominantly divided along an enablement/burdening dichotomy. Over the years, some more critical and in-depth analyses of TRIPS and global IP have appeared, several of which I refer to throughout this book, and the field has progressively become richer (e.g. Halbert, 2005; Deere, 2010). The global movements that animated TRIPS and resistance to TRIPS have been particularly rich fields for critical engagement with IP in its transnational dimensions (Sell, 2003; Halbert, 2005; Deere, 2010; Klug, 2010). Similarly, processes of implementation of TRIPS have progressively been looked at in more detail. The narrow range of case studies that were originally selected when looking at the links between patents and health in so-called developing states also broadened progressively. While early studies focused essentially on the states that had been most vocal in their opposition to TRIPS, a broader diversity of case studies has gradually been provided (Shadlen et al., 2011).

Nonetheless, many questions remain underexplored in this domain. This is particularly problematic given the urgency of some of the themes of these debates and the complexity of the links between each of the main actors that interact. Specifically, in-depth qualitative studies of local practices and the entanglement of IP into the everyday are rare. Their exceptions are to be found mainly in medical sociology and anthropology and do not usually take TRIPS as their central point of analysis (Hayden, 2007; Ecks and Basu, 2009; Hayden, 2011). As a result, a large part of the literature has not closely engaged with the mechanisms that shape the experience of prescribing, buying and receiving medicines, nor with the mechanics of the deployment of particular legal tools when assessing the links between patents and health (e.g. Watal 2000; Correa, 2003; Matthews, 2004b; Sun, 2004). The boundaries between official and non-official methods of ordering have not always been teased out. Consequently, much of the literature on IP and access to medicines has only had limited engagement with the many contingencies and events that shape how drugs are deployed in particular localities, and in turn how they reach or do not reach patients. The potential discrepancies between legal tools, legal requirements and legal possibilities and the response of individual networks to the law have rarely been questioned in this particular field, beyond the exploration of mechanisms of implementation and compliance. Other themes of importance to this area, such as issues of expertise, or the entanglement of IP with emerging discourses on the nature of health crises, have also been relatively understudied.

In terms of creating a deeper understanding of the mechanisms linking IP and health, this has been aggravated by the relatively limited attention given to sub-Saharan Africa in academic literature (beyond the case of South Africa), in spite of the well-known tragedies it is regularly facing. Much of this is related to the fact that, for a long time, research focused on the states that had more actively engaged with IP and often raised concerns about the impact of TRIPS on health. Although this has progressively changed, and the policies and responses of a wider number of states have been explored, in-depth empirical research on sub-Saharan Africa is still too limited. Similarly, least-developed countries (LDCs) have in general only been given limited attention in much of this literature. Overall, our understanding of the complex links between legal tools and their deployment, in contexts where the official and the unofficial are often difficult to separate, where rules and their practice are often divergent, is still limited by a lack of in-depth engagement with localized practices. More than just a theoretical problem, this is also a political one, in which the events that lead to aggravated sufferings, exclusions and burdening of significant parts of the world are not always given the detailed attention they deserve.

In this research, I aimed to return to some of the issues linking IP and access to health that have been left aside in much of the literature on TRIPS. I do not claim to answer all the questions that are still to be answered, but to make a contribution to this field by looking at places that have been relatively understudied, and adopting a methodology that differs from the predominant approach to understanding the law of IP and its deployment in so-called developing states. I turn to practices, and to localized events, to question what TRIPS and what pharmaceutical patents have meant for some of those who engage with them in their day-to-day lives. I also revisit the very nature of both TRIPS and patents and, as a result, re-examine how we should approach them empirically. In the process of this interrogation, the very boundaries of the law and of legal objects have become very blurry, and at times meaningless. Practices and events appeared to often bear complex, unexpected and sometimes contradictory relationships with the letter of the law. Overall, this book aims to demonstrate some of this complexity, and seeks to invite further reflexions on how we can approach this complex phenomenon and give to local events the attention they deserve in their diversity and contingency.

Ghana and Djibouti

With the examples of Ghana and Djibouti I hope to offer new standpoints from which to explore the meaning and deployment of global IP and pharmaceutical patents. In particular, these case studies provide two different perspectives on the unfolding of TRIPS and patents in sub-Saharan Africa, adding to the limited set of in-depth case studies carried out so far in the continent and outside South Africa. In addition, Djibouti provides an example of an LDC and illustrates the transformations of TRIPS in one of the smallest and poorest countries in the world in contrast to the situation in the more prosperous countries in which this has usually been studied. The choice of these case studies was therefore partly guided by a desire to engage with the deployment of TRIPS in new and highly relevant settings. In particular, I wanted to move away from a dominant discourse in which generalizations have been drawn on TRIPS in 'developing countries' or 'the global South'. Although many patterns are shared, and their commonalities have been useful in galvanizing the global networks of opposition that surrounded the access to medicines campaign, the discourse has its limitations. In particular, the peculiarities and uniqueness of localities can become lost in this effort to generalize. The tendency to assimilate all cultures and spaces in the developing world under one label is one that is often repeated to the detriment of an attention to context and details that is essential to the richness of academic and political knowledge. Critiques to categorization in this domain have not always been taken into account in literature on TRIPS.

I started this research several years ago by studying the deployment of TRIPS in Djibouti, in an environment to which very little attention is generally given in literature, but that provides nonetheless a good illustration of many of the practical difficulties that international legal instruments may meet when travelling around the globe – and a country with which I had a number of personal connections. This example raised many areas of contrast with the phenomena that had been highlighted in most of the literature on TRIPS, and called for further attention. After having investigated some of the peculiar effects of patents and TRIPS in Djibouti, I turned to a second case study, in Ghana, to give more substance and depth to the complexity of the links between patents and access to health, by looking at an example that provides a useful contrast with Djibouti in terms of cultural, regional and economic positioning. The two case studies taken together offer an illustration of some of the many patterns that are at play in sub-Saharan Africa when patents and health systems are brought together – and other case studies would undoubtedly illustrate other phenomena that were not explicit here. The contrasts between the two examples also illustrate some of the diversity not only of 'developing states', but also of Africa, and I hope that throughout the book the examples respond to each other to show some of this diversity in spite of many shared experiences.

A few words on each of these countries illustrate this diversity. Djibouti is a small LDC in East Africa, of around 800,000 inhabitants (although estimates vary greatly), with almost no local industries, and no local pharmaceutical industry, few natural resources, and an economy based essentially on tertiary sector businesses, facilitated by its geographical positioning at the crossroads of Africa and the Middle East. It had almost no history of IP pre-TRIPS. It is also a unique site from which to explore the (post)colonial relationships of France with its former colonies. The last of the French former colonies to gain independence, in 1977, Djibouti still hosts the largest French military base abroad, and its governmental institutions are still heavily reliant on the French co-operation programme, as is its health system. The cultural make-up of Djibouti is highly mixed, having been built around movements across Djibouti, Somalia, Ethiopia and Yemen as well as a large European population, both settled and in medium-term employment.[1]

In contrast, Ghana is a middle-income West-African state, of over 20 million inhabitants. Its capital Accra is an African metropolis of over 3 million inhabitants. It has a strong industrial sector, including an established generic pharmaceutical industry. It was also one of the first African states to gain independence, in 1957. It is actively present on the international scene, and more visible than Djibouti has ever been. It shares with Djibouti, however, a rampant poverty, and the difficulties in answering the basic needs of their populations are shared across both countries. The two case studies also benefit from being told alongside each other (and I am careful to avoid the term 'comparison' here, as I do not intend this book to be a 'comparative study', and cannot, methodologically, claim that it is). This is particularly so because they illustrate diversity and variety and in spite of commonalities remind us of the specific lives that are adopted by TRIPS, by patents, by drugs or diseases in different environments, and how each object adopts as most actor-networks a multiplicity of realities. They provide opportunities to engage with a broad range of interactions and in different elements of the construction of 'TRIPS' as a complex socio-legal technology.

Exploring local networks

The methodology used in this project also responds to the current limitations of scholarly engagement with TRIPS. Although some careful engagement with the processes of implementation of TRIPS, its political significance and its economics has emerged in recent years, socio-legal scholarship, and qualitative research, is still relatively marginal in this area. The growing critical engagement with IP as a whole has not yet been echoed in much of the scholarship on IP and access to medicines in its understanding of the relationship between legal and social transformations (e.g. Watal, 2000; Matthews, 2004a). Similarly, the engagement of medical sociology and science and technology studies with the complexity of pharmaceutical and medical processes has had little effect on much of this literature. Finally, the complexity of the links between legal rules and social practices that socio-legal scholarship has progressively demonstrated is rarely engaged with in this area. As a result, the multiple impacts of TRIPS within the networks surrounding health and

---

1 Nowhere is the social and cultural make-up of Djibouti captured as precisely as in Abdourahman Waberi's novels (e.g. 2002; 2003).

access to medication have remained largely undertheorized. By following TRIPS and its processes of deployment on the ground in Ghana and Djibouti, I have tried to bring some of these insights into these debates to retell a story of complexity, and at times of messiness.

This research is based on empirical data collected between 2004 and 2012 in Djibouti and Ghana. The methods I used were primarily inspired from ethnography and based predominantly on in-depth, loosely structured interviews (Hammersley and Atkinson, 1995). Interviews were carried out in French in Djibouti and in English in Ghana; interviews held in Ghana were recorded and transcribed; interviews in Djibouti were not recorded (as this would not have been suited to the local practices and political sensibilities) but thorough notes were taken during all interviews. Observations were also recorded on detailed fieldnotes, and phone interviews and email follow-ups were used to complement the main data collection once back in the UK. The participants in this research were selected very broadly, in order to explore the various sites to which patents and TRIPS could matter in some way; this wide approach was essential in designing a project in which the broad networks that enlisted – or failed to enlist – TRIPS and pharmaceutical patents could be explored. Overall, I interviewed 48 participants, split between Djibouti and Ghana. This included policy-makers both working on IP (in Djibouti, in the Ministry of Trade and Industry, and in Ghana, in the Attorney General's Chambers) and on public health (in Djibouti, in the various departments of the Ministry of Health and the World Health Organization, and in Ghana, in specialist agencies such as the Pharmacy Council, the Food and Drugs Board and the National Drugs Programme). More broadly, I aimed to retrace the various relevant networks of practices of public health through interviews with their key actors – pharmaceutical importers and wholesalers, pharmacists (private and hospital), doctors, representatives of global programmes on health in both Djibouti and Ghana, and in Ghana academic and policy researchers. The interviews carried out were loosely structured and, although general themes that I would try to discuss were identified before each interview, the discussion was kept open in order to avoid performing the relative importance of particular issues, or leading the interview away from what appeared relevant to each informant. Fieldwork in both cases was often chaotic and the informal setting of many institutions and difficulties in identifying names or details from (sometimes non-existent) websites made the sampling a clear example of snow-balling. Both in Ghana and Djibouti, I was lucky enough to receive a lot of help. Most significantly, the Ghanaian fieldwork was carried out with Dr Jemima Agyare and many of the contacts we obtained would have been difficult if not impossible to identify had it not been for her own positions within policy (at the Kuofor Foundation) and academic circles (at the Ghana Institute of Management and Public Administration). As in most projects, there were limits to these methods: interviews with patients were not carried out and could, in hindsight, have enriched some of stories of the local markets, in particular. In Ghana, all interviews were also carried out in Accra, due to time and practical constraints. Many of the actors interviewed, however, had experience of working with or engaging with other districts, bringing insights and comparison throughout. When using this data, and throughout the book, I use interview quotes extensively, in an effort to remain close to the discourses of participants themselves, and also to try to convey some of the undertones of many of the discussions we had. I was somewhat constrained in providing specific details about interviewees due to the size of the local institutions and the need to maintain their anonymity, but I provide some basic information in order to locate their insights. As traditionally done in qualitative research, and in particular those inspired by ethnography as was the case here, the research process was largely guided by participants, and its scope evolved accordingly throughout the course of this research.

This empirical work was guided and enriched by my simultaneous engagement with ANT and its particular approach to ethnographic exploration of heterogeneous networks (Latour, 2005). I explain in detail the significance of this approach for this project in the next chapter. In brief, however, the method resulted in the framing of the mechanisms observed here as fluid and complex processes, in which localized practices come to slowly constitute what become perceived as global phenomena. The fluidity at play also invites a challenge to traditional boundaries, and my understanding of the law, and of legal objects, has similarly become increasingly uncertain over the years. In the course of this research, drawing clear boundaries between written rules and practices, expectations and effects, intentional and non-intentional forms of regulation, formal and informal, all became increasingly difficult to unpack. Instead, processes of ordering, of texts, habits, pressures and connection, were retraced in ways that may illuminate a field that has often been characterized by the attachment of fixed expectations to legal texts. In this research, I also became interested in the materiality that shapes access, and of the relative enrolment of IP rules within these materials, or heterogeneous networks.

I hope that this approach, and the empirical data collected throughout this project, enable this research to have implications beyond the specific context of TRIPS, medicines and of ANT. In particular, the entanglement of regulations in the day-to-day and multi-layered deployment and transformation of legal tools into practice that emerged through this research brings broader questions about the significance of law itself, and its contingency. Observing the displacement of tools, constructed predominantly outside the African context, into the localized sites where they travel, or are expected to travel, also invites questions about the positionality and constitution of different nodes of so-called 'global networks', and about the very concept of 'globality'. Finally, the making of power, and the persistence of relationships of dependency that transpires by looking at the example of pharmaceuticals and access to health (and to life) speaks more broadly to debates on the nature and constitutions of socio-economic networks in a world still riddled with inequalities. This book suggests that attending to the complexity of these relationships, and to the importance of the localized and the day-to-day in their making, enables a richer understanding of those networks of inequality.

Overview

In Chapter 1, I introduce in more detail the conceptual approach that is adopted throughout and some of its consequences for the way I understand TRIPS as an actor in the access to medicines campaign. I introduce the significance of ANT for this research, and explain how it leads to imagining TRIPS as a complex, fluid and indeterminate object that can be unpacked both in its making and its deployment.

I then turn to exploring the translation of TRIPS, and pharmaceutical patents, as a set of rules into the daily practices of those that engage with the policies and politics of health in Ghana and Djibouti. I start in Chapter 2 by following the 'legal implementation' of the text and the challenges it raised in both countries. I emphasize the process as one in which micro-interactions shape what becomes of international law, and where the fragility of local expertise significantly transforms the very nature of IP, from a highly specialized field of transnational regulation to an uncertain and small policy area, and from global politics to local possibilities.

In Chapter 3, I follow the theme of 'translation' further, by exploring how the national efforts to integrate TRIPS and pharmaceutical patents into national laws and practices are responded to by public health networks. Here I highlight the difficulties for governmental actors, and for the WTO, in fostering responses from those on whose practices the effects of pharmaceutical patents are most dependent.

Having described the key aspects of the translation of official rules on pharmaceutical patents into practice, I turn in Chapters 4 and 5 to the less official, and more discreet, roles that patents play in the healthcare systems of Djibouti and Ghana. By looking at the pharmaceutical markets of each country, I interrogate the effects that the unique place innovator brands play in the practice of healthcare has on the availability and distribution of generic medicines. In Chapter 4, the Djiboutian market illustrates how a system from which pharmaceutical patents are officially absent became heavily reliant on innovator brands, becoming ordered more strictly to favour branded medicines than many states in which patents are protected.

In Chapter 5, I turn to the pharmaceutical market of Ghana to demonstrate how efforts from the government to enrol generic medicines into practice, although more effective than they ever were in Djibouti, are constantly faced with resistance. In particular, I question the role that counterfeits and discourses on counterfeits play in leading doctors and patients towards a return to branded medicines.

In Chapter 6, I return to some of the global movements generated by TRIPS and argue that the links between IP and health cannot be fully explored without questioning the effects of the access to medicines campaign on localities. Arguing that TRIPS is best understood as an assemblage that triggered, and inherently entangles, the access to medicines campaign, I question how global responses to TRIPS have participated in reshaping the landscape of healthcare in Djibouti and Ghana.

I conclude by drawing these different insights together and suggesting that the links between IP and health are complex and contingent and that an evaluation of the effects of TRIPS, and of its politics, is best addressed by a critical questioning of the ways in which certain medicines, and certain producers, manage to act from a distance in the daily practices of health in Africa.

1
TRIPS as Assemblage

In this chapter, I explore some of the conceptual ideas that guided this research. In particular, I question the significance of its grounding in actor-network theory (ANT), and what this means for the way the Trade Related Aspects of Intellectual Property Rights (TRIPS) agreement, intellectual property (IP) and pharmaceutical patents are conceptualized in this research. I start by explaining in some detail the key ideas of ANT, focusing on the elements that are particularly relevant to this research, and on some of its controversies. I then turn more specifically to TRIPS and question its historical constitution as an assemblage, and how it has become shaped over the years into the complex multidimensional entity that now travels the globe. I conclude by summarizing the way in which this conceptualization of TRIPS and patents is played out in the following chapters.

Material societies and the fluidity of the 'legal'

ANT has been used in many different contexts and defined many times both by its creators and its other users. Definitions have of course varied, but they all emphasize a common set of characteristics that this chapter aims to bring together. A useful starting point in understanding contemporary views of ANT is this quote from John Law:

> Actor-network theory is a disparate family of material semiotics tools, sensibilities and methods of analysis that treats everything in the social and natural worlds as a continuously generated effect of the webs of relations within which they are located. (2008, p. 1)

This quote highlights quite explicitly the fluidity of ANT, and the variety of its uses and understandings. At the same time, it covers at least two of the most central characteristics of the method, including the concepts of indeterminacy and heterogeneity that have made this tradition stand out from other approaches in social science and other philosophical traditions (Harman, 2009). ANT has also undergone some significant rethinking over the last decade, triggered in part by at least three different movements: its enrolment in new disciplines, including law; a movement away from the original form of ANT by some of its founders; and a more extensive engagement with the philosophical underpinnings of ANT, in particular in the work of Bruno Latour.

This section considers the core aspects of ANT in some detail, before questioning its recent evolution, and how ANT has been transformed over the years. It will then explore more specifically: what ANT means for this project, focusing on ANT's approach to health and disease, and how this enables a particular conception of medicines relevant to questioning their deployment; the study of the law, which questions it raises and what an ANT approach to transnational legal tools might mean; and finally some of the possibilities and limitations of using ANT in the postcolonial context.

Introducing ANT

The origins of ANT are to be found in the sociology of science and technologies, and in particular in the thinking of Bruno Latour, John Law and Michel Callon. In its origins, ANT was deployed to understand the life of scientific objects within and outside the laboratory (Latour and Woolgar, 1979; Latour, 1988a; 1993). Scientific objects were therefore the centre of the analysis, and ANT was developed as a sociological method to understand their roles and modes of action. Although it has since then been integrated in analysis covering a much wider range of themes, the origin of ANT as a method to understand the making of science remains one of its key features, and has influenced its development and transformations. One of the strengths of early ANT has therefore been that it has become, arguably, a tool to enable us to analyse the process of construction of scientific facts and events and the emergence and action of scientific objects, in the way any other social phenomenon could be described. Its original context has been determinant in providing ANT with the range of case studies that have cemented its ideas, including its focus on materiality. Progressively, however, ANT broadened its scope beyond science and became a method of analysis that could then be applied and extended to the processes surrounding the making and unmaking of a much broader range of material actors; as well as disease, medicines, technological devices, ANT-inspired studies, for example, on expertise and participation (Barry, 2001; Callon et al., 2009, markets (Callon, 2007), law (Cloatre, 2008; Cowan and Carr, 2008; Pottage, 2012) and space (Law, 1997a; Murdoch, 1998; Law, 1999a).

Indeterminate actors

As a starting point, ANT questions the stability of any social entity, and suggests re-imagining the social as a network of fluid and mobile connections, in which every actor is indeterminate and co-dependent on its relationships with others. The social therefore becomes understood as a series of temporary and fragile arrangements, or agencements, in which actors fluctuate and are permanently revisited:

> All entities, it says, achieve their significance by being in relation to other entities. This means that in ANT entities, things, people, are not fixed. Nothing that enters into relations has fixed significance or attributes in and of itself. Instead, the attributes of any particular element in the system, any particular node in the network, are entirely defined in relation to other elements in the system, to other nodes in the network. And it is the analyst's job, at least in part, to explore how those relations – and so the entities that they constitute – are brought into being. (Law, 2000, p. 4)

Derived from semiotics and the emergence of meaning from relations, ANT aims to understand how associations and connections make actors what they are, and act the way they do (Akrich and Latour, 1992). It is based on the notion that nothing is truly stable and pre-defined, but always co-dependent on what surrounds it; in other terms, actors do not hold any specific 'essence', but are only characterized and defined through 'connections', being enacted and re-enacted; actors are events that happen only once (Latour, 1988b, p. 162; Harman, 2009, p. 17), and are constantly made up of multiple realities (Mol, 2003).

A world of 'things'

In these processes of making, unmaking and re-making, materials play a central role, and the emphasis on the role of materials in the social world has probably become the best-known dimension of ANT (Law and Mol, 1995; 2002). The claim is that, in any network, materials act as much as humans, and humans and non-humans need to be considered symmetrically – a position that was challenged by ANT's early critiques.[1] So when Bruno Latour looks at Latour (1988a), in one of the founding texts of ANT, he refuses to stop at the description of him as a 'great man', but describes how he emerged as such by the agencements of a whole range of actors, from labs to bacteria, to devices etc. When Michel Callon (1986a) looks at production lines of scallops,

---

1 See, for example, Amsterdamska (1990) and Yearley and Colin (1992) and, for responses, see Callon and Latour (1992), Callon and Law (1995) and Latour (1999b).

in another classic story, he compares how fishermen deal with scallops and how scallops constrain the action of fishermen, by shaping their activities in a certain way. For ANT, society and sociology are not about humans, they are about 'stuff' – which includes humans, but not exclusively.[2]

These ideas of materiality and indeterminacy are captured in the very notion of 'actor-network', by which actors are always only gatherings of connections, therefore constituted through inherent interactions, and part of a broader set of linkages with others. Actor-networks are both constituted and constitutive of 'society', whose nature itself becomes redefined by this emphasis on fluidity, movement and interaction:

> The network pole of actor-network does not aim at all at designating a Society, this Big Animal. It designates something entirely different which is the summing up of interactions through various kinds of devices, inscriptions, forms etc, into a very local, very practical, very tiny locus. (Latour, 2004, p. 2)[3]

ANT studies have paid particular attention to processes of stabilization – of actors into blackboxes (Latour, 1987, pp. 108–21; Harman, 2009, pp. 50–1), of controversies into settled belief (Epstein, 1996; Barry, 2001) – and endeavoured to unpack the complexity and multiplicity of technologies (Mol and de Laet, 2000). The 'translation' of multiple connections into a new actor with a sense or appearance of stability is at the core of much of this research. Processes of enlisting, interessement[4] or enrolment are under particular scrutiny on these studies, where the ways in which stability is achieved by any particular actor is dependent on its gathering of others and ability to generate links elsewhere.

In each of these studies, actor-networks are characterized as a constant process of co-constitution between the whole and the parts (Callon and Latour, 1981). Any event is only understood as the result of further connections happening elsewhere and of the embedment of associations and actors into what appears temporarily as a stable hybrid (Latour, 1993). In this fluid movement, whole and parts, specific and diffuse, global and local, become impossible to isolate or observe separately from one another:

> Actor and network...designates two faces of the same phenomenon, like wave and particles, the slow realization that the social is a certain type of circulation that can travel endlessly without ever encountering either the micro-level – there is never an interaction that is not framed – or the macro-level – there are only local summing. (Latour, 2004, p. 3)

---

2 For some further implications, see Latour (2009b).
3 Positioning the use of the term network in ANT very differently to how it has been used in other conceptualizations of the term, for example, Castells (1996; 2000).
4 For the original use of the concept, see Callon (1986).

Irreduction

Inherently, because of its particular understanding of the making of social connections, ANT is *irreductionist* (Latour, 1988b). In other words, if everything is only an effect of fragile connections, nothing can ever be reduced to anything else, and it is therefore never possible to explain a phenomenon, or an actor, simply by referring to another explanatory category. Examples of notions that are rejected by ANT authors as explanatory categories are the notions of power, knowledge, or capitalism. ANT does not deny that these exist, but they are themselves effects rather than causes, they are part of the 'explained' or 'to-be-explained', rather than the explanatory – and this is significant to ANT's ontology and epistemology. Any of these are in themselves the result of a certain form of agencement, of a certain set of connections. So for Latour:

> We need to get rid of all categories like those of power, knowledge, profit or capital, because they divide up a cloth that we want seamless in order to study it as we choose...The question is rather simple: how to act at a distance on unfamiliar events, places and people? Answer: by somehow bringing home these events, places and people. How can this be achieved, since they are distant? By inventing [methods] that (a) render them mobile so that they can be brought back; (b) keep them stable so that they can be moved back and forth without additional distortion, corruption or decay and (c) are combinable so that whatever stuff they are made of, they can be cumulated, aggregated or shuffled like a pack of cards. If those conditions are met, then a small provincial town, or an obscure laboratory, or a puny little company in a garage, that were at first as weak as any other place, will become centres dominating at a distance many other places. (1987, p. 223)

Michel Callon focused specifically on revisiting the usefulness of the notion of capitalism in much of his writing (Callon, 1998; 1999). When asked about the role of concepts such as capitalism in his analysis, in an interview with Andrew Barry and Don Slater, he summarizes what is also the more general understanding of ANT on such notions:

> I would say that we no longer have macro-structures. The idea of the existence of macro-structures is very far from the description we are trying to give. As I said, it doesn't mean that there are only local localities, because what is provided by this description is precisely a double logic of local framing and connections between localities. In these terms, some localities

are able to control other localities. So what has to be explained is precisely the progressive construction of connections, and of localities that are able to control other localities...So I would not say that you have structures and that you have positions within these structures, and from this position you can deduce or explain some opposition or some conflicts about how to structure economic markets given the fact that this structuration depends on how configurations which mix property rights, certain forms of technological developments as well as other things. It doesn't mean that there is no structuring process, but that the structuring process as such is at stake. (Barry and Slater, 2002, p. 295)

Power, knowledge and capitalism are all themes that have been important in my research too, and my approach has been to unpack some of their own making and nature through the example of IP and health that I have chosen here. Rather than explanations, these concepts become research questions, likely to become redivided and redrawn with each research project that interrogates them.

A methodology more than a theory?

This particular ontology has significant implications in terms of methods, and in terms of research process. This co-constitution of actors has been primarily understood as an empirical matter, and ANT is actually a particular form of ethnography. The vocabulary it uses, and its reluctance to draw patterns beyond defining the social as a constantly shifting set of relationships, makes it almost inevitably dependent on a careful, empirical observation of these very connections and of carefully selected actors.

ANT remains first and foremost a toolbox aimed at empirical work, and the core of ANT research has been focused on demonstrating the implications of these claims for studies of practice, and studies of objects as deployed in social life. Although the philosophical implications have been increasingly scrutinized, and Bruno Latour's work (including his most recent work) is heavily grounded in philosophical thought (while remaining interested in the 'specific') (e.g. Latour et al., 2012), the main corpus of ANT research, and arguably its main value, is to guide the empirical to facilitate the questioning of its multiple complexity: 'it is possible to describe actor-network theory in the abstract...but this misses the point because it is not abstract but is grounded in empirical case-studies. We can only understand the approach if we have a sense of those case-studies and how these work in practice.' (Law 2008, p. 141)

While its relation to post-structural thoughts has become broadly acknowledged and increasingly questioned, its full potentiality is best deployed as a toolbox bringing poststructuralist ideas with empirical localities. For John Law (2008, p. 145):

> The logic is not far removed from Foucault's. It can also be understood as an empirical version of Gilles Deleuze's nomadic philosophy (Deleuze and Guattari: 1988). Latour has observed that we might talk of 'actant-rhizomes' rather than 'actor-networks', and John Law has argued that there is little difference between Deleuze's 'agencement' (awkwardly translated as 'assemblage' in English) and the term 'actor-network' (Law: 2004). Both refer to the provisional assembly of productive, heterogeneous and (this is the crucial point) quite limited forms of ordering located in no larger overall order. This is why it is helpful to see actor-network theory as a particular empirical translation of post-structuralism.

Translations of ANT

Aside from these core concepts, ANT has been a fluid project, translated and rewritten with each of the stories that it has inspired. The term has been challenged by the small group of scholars who first coined it. For John Law (2008, p. 142), 'it is better to talk of "material semiotics" rather than "actor-network theory". This better catches the openness, uncertainty, revisability and diversity of the most interesting work.'[5] Bruno Latour had denounced the term ANT as early as 1999, and in his more recent work referred more extensively to the term 'sociology of association' to capture the essence of ANT (Latour, 1999a; 2005). Meanwhile, Michel Callon in his latest work, although still strongly influenced by ANT in his thinking, and openly relating his ideas to the method, commonly refers to it in the past tense, and has moved away from some of its key concepts and taken them forward to enable him to optimize the method for its use in the sociology of economics. For example, referring to one of the key concepts of ANT:

> The notion of embeddedness has been very useful, but now we have to get rid of it. The metaphors of entanglement and dis-entanglement are more productive because they allow you to describe the omnipresence of commercial transactions and other types of relations and, in the same movement, the process of boundary shifting...I see science and technology as some of the media through which the process of disentanglement and entanglement is not only made possible, but enhanced and made easier. In actor-network theory, the emphasis was put on

---

5 For an earlier engagement with the transformations of ANT, see Law (1997b).

these links, but not so much on the process of entanglement and dis-entanglement. (Barry and Slater, 2002, p. 9)

The term 'post-ANT' has commonly been used to refer to the large amount of research that has built on some aspects of this tradition, and developed it further, in new disciplines or for new purposes (Moser, 2008). The fluidity of the method itself makes it difficult to claim that any project is ever a pure 'ANT exploration' and this research is no exception.[6] While borrowing from many of its ideas and grounded in literature that is itself affiliated with ANT thinking, or that shares some of its key characteristics under different labels, I certainly take some liberties with my handling of the concepts. At times, this has had the result of attempting to stretch ANT into the new territories of transnational law, of Djibouti or of Ghana; at others, it has resulted in unavoidable compromises in having to limit and tidy a project that the precepts of ANT could have made endless.

Using ANT to study IP and health in Africa

In this section, I consider more specifically aspects of ANT that need to be teased out or explored and that are of relevance to this project. There are three particular nodes of my own 'ANT-network' that I wish to explore here. First, I want to briefly review some of the insights that ANT has brought to the understanding of diseases, and how these feed into my questioning of pharmaceuticals. I then turn to an emerging aspect of ANT, namely its meaning for conceptualizations of the law. Finally, I turn to the more controversial issue of what it means to use ANT in the postcolonial context, and what are the possibilities and limitations of its particular ontology.

Rethinking diseases and drugs in debates on access to medication

A significant number of classic ANT stories emerged in relation to the making and deployment of disease and treatment and have formed the basis of some of the understandings I build on in the remainder of my analysis.

In one of the classic founding tales of ANT, Bruno Latour (1988a) revisits the story of Pasteur and the spreading of his discoveries across broader public health practice in France – and later the rest of the world. In this analysis, relationships within the laboratory and around the laboratory where Pasteur researched are explored, in order to retell the story of his discoveries as constituted from a myriad of material and political enrolments. Scientific practice and the concept of discovery are revisited, and a key moment in the development of Western medicine is reassessed as the heterogeneous combination of disparate elements. The permeability and contingency of biomedical science

---

6 The vocabulary and some of the conceptual insights of the methods also link into other rich recent analyses of the entanglement of nature and society (e.g. Barad, 2007).

is explored in several other ANT studies, or stories inspired by ANT. Steven Epstein (1996), for example, provides a thorough analysis of the making of AIDS as a disease and of the politics of its treatment. This work is illuminating in describing the complex and multiple processes that are at stake in understanding the happenings of diseases and developing strategies for treatments and associated ethics. The production of scientific 'certainties' and the settlement of controversies are shown as contingent of fragile processes, always open to challenges and scrutiny. The very nature of disease itself is also a classic focus, explored, for example, by Anne-Marie Mol (2003) in her study of the day-to-day constitution of atherosclerosis. In this seminal study, disease is shown to be both multiple in its making, experience and translation, and stabilized in its holding together of its many constituents. Its management in the hospital that she explores is made possible by the stability of the blackboxed disease that is constituted. The transformations of the disease are both what makes it difficult to seize and understand, and what will make it ultimately open to solutions and treatment.[7]

In these various studies – those quoted above being only some of the most notable examples – contingency and fluidity are constantly emphasized. One of the aspects of these studies is the revising of the boundaries between the 'outside' and the 'inside' of science into a permeable continuum. This in turn opens new questions about the nature of expertise and contested knowledges in the biomedical field. This questioning of expertise participates in demonstrating how the medical sphere and medical knowledge are no longer the terrain of a few experts, and that the question of who makes healthcare is constantly reshaped and renegotiated by new participants, new actors.

This body of work opens up new avenues in the analysis of both disease and treatment, as contingent on interactions and connections and as dependent on the ability of networks to become stabilized, or blackboxed. This contingency permeates the research I carried out here, and the issues I explore build on the understanding of the permeability and fluidity of networks of disease and treatment. In this book, multiple stories of health and their contestation are produced in a variety of sites, ranging from local hospitals in Africa, to the offices of the World Bank, through villages, non-governmental organizations (NGOs) and European and African bodies, and at each stage the fragile nature of disease, medicines and medical certainties is challenged. Diseases become fluid actors whose very nature seems to vary and be transformed in the discourse and practices of those encountered, in their translation in international policies and in the experience of local practitioners and patients. The politics of treatment are constantly being revisited and questioned as they travel to new localized networks. Finally, challenges emerge repeatedly to the

---

7 See also Law and Singleton (2000a).

stability of apparently settled networks, in the form of patients' demands, medical practices, or patents and new medical entities. Medicines, specifically, are understood here as the result of a highly political and fluctuating set of relationships. The politics of treatment, like the politics of disease, become contingent on their enrolment into networks that may make them accepted or rejected, successful or not successful, successful in some of their aims and clear failures in others, or partial winners against diseases that may become displaced if not transformed in the face of treatment. Pharmaceuticals are complex in their shaping as well as in their deployment.

In their shaping, an understanding of drugs based to any extent in ANT will situate them as the outcome of multiple events and scripts that they embed and carry to new spaces and networks (Barry, 2005). Drugs produced by research-based industries in Europe will travel with political implications that differ radically from those produced by an emerging industry in a developing state.[8] They will also travel differently – and sometimes will not travel at all, as we will see in the context of Djibouti where some drugs struggle to reach patients if they are not of the right type or with the right script. In their deployment, drugs also follow messy trajectories – challenging the possibility of identifying straightforward patterns. Importantly, drugs can also be powerful devices (Law, 1994); power that is not inherent, not necessarily fixed, but fluctuating in different contexts. But drugs in their most material form, in their packaging, in their labelling, are influential and symbolic actors, and some drugs stabilize as more influential than others, as I will illustrate by looking at the organization of the public health systems of Ghana and Djibouti.

ANT and the law

The second specific set of questions that this research is asking is about the law, and particular forms of movements that create and surround what comes to be known as legal, or produces effects that are approaching the legal. In this, it feeds into an emerging interdisciplinary legal scholarship that has explored ANT as a method of analysing the making and deployment of law and legal objects. In this project, I explore what ANT means for the question of law, and whether a theory of law in ANT can be extrapolated from existing scholarship. I am particularly interested here in what ANT means for the study of transnational legal tools, such as TRIPS, that are fluid by nature and travel through a vast set of cultures and institutions, but also of travelling tools such as patents. The question here is what ANT's contributions, be they on the heterogeneous nature of social networks, on the principle of

---

8 And the intricacy of the sets of interests at play are more complex than a straightforward public/private, developing/developed divide (Hayden, 2011).

irreduction, or on the indeterminacy of the social, can teach us about the law. Methodologically and conceptually, the emphasis that ANT brings to the complexity and interdependency of the social creates many epistemological and ontological questions for the study of the law. This issue builds on a small but growing literature that has sought to explore the relationship between ANT and legal constitution. The leading work of Annelise Riles has provided rich instances in which the heterogeneous production of the law and the entanglement of networked agencies in this process are explored through the lens of technical materialities (e.g. Riles, 2000; 2010; 2011). The focus here is on networked technicalities in the constitution of legal spaces and practices. The relationship between law and ANT has also been explored in a few key papers by law and society scholars in the past few years (Silbey and Ewick, 2003; Levi and Valverde, 2008). Nonetheless, the field is still nascent, and the theoretical significance of ANT for understanding legal processes – in the making and travels of legal objects – is still being mapped out.

One of the most explicit ANT explorations of law is Bruno Latour's *The Making of the Law* (2010). Central to this particular project is an exploration of law in its materiality and Latour adopts in this book the ethnographic tools he deployed in studying the making of science to analyse the processes by which law becomes enunciated in the French Conseil d'Etat. The book is a clear continuation from the project that ANT started several decades ago, in examining how law becomes produced, and carefully analysing the 'things' and practices that generate the law as a particular form of social netting.

The possibility of defining the legal as a determined or determinable domain outside of the specific institutions that produce it is a different question, and one I explore in this project. Here, we need to interrogate the manifestations and movements of the law once enacted as a particular textual and institutional actor. Centrally, the irreductionist approach of ANT, and its emphasis on fluidity, makes the very existence of a definable 'legal space' and of identifiable 'legal actors' potentiality problematic. I argue that the premises of ANT should in fact encourage us to rethink more radically the very existence of the law as a definable entity, and in doing so wish to engage with questions raised elsewhere by Alain Pottage (Pottage, 2012). In particular, although a self-definition of the law as a particular network is commonly performed by lawyers and others, a broader analysis of legal objects, both in their making and their deployment, suggests a revisiting of the boundaries of the law.

If the methodology reconceptualizes society as a set of fluid interdependent and co-generative assemblages, the idea that we can presume that the 'law' has a set of fixed characteristics, beyond those that lawyers allocate to it and expect from it, becomes problematic. Instead, legal texts should be followed through their entanglement with other social assemblages and the processes of repeated blackboxing and translation that occur around legal texts. Texts become loaded materials, complex assemblages in themselves, entangled within pre-existing controversies, institutions and material possibilities, that go on to inscribe and carry with them the scripts that produced them (Cloatre and Dingwall, forthcoming). Their deployment is multi-directional, and contingent on the connections set with others that creators may have anticipated or not. One of the effects of ANT becomes to challenge the assumption that law holds characteristics that travel in a particular shape. Focusing on moments, on the empirical, and on practices as well as discourses enables us to deconstruct the effects and movements that are co-produced, generated, or impacted on, by legal texts, by expectations linked to these, by misconceptions, by interessement or non-interessement (Callon, 1986). The notion of indeterminacy of the actor suggests that we need to move from the stability of the law, law as a special form of institution, to something that only acquires this particular meaning under specific circumstances and as a specific text, for example, is successful in mobilizing key actors. The very definition of a definable legal space becomes problematic. In other words, the law becomes an object of inquiry, a social technology to be questioned and unpacked, rather than a stable and explanatory category. Legal tools participate in generating forms of ordering that may not inherently differ or be separated from alternative, including material, forms of regulations (as I explore in particular in Chapter 4).

In this project, this approach to the law is particularly useful because of the cultural and geographical travels of the objects I followed. Exploring their traces in processes of ordering, and the potential discrepancies that occur between the supposed nature of the law and its actual workings, allowed me to visit the various processes through which they act in unexpected ways.

ANT in a (post)colonial context

ANT has been the subject of many critiques, and I want to conclude this section by engaging in some depth with one of the common criticisms that has been directed towards it, and that I have been asked about many times when presenting this work: namely, whether ANT can accommodate an acknowledgment of the postcolonial context. More generally, the question here is about ANT's engagement – or lack thereof – with critical scholarship that has demonstrated repetitive patterns of exclusion and dominance – both feminist and postcolonial. Here, I consider specifically the issue of the postcolonial within ANT, or the question of *if* and *how* ANT analyses offer space to acknowledge the historical and systemic experiences of the (post)-colonial. My position is that, although ANT has so far only offered a limited engagement with subaltern voices and persistent relations of power, it offers tools that can illuminate new aspects of the constitution of such patterns. The critiques are significant, nonetheless, and deserve further attention in order to justify my hopeful position on the relevance of ANT to the postcolonial context, and its pertinence in drawing in voices traditionally excluded by persistent historical patterns of power. The issues at stake here are also central to the themes of this research. The spaces studied in the course of this research are the first and most obvious reflection of this, though Ghana and Djibouti have very distinct pasts and presents in their relationships to the former colonial powers. Science and technology are areas that have historically been particularly tightly linked to state expansion and powerful reliance on Western knowledge systems. Specifically, global health practices have been illustrative sites of the persistence of forms of power inherited from the colonial era, and the current practices of the global pharmaceutical industry have been criticized for producing new forms of imperialism.

In spite of the significant historical and current relevance of technoscience to colonial and postcolonial relationships, Northern science and technology studies (STS) (as Sandra Harding, 2008, has labelled them) have been slow to engage explicitly with the postcolonial. Calls for alternative understandings of modernities have been issued repeatedly by voices in the South, but until recently have had little impact on Euro-American writings on science and technology. This has started to shift quite recently, and postcolonial STS has emerged as a sub-discipline with its own set of questions and own framework of analysis to understand the social workings of science (Harding 1998; Anderson 2002; Anderson and Adams, 2008). These have often worked to challenge understandings of modernity and the division between 'traditional' and 'modern' forms of knowledge, producing symmetrical analyses of competing or co-existing knowledge systems. In addition, postcolonial STS has progressively worked to demonstrate the role of science and technology in empire-building and in maintaining relationships of power. From there, critiques of current patterns of exclusion have been voiced, and the role of science and technology in producing and maintaining the exteriorization of particular groups from mainstream society has been highlighted.

Returning more specifically to ANT, one key critique has been its obscuring of the very patterns of exclusion that postcolonial scholarship has highlighted (Mallavarapu and Prasad, 2006; Ray and Selinger, 2008). The critiques stemmed both from the lack of engagement of Bruno Latour with this body of work and from the apparent refusal of ANT to accept 'patterns' or structural movements of any kind that are inherently at the heart of these writings. Indeed, Latour's work has made little effort to engage with the work of postcolonial scholars (or feminist scholars); in fact, ANT has always developed in something of a vacuum and the origins of ANT in the thinking of Foucault or Deleuze, for example, have been pointed out repeatedly from outside ANT more commonly than by ANT authors themselves. The second point is both a methodological one and a political, or normative, one. On the one hand, the critique questions Latour's politics and whether his work can address the current limits to democracy that he explores in relation to nature. On the other hand, there is a methodological question: if we are to understand ANT as a way to explore the (fluid) social, does the approach enable us to understand what creates, constitutes or maintains processes of exclusion and violence?

Processes of inclusion, exclusion and normalization or stabilization have certainly been a concern for ANT since its early days, and the rooting of some of its thoughts in ethnomethodology are illustrative of this (Latour and Woolgar, 1979). Explicit efforts to engage ANT with postcolonial literature are still rare, however, and have just started emerging. Matthew Watson (2011) argues, for example, that the views of Latour, in particular in his concept of cosmopolitics, can interestingly be conciliated with ideas of Chakrabharty (2000) in relation to the subaltern pasts. Reviewing the principal critiques of ANT as silencing the voices of the subalterns (including the views of Haraway and Harding), Watson goes on to argue that the position of Latour is not necessarily inherently incommensurable with the calls of postcolonial authors for a more effective engagement with the violence and exclusionary processes involved in the historical deployment of scientific and technological knowledge. Underlying some of the critiques of Latour summarized by Watson is the lack of normative engagement of Latour's theory with the performed exclusions of past and current practices, and the resulting call of postcolonial scholars for a renewed attention to the necessity of inclusionary strategies. Latour's cosmopolitics have a significant descriptive dimension, by which the stories of exclusion and return of particular entities into the political and the democratic sphere are retold. But his underlying assumption that actors are inherently symmetrical and may in comparable ways become excluded or re-included into the participatory sphere he imagines allows limited space, in itself, for claims to shift positionalities. It can be argued, however, that Latour's particular reading of externalization processes can be enriched and reworked with a more careful questioning of what become persistent exclusionary patterns that make re-inclusion more problematic for particular groups than others. In other words, a more political and normative reading of the notion of cosmopolitics in particular, but also of Latour's and others' ANT projects, is not only possible but also promising. Watson proposes to do this by bringing together Latour's statements on the need to bring sciences within politics with Chakrabharty's analysis of histories of marginalization of subaltern forms of knowledge and experiences. The strength of Latour's project and its contribution to postcolonial thinking of science, on the other hand, is located in its radical rethinking of the heterogeneity and fluidity of the social. This not only adds to, for example, Chakrabharty's exploration of gods and deities as actors by multiplying the range of objects that form social nettings alongside traditionally understood 'humans', but also enables a rethinking of the production of forms of knowledge-power that powerfully explain processes of entanglement, disentanglement, inclusion and exclusion.[9]

Amongst founding ANT texts, few references can be identified to non-Western contexts. In *We Have Never Been Modern*, Bruno Latour makes the following critical statement of our engagement with the 'non-Western':

> The great divide between Us – Occidentals – and Them – everyone else, from the China seas to the Yucatan, from the Inuit to the Tasmanian aborigines – has not ceased to obsess us. Whatever they do, Westerners bring history along with them in the hulls of their caravels and their gunboats, in the cylinders of their telescopes and the pistons of their immunizing syringes. They bear this white man's burden sometimes as a tragedy, but always as a destiny. They do not claim merely that they differ from others as the Sioux differ from the Algonquins, or the Baoules from the Lapps, but that they differ radically, absolutely, to the extent that Westerners can be lined up on one side and all the cultures on the other, since the latter all have in common that they are precisely cultures amongst others. In Westerners' eyes, the West, and the West alone, is not a culture, not merely a culture. (Latour, 1993, p. 97)[10]

Although this point is not elaborated in much more detail, it is nonetheless fundamental in its implications for the type of analysis that ANT is critical of. The quote illustrates how a return to specificities of the 'Other' is essential for Western thought. The inherent criticism is for the Othering process in itself, and for the consequence that this has in the production of Eurocentrism, and the permanent reinvention of the Westerner as the starting point to which others will be compared and contrasted, not as unique in their difference, but as bundled in a whole within which distinctions cease to matter. Latour's analysis is principally interested here in challenging our understanding of modernity, and the process he is focusing on in the chapter that surrounds this quote is the distinction between nature and culture that has become constitutive of the concept of modernity that he challenges. Modernity in this sense, and the separation of nature and society that it relies on, is what participated in creating the Eurocentrism in which the Westerner becomes the only one to have 'progressed' to a new stage of human civilization. The project of ANT, challenging this very

---

9 For an interesting parallel, see Latour (2009b).
10 See also, for a further analysis of this book with a focus on the positioning of Western science in global relations, Elam (1999).

conceptualization of modernity that is one of the foundations of Western specificities, therefore has a great deal to respond to issues that touch very closely on postcolonialism. Marilyn Strathern has taken the analysis further in an attempt to revisit familiar dichotomies and question the concept of heterogeneity and the making of humans as heterogeneous beings. Of the early ANT authors, she has made the most significant contribution to questioning the meaning of ANT in a non-Western context. Again, the relevance here is on the fringes of what postcolonial studies may be interested in, but her research nonetheless suggests a radical rethinking of the making of the heterogeneous netting of society that enables social analysis to account more effectively for the cultural specificities of heterogeneous relationships. The voices of particular societies and the correlated making of individuals and communities are rendered visible in a subtle way in her extensive work. This questioning of modernity is constructed by paying attention to localized movements and creates a significant challenge to the generalizations that lead to much uncritical writing. In her critique of ANT, Sandra Harding acknowledges that there are indeed some positive contributions to critiques of modernity in the project started by Latour. But it is also useful to look beyond Latour to demonstrate that ANT as a whole has the tools to provide useful contributions to this debate, political sympathies that enable it do so, and an interest for critique that is shared by those traditionally engaging with the socio-cultural context of past-colonies and the persistent patterns of power that they display.

ANT has engaged with the process of making 'empires', both in very literal terms (Law, 1986) and in more metaphorical ones (Latour, 2002). The irreductionist approach of ANT has invited its authors to focus on the specific material connections that enable the production of networked patterns of power and the maintenance of relationships of dominance, or control, at a distance. The refusal of ANT to rely heavily on notions such as that of capitalism, commonly understood to be at the root of many current patterns of exclusion, is not, as I have explained, a denial of the movements that may be captured in this term. Instead, ANT suggests engaging with the *hows* and the *whats* of these concepts, by returning to a detailed analysis of the sites and processes of constitution of what becomes simplified by labelling. Far from denying the existence of movements that maintain or generate exclusion or violence, the challenges to dichotomies, fixed categories and a pre-defined social that ANT argues for suggest a return to the mechanics of control and empire-building. The attention to materials and the fluidity of technologies has also been a rich ground for demonstrating both the successful enrolment of some technologies in new contexts and the relative failure of others to adapt. In a classic example of the former, Marianne de Laet and Anne-Marie Mol (2000) follow the deployment of a particular waterpump across communities in Zimbabwe. In the process of doing so, they observe how the adaptability of the technology means that it is constantly revisited and transformed by villagers, to the point where transformation is so radical that the object is barely recognizable. The fluidity of the pump is what makes it particularly successful, strong and resistant. Most interesting is the significance of this story for the relationship between technology and material knowledge systems; the strength of the technology is its ability to adapt to different forms of modernity: a technology designed within a particular system of knowledge production is deployed in an environment in which constituted/constitutive knowledge and possibilities are different. The local users, faced with a temporary failure of the technology as originally built, deploy their own skills, experiences and material potentialities to address this failure and make the technology their own. The strength of the technology itself is to be adaptable to the various resources available to its users, and in this sense avoids the dependability that more rigid technologies would have on a particular form of knowledge. In the process, users also make the acquired knowledge their own and create their own heterogeneous technological knowledge. The normative agenda proposed in this paper in rethinking technology is pursued in other more recent examples of ANT analysis of technologies travelling across socio-cultural contexts. In a recent analysis, for example, a close look at a dairy farm in East Timor offers some critical insights on the practices of development, and more specifically on the links between technoscience and development – an issue related, albeit different in its matter of inquiry and approach, to that of the postcolonial (Sheperd and Gibbs, 2006). The careful ethnographic analysis provided, of the transformations followed by the technology under scrutiny and between creators' expectations and users' practices, engages closely with some of the repetitive patterns of power that animate the more general field of international aid in the form of technology transfer. The dairy farm 'should' work in a certain way, for its developers, and any deviation from this model is understood as a failure, and a failure, in this case, of the Other. A close attention to the cultural assumptions of technology and the patterns of power and/or dominance they embed enables a real normative engagement with technologies and the socio-cultural scripts that they carry. Nonetheless, the political message is not always made explicit beyond its technological implications. For Anderson:

> A sort of semiotic formalism seems to supervene on the analysis of such local sites: the 'local' can seem quite abstract, depleted of historical and social specificity. The structural features of the network become clear, but often it is hard to discern the relations and the politics engendered through it. (2002, p. 649)

Without it being inherent to ANT, it is one of the strands of the method that can still be developed further – and the balance between localized, empirical and historical and political contextualization are at stake here.

The deconstruction of postcolonial relationships is an important step in understanding their constitution, their persistence and their modes of establishment. A significant focus of ANT is on understanding ordering, in deconstructing patterns of repetition that result in the stabilization, over time, of relationships of power and codependency. It calls for a return to asymmetrical analysis of traditionally divided categories and asymmetrical approach to knowledge systems and cultural specificities. In these aspects of its aims and underlying politics, it provides tools that are indeed of high relevance to decrypting the mechanisms that lead to the persistence of historical relationships.[11] If ANT is to be conceived, as it often is, as a project that is still under construction, and permanently being reshaped, the space it provides for postcolonial critique is one the themes that needs to be teased out and discussed. Its call to return to the local and the empirical, and to describe social events and processes of ordering without assuming a stable pre-existing context, is both its most problematic and its most promising dimension in relation to the postcolonial. ANT's challenges to the idea of a pre-existing context, however, do not preclude it from engaging with culture, history, or repeated processes of ordering – and indeed this has been done in much ANT scholarship. It calls, however, for an understanding of ordering as always fragile and open to challenge, but the seemingly descriptive approach of much ANT scholarship does not preclude normative claims, conclusions and strategies to be drawn from examples – and indeed subtle political projects are included in much recent scholarship. In fact, this attention to detail and the irreductionist approach of ANT is also potentially what makes it a most useful player in the study of the postcolonial and of underexplored localities. In the words of Escobar quoted by Anderson (2002):

> Instead of searching for grand alternative models or strategies, what is needed is the investigation of alternative representations and practices in concrete local settings, particularly so as they exist in contexts of hybridization, collective action and political mobilization. (Escobar, 1994, p. 223)

The non-essentialist and empirical approach of ANT and its ontological position calling for a rethinking of the very nature of the social have significant potential for questioning the relationships at play in postcolonial contexts and in the deployment of particular events that determine and influence

---

11 See also Schegloff (1997) for an exploration of the relationship between academic critique and the enablement of actors to display their own politics.

contemporary processes of repeated exclusions. As a method, it is very well positioned to 'destabilize imperial and colonial categories, and reconstitute encounters through the concentrated examination of particular historical, political and cultural contexts' (Anderson, 2002, p. 647).

Unpacking TRIPS

This book explores the workings of global IP in Djibouti and Ghana and responds specifically to questions raised about the impact of the TRIPS agreement on 'developing states'. I want to start by returning briefly to the construction of TRIPS and draw a picture of its conflicted nature. As emphasized many times in ANT case studies, the constitutive pieces of a network often come to be made apparent when the network collapses or is challenged in a new way. The history of TRIPS is an interesting example of this, in which the public health aspects of TRIPS managed to remain discreet during most of the drafting of TRIPS, before coming to light in response to a number of external events. The nature of TRIPS and patents is also important to question here as it will tie in closely with the many discourses, questions and assumptions that are being carried and translated both in Djibouti and in Ghana. This section also explores what an ANT approach to both sets of instruments implies and how they are conceptualized in this research. I draw attention to aspects of the political history of the creation of TRIPS and to the stabilization of a set of IP rules into a legal blackbox. I then go on to question some of the significance that TRIPS has had in global discourses and its speedy enrolment into public health networks (issues that are explored further in the following chapters).

Throughout, I interrogate what it means to reimagine TRIPS drawing on the ideas of ANT. IP is not a complete stranger to ANT; Marilyn Strathern (1999), for example, has explored aspects of IP in the context of Papua New Guinea. From a different perspective, Marianne de Laet (2000) has followed patents as travelling objects. The exploration of the concept of 'invention' in Pottage and Sherman's *Figures of Invention* (2010), though not drawing explicitly or exclusively on ANT, is closely associated with the focus on assemblage and socially constructive fluidity that ANT has developed. But the re-exploration of TRIPS also engages with a transnational instrument and its translation in a variety of explored and non-explored local networks.

The story of TRIPS is one that is played out at a variety of levels and engages a broad range of socio-legal material and immaterial actors. At the most introductory level, investigating TRIPS in its public health dimensions means focusing on the making and stabilization of TRIPS as a text of law, and as a series of scripts designed to travel globally and transform networks and practices.

Both the construction and translation of TRIPS are at the core of explaining what it does for and to health. But the definition of TRIPS, its boundaries and constituents, is in itself problematic – as well as a text, set of rules and scripts, TRIPS embodies a particular history, certain notions of expertise and a materiality that makes it more easily accessible for some than others. Its travel and deployment are similarly constrained by material possibilities and by its ability to become enrolled in appropriate networks – its relative entanglement or non-entanglement will determine precisely what it is able to do, and therefore what it is (a text with a variable (in)ability to order, transform and act at a distance). But exploring the impact of global IP on health also requires a careful analysis of pharmaceutical patents, whose relationship to TRIPS cannot be derived exclusively from the blackletter of TRIPS – and, throughout the empirical sections of this book, I illustrate this in specific instances. While patents are intrinsically linked to TRIPS in the scripts and requirements set by global intellectual property, they are a market tool as well as a socio-legal one, and therefore travel across markets and, in their inscription within drugs, in ways that are potentially independent from TRIPS and other legal regulations. Finally, the story of TRIPS and of patents is also a story played and replayed at different levels, in which global negotiations, pressures and resistance have all impacted in complex and interrelated ways on what happens at the localized levels of the networks in which drugs are deployed – or fail to be deployed.

Retelling the story of TRIPS, pharmaceutical patents and their impact on markets and access to medicines in the light of ANT invites us to question and empirically reconsider these various nodes and connections and how they interact with each other. Doing this without assuming the inherent quality of any of the surrounding actors, be they the 'global industry', diseases or drugs, also involves a messy and constant questioning of the different nodes in which patents and TRIPS come to play a role or reorder practices and objects. The nature of TRIPS here is understood as being more than a 'flat' text. Rather, it is a textual and institutional assemblage. But its fluid nature also means that the limits to its action are inherent. It only becomes an actor if it encounters appropriate networks that it has the realized ability to influence. Consequently, its potential and actual effects cannot be predicted nor generalized, but will depend on its interactions with others.

In those different aspects of TRIPS that ANT would suggest need to be unpacked, two main elements appear. On the one hand, recalling the 'making' of TRIPS will provide some of the background to understanding what constitutes it, and how it came to be generated in its particular form and associated with a series of expectations. On the other hand, the complexity of its deployment and of its effect on pharmaceutical patents is to be closely unpacked through their daily practice. The process of making TRIPS does not end in its drafting in a textual form: and, in fact, TRIPS became transformed and revisited by the various campaigns that it generated to a point where its very nature appeared transformed. In the following section, I question this process of production, from the making of a new text to the production of a new key actor in the access to medicines campaign – from TRIPS as the stabilized version of certain demands on IP to its stabilizing of demands in the public health field. I then turn briefly to explaining the approach undertaken in this book to TRIPS deployment in new networks and localities, returning to questions relative to patents and their travels (de Laet, 2000).

TRIPS in the making

The creation of TRIPS is the fascinating story of the stabilizing and black-boxing of a complex set of power relationships and the interests of a few into a global regulatory instrument. TRIPS is a particular localization and a particular moment in the settlement of demands and pressures that had pre-existed it and continue to persevere alongside it, as well as within it. In the same way as science in the making can be analysed, law in the making shows us how we move from the uncertain, the 'possible', the optional, to the production of stability and objects shaped and perceived as being definite and authoritative. TRIPS and the making of TRIPS have been analysed in great detail elsewhere, and here I want to concentrate essentially on recalling key aspects of its history, and more particularly its social and political history. The history of TRIPS can be retold as one of mobilization of some actors by others that enabled them to find new ways of acting at a distance. Global IP has often been used as an example of the new forms of imperialism that are deployed in the so-called 'globalization era', and indeed it is interesting to keep in mind ANT's engagement with the role of 'things' in empire-building when questioning the role and effects of TRIPS (Law, 1986). How did some already powerful actors manage to produce a new emerging tool that enabled them to project their influence to new spaces and territories and through the language of the law? When looking at the history of TRIPS, the range of elements that came together successfully to produce this new powerful tool is very broad – from partner industries to particular discourses (from equity to industrial development), legal tools and institutional momentum. As a result, what was a small but highly powerful group of entities managed to settle their claims into a new form that would give them a renewed ability to act at a distance. TRIPS became the key actor in this process of acting at a distance and the history of TRIPS is one of enablement, of making this possible by creating this new legal technology.

The asymmetrical emergence of patents

The diversity of approaches to pharmaceutical patents that existed prior to TRIPS reflects the multiple nature of pharmaceutical patents and the particularities of medicines as objects in their creation and 'protection'. Although commentators have often emphasized a broad 'developing'/'developed' countries distinction, the role that patents played or were expected to play in different localities was spread across a very broad spectrum – so, a broad tendency to extend the field of pharmaceutical patents in the most industrialized states can be seen while they have generally tended to be less relied upon in less industrialized states. I will start here with one of the peculiarities of drugs as objects of protection. Drugs are an interesting example of multilayered heterogeneous assemblages (Jeffery et al., 2007). At one level, they could be defined as very 'simple' materials – molecular structures that are relatively easy and cheap to produce and replicate in most cases. However, each drug is also the result of a very complex process that becomes inscribed into each of the tablets that is produced, and each tablet carries with it significant implications in relation to health and life, but also in relation to the future production of other drugs.

Therefore, the development of any individual drug is entangled within complex processes of production that become dependent on technical abilities to research and significant regulatory demands. 'Creating' a new drug is therefore a fundamentally different process, very different in nature from 'replicating' a drug that has already been developed and tested (Grubb, 1999). Admittedly, the regulatory requirements that are placed on drug developers are lengthy and expensive and, as a result, the cost of 'inventing' a drug and taking it to the market are much higher than the costs of making a drug. Interestingly, the same 'tablet' can therefore acquire significantly different meanings depending on its situatedness in networks of production. At the same time, the technical networks that are necessary to enable the development of a new drug are rare, limited and tend to be geographically situated in a few states only – creating a geographical dimension to the multilayeredness of patents (Crampes, 2000; Grabowski, 2002). From this contingent nature of medicines emerged at least two sets of approaches to pharmaceutical patents, and how they are understood or used. On the one hand, those who are technically able to invent new medicines have framed patents as an essential tool to ensure that the value that they have inscribed in any drug through the significant investments made to turn a tablet into a marketable 'medicine' can be reflected in its price. Their argument is that the financial value of a new medicine is more than that of the tablet, and that only patents and the temporary monopoly they allow can guarantee its recovery. As a result, pharmaceutical patents become understood as an essential incentive to research – if medicines are understood as thick materials whose added value can only truly be reflected by a temporary monopoly, patents become a key tool in incentivizing researchers to develop new drugs (Bale, 1997; 1998; Scherer, 2000; Dimasi et al., 2003). Critiques will emphasize that the significant profits made by the global pharmaceutical industry mean that patents demonstrate that this logic could be achieved with a more contained set of incentives, and the contingency of this on a particular form of social and economic construction of pharmaceutical research has been highlighted (Light and Warburton, 2011).

When starting from the point of view of producing industries, or states that host such industries, the meaning of patents, however, can be very different. Framing patents as a necessary incentive for research and innovation is contingent on an ability to research, which is present only in a very limited number of countries (Crampes, 2000; Grabowski, 2002). An alternative framing of patents is to reflect on the role that their presence or absence may play for the development of a pharmaceutical industry. The questions here are intimately linked to issues of development and decolonization processes and are not unique to the pharmaceutical industry, but made particularly salient by the highly specialized nature of this industry (Vaistos, 1971; Drahos, 2002). If reimagining patents within the broader issue of industrial and technological development, they create limitations as to what can be produced or made (Nogues, 1990; 1993). The regulatory constraints that industries have to negotiate in the process of 'inventing' drugs become displaced by the process of 'making' or 'producing' drugs, therefore making the activities of the generic industry more constrained and limited. To the extent that only very few countries have an industry considered to have inventive capacities, and can thus be expected to offer an important part of their patents to their own nationals, the constraining rather than enabling role of patents becomes a prime concern in many locales (Keyala, 1999; Shadlen et al., 2011). The debate in this field has been strongly grounded in the example given by some countries which now have a strong and competitive pharmaceutical industry, but had chosen in the past to exclude pharmaceuticals – or pharmaceutical products only – from the patentability field. Switzerland, Italy (Challu, 1995) and India (Henderson, 1997; Seeratan, 2001; Chauduri, 2005) are amongst the most commonly mentioned of these.[12] These different examples have proved that it can be economically beneficial for a country to limit pharmaceutical patents in order to give a sound basis to its local industrial capabilities and to introduce pharmaceutical patents only when a certain level of innovative capacity has been reached. Aiming for the development of a generic industry can thus become a strategy for the progressive development of future research capacity.

As a result of these various sets of considerations, and until TRIPS was adopted, the regimes applied to pharmaceutical patents varied widely across the globe. While, on the one hand, countries with a strong research-based

---

12 See also, for example, Kirim (1985), Park (1993) and LaCroix et al. (1996).

pharmaceutical industry were willing to see pharmaceutical inventions strongly protected, countries with only a generic industry limited the potentially negative impact of strong pharmaceutical patent rights on their industrial development – either by, for example, excluding pharmaceutical patents from the field of patentability altogether, or authorizing only the patenting of pharmaceutical processes as opposed to products. Shifts in strategy were then performed in a number of states after a certain stage of development was reached by the pharmaceutical industry. Alongside these well-defined if divergent strategies, it is also worth noting that in some contexts, such as that of Djibouti, there was very little engagement with IP of any type, including pharmaceutical patents, until new obligations appeared in the form of TRIPS.

From diversity to discontent

From the 1980s, the non-generic pharmaceutical industry – located in a handful of countries – started lobbying against the approach of what they called 'free-riders' – states and generic companies that were using what they considered to be 'their' inventions. In the US, in particular, the industry lobbied the government heavily into taking unilateral measures against countries that were deemed to have excessively weak protection for patents (Sell, 2003). This growing pressure was not limited to the pharmaceutical field and arose in a number of key areas. The pharmaceutical industry was particularly proactive but the lobbying nonetheless needs to be understood as a whole, within an overall disagreement amongst governments, and between the industry in different sectors and states, as to what should be considered as an 'appropriate' IP regime. Overall, by jointly lobbying for a stronger protection of IP worldwide, different sectors of the industry, essentially in Europe and North America, organized into a strong policy network in which national governments became key players.[13] The gathering of those various powerful entities into a strong and effective pole of power and influence was also facilitated by the use of particular tools and instruments over the years, prior to the negotiation and adoption of TRIPS. An example of the type of pressure that they exerted, and of the support they gained from their own governments, can be found in the commercial action of the US against states with a 'weak' IP system. The pressure put on countries with weak IP protection, and in particular in the pharmaceutical field, was maintained for several years. Although this enabled this newly blackboxed lobby group to reach new areas around

---

13 Mobilizing, in particular, the International Intellectual Property Alliance, the Pharmaceutical Manufacturers Association, the Chemical Manufacturers Association, National Agrochemical Chemicals Association, Motor Equipment Manufacturers Association, Auto Exports Council, Intellectual Property Owners, Inc., the International Anti-counterfeiting Coalition and the Semiconductor Industry Association.

the world, the approach remained limited and some places unreachable. In particular, some states resisted the pressure they were put under by the use of commercial measures. The legitimacy of the approach was also soon questioned as the use of unilateral commercial actions to enforce standards of IP on countries that had no legal duties to respect them began to be questioned. As it became evident that the use of non-legitimized pressure was a limited tool for expansion, it appeared that the most sustainable way to reach those new places would be to negotiate a set of international standards that would respond to and reflect the demands of the industry.

In 1986, a significant step was taken when the corporate executives of 12 US-based companies gathered to create a new negotiating blackbox – the Intellectual Property Committee (IPC). The IPC then proceeded to produce the textual material that would enable its interests to travel to the World Trade Organization (WTO) and then reach out worldwide into new spaces, in the form of a proposal for a new global agreement on IP that would sow the seeds of TRIPS. As highlighted by Susan Sell (2003), the story of this process is one in which an industrial network successfully transformed and stabilized its demands into public law. Progressively, the work produced by the IPC, and the demands of the industry in their more precise 'proposal' form, gained momentum and found a global platform for discussion in the Uruguay Round as part of the questions that needed to be tackled in order to limit barriers to free trade. In the Uruguay Round itself, negotiations were constrained, partly because of the format of the discussions and partly because of the broader entanglement of IP with global trade issues and membership of the WTO:

> The negotiations on TRIPS are often said to have begun properly in the second half of 1989, when a number of countries made proposals, or the first part of 1990, when five draft texts of an agreement were submitted to the negotiating group. A more sceptical view is that the negotiations were by then largely over. An even more sceptical view is to say that no real negotiation ever took place. Developing countries had simply run out of alternatives and options. (Drahos and Braithwaite, 2002, p. 139)

With the adoption of TRIPS, pharmaceutical patents became compulsory tools in many new legal spaces. TRIPS does not allow for pharmaceutical products to be excluded from the field of patentability and creates a requirement for every member state of the WTO to make pharmaceutical patents available in their national system for a minimum of 20 years, answering the claims of the pharmaceutical industry (Otten, 2000). Article 27(1), which sets the broad definition of the domain of patentability to forbid the exclusion of pharmaceutical patents, was a crucial aspect of the TRIPS negotiation and considered 'the reason of being of the whole TRIPS agreement' (Pires de Carvalho, 2002, p. 141). Although states were given an implementation period for TRIPS, pharmaceutical patents were required to become part of a mailbox system (Article 70(8)) for applications to be submitted before the end of the implementation period in order to accelerate the process of granting them. Safeguards were integrated and, in particular, the possibility for states to adopt compulsory licences, under strict conditions (Article 31(f)), gave them a certain margin of action in responding to the immediate needs of their own populations. Compulsory licences are authorizations granted by the state to a producer to produce patented medicines before the expiration of the patent-owner's rights and without their authorization, if necessary, in the public interest. Consequently, they are thought to be potentially useful in cases where patent rights are a threat to public health and have, indeed, occasionally been used by states to produce medicines that their own population needed. Often, however, these efforts have resulted in political pressure and opposition from patent-holders or their governments. In spite of these limited safeguards, overall, the changes generated by TRIPS in relation to pharmaceutical patents were significant. Interestingly, they were also originally essentially framed in terms of industrial development. Shortly after the adoption of TRIPS, however, a reshaping of pharmaceutical patents occurred, by which they switched from being perceived as a tool for industrial development (or an obstacle to industrial development) to being a public health matter.

The (re)making of TRIPS as a public health actor

Soon after the adoption of TRIPS, opposition to the text for its potential impact on public health and access to medicines galvanized, articulated around several key moments and events. I want to suggest that the access to medicines campaign significantly reshaped TRIPS itself, turning it into a key public health actor. In Chapter 6, I will explain how the effects TRIPS has on specific localities need to be assessed and understood by also acknowledging its entanglement with the campaign, illustrating how a particular object can demultiply, take a new shape, adopt new dimensions and become transformed beyond recognition. TRIPS became much more than a stable text of law and moved from being a largely unchallenged text, flowing from private to public domain, to being the subject of intense attacks and the focus of a new form of democratic engagement. IP moved from the forums of specialist lawyers and economists to new scenes in which actors with different sets of expertise and interests became involved, and into fields in which citizens started having a voice. In this process, we can observe the making of 'multiple TRIPS' and understanding 'TRIPS' and its impact also means understanding TRIPS there, as it emerged whilst generating new alliances and new lobbies.

Entanglement of pharmaceutical patents and public health

By their very nature, and as mentioned earlier, patents allow producers to market their products for the price that the market will tolerate without having to consider elements of competition. In the pharmaceutical field, this means that drugs will often be much more expensive than if they were produced by several competitors (Bala et al., 1998; Rozek and Berkowitz, 1998; Bala and Sagoo, 2000). The potential impact of pharmaceutical patents on the cost of medication has become a highly controversial issue in recent years, accentuated by the impact of specific health-related scandals (Bass, 2002). The worsening AIDS crisis in many developing countries and the difficulties experienced by poor populations in buying anti-HIV/AIDS drugs that are still under patents have made the controversies around pharmaceutical patents stark. Similarly, the argument made by pharmaceutical companies for rights over their inventions has been challenged increasingly by arguments built around the right to life (Sell, 2002a). The debate around TRIPS grew to include a range of health and development NGOs arguing for the need to improve access to medication on the one hand and, on the other hand, drug companies insisting on the pressing necessity to improve IP standards in order to maintain a high level of research and investment. Overall, the action of health activists soon started making the links between patents and health in developing countries appear as stable and rather simple – pharmaceutical patents were likely to make drugs more expensive and, therefore, to have a negative impact on access to health. AIDS was presented as the clearest example of this:

> consumer and health groups on the front lines of the anti-HIV/AIDS pandemic mobilised to protest the high cost of HIV/AIDS drugs, the subsequent lack of access to the drugs, and the dangers of overly strong intellectual property protection as embodied in TRIPS. They presented an alternative framing of IP as a public health issue, not a trade issue. (Sell, 2002a, p. 497)

TRIPS was made possible largely because the dominant discourse on IP that preceded its adoption was based on innovation and economics and the closed-doors approach to the negotiations was both the cause and the result of a limited involvement of citizen groups in what was still conceived largely as a technical issue. In the words of Drahos and Braithwaite: 'Had TRIPS been framed as a public health issue, the anxiety of mass publics in the US and other Western states might have become a factor in destabilizing what US business elites had built around TRIPS.' (2002, p. 576) Soon after its adoption, TRIPS would shift significantly to become a much more open and questionable field of public policy as it became reframed as a public health concern. Therefore, the signing of TRIPS/drafting of TRIPS is only one side of the story of TRIPS in the making – and TRIPS is a good example of why Latour may say that actors are accidents that only happen once, at a specific point in time. Immediately after its signing, TRIPS was already something new and different as it became seized and retold by groups reading it through a public health lens. The process by which the access to medicines campaign stabilized is a complex one, told in greater detail elsewhere and only a brief reminder of key turning points and key moments is needed here. It is interesting to note, in particular, that the opposition to TRIPS that emerged was greatly facilitated by the pre-existence of well-established networks with relevant interests, in particular, consumer groups based in the US. Those groups, for example the Consumer Project on Technology, were already in a position to act as they had established the key connections that they would need for that purpose. Similarly, the networks that had developed around AIDS in the US had created the basis for what would become a well-established global movement. The original focus of these groups responded to broader concerns regarding the price of drugs within the US. The conflicts between equitable and affordable access to drugs on the one hand and the demands of the pharmaceutical industry for an ever-increasing protection of their inventions on the other progressively moved from US to global debates and grew to include more actors, in a broader set of locations. In 1996, Health Action International became involved, giving a new global spin to the campaign (Sell, 2003, p. 148), and were joined in 1998 by Médecins sans Frontières (MSF). Ellen t'Hoen (2010) recalls in particular how the World Health Organization (WHO) and health NGOs became involved in IP issues when revising the WHO's drugs policy. Whilst the WHO had, since the 1970s, been involved in drafting essential medicines lists, which would guide states as to which drugs should be given priority in their procurement and distribution policies, it had had very little involvement in issues of IP. In other words, IP had remained a specialist area in which global health actors had very limited involvement. Things changed, however, with the adoption of TRIPS. At the 1995 World Health Assembly, the links between essential medicines and patents started being drawn. Whilst the WHO had been advocating local production and the use of generics, international trade negotiations were making this increasingly difficult. As international health NGOs were becoming more interested in the links between IP and health, the WHO also seized on the issue (Klug, 2010). The complexity of the links between IP and health within the WHO policies is a highly interesting issue in its own right (and I come back to the question of essential medicines lists and how this tool is constituted in Chapter 4; the role of patents in shaping this list through the attention that is paid to 'cost' when drawing it up is of particular interest).

The (re)making of TRIPS into a public health agent was intertwined with the (re)making of other key actors of the access to medicines campaign. Specific diseases emerged as powerful players in the campaign and as being particularly central actors in the processes of inclusion/exclusion that were deployed in the gathering of the campaign. AIDS in particular, one of the most central focal points of the access to medicines campaign, was transformed radically in its international politics (Ford, 2003). Although it had been devastating segments of population across the world for around a decade by the time TRIPS was adopted, the realities of drug development, pricing and IP, as highlighted by the campaign, meant that it was now a manageable disease – but only for some. From being a death sentence in Africa, AIDS continued to be a death sentence in Africa *because* of IP rules and the behaviour of the global pharmaceutical industry in transforming legal requirements and possibilities. In turn, this created a very different place for AIDS both in Africa and within global public health fora. Similarly, medicines became entangled with global networks in new ways, with repercussions travelling to and from new localities. Throughout the growth of the access to medicines campaign, the enabling power of drugs appeared in newly contingent ways: the intertwining of pharmaceuticals, their delivery within patients' bodies and global regulations were highlighted in new ways that transformed the place of drugs and drug policies in the political space. Correspondingly, specific drugs came to become central actors in strengthening the access to medicines campaign around specific events. For example, the announcement by CIPLA that it could provide antiretrovirals for just under $1 a day was a key turning point in the campaign – and a symbolically strong moment in showing the direct links between patents and patients (Sell, 2002b, p. 510). Through this drug and the new possibility it opened, IP in turn became something still slightly new and different: it became 'something' that could turn a $350-a-year medicine into a $10,000 one. This announcement by CIPLA was a key moment in transforming TRIPS and bringing it to the centre of public health networks while similarly redefining the global position of the pharmaceutical industry. Other such moments have also been widely mediatized – for example, the Pretoria trial in South Africa in which global corporations challenged the South African government's Medical Act for breaching TRIPS, before withdrawing their complaint under significant public pressure (Barnard, 2002).[14] The outrage generated by the US and Canadian governments' declarations on compulsory licences in the midst of the anthrax scare was another such moment, in which new forms of inequality in global health came to the public's attention (Mullin, 2002; Sun, 2004; Klug, 2010).

In the unfolding of the history of TRIPS and the access to medicines campaign, a number of moments and incidences created a new social reality

---

14 A significant literature has focused on these movements surrounding IP in South Africa; e.g. Bond (1999), Dolmo (2001) and Halbert (2002).

of what sort of actor TRIPS is, of the meaning and role of drugs (and specific drugs), of the social significance of particular diseases, and of the nature of 'Big Pharma'. ANT's emphasis on materiality and cogeneration reminds us that the centrality of those materials and the impact of their (re)making is as productive and determinant to social ordering as an (imaginary) isolated human action. In this process, several realities of TRIPS also emerged. On the one hand, there was TRIPS as a strong legal tool, stabilized by a specific process of legal drafting and the powerful networks built around it, but also by the work of lawyers after its adoption – through courts and legal commentaries. At the same time, a different reality of TRIPS emerged in circles interested in access to drugs. There, TRIPS became all at once a symbol of the hegemony of Big Pharma, a barrier to health for all and a dubious text that deserved to be challenged for not promoting the appropriate sets of rights. Those two realities also contributed to performing and maintaining each other and, for example, the very nature of TRIPS as a legal tool became reshaped by its concomitant rewriting as a public health actor. Some of this transformation is very literal and, as a result of the access to medicines campaign, parts of TRIPS were literally transformed. I briefly recap these transformations here, before returning to the performance of the multiple production of TRIPS.

Response to and reframing of the links of TRIPS to health

The transformation of TRIPS into a public health actor resulted in the literal remaking of its official content. I will briefly summarize here some of the key elements of this rewriting, to the extent that they are relevant to understanding the context of my case studies, but they have been studied in very precise details by others. The key turning point in settling the public health dimension of TRIPS and its consequent rewriting was the Doha Declaration on TRIPS and public health signed in 2001 (Abbott, 2002; Engelberg, 2002; MSF, 2003a; 2003b; 2003c). The declaration did not radically transform the substance of the text of TRIPS per se, but one of its concrete outcomes was to create new extended deadlines for developing and least-developed countries (LDCs) in relation to the implementation of the protection of pharmaceutical patents in national legislations. It also stated the importance for developing states of using particular safeguards, as detailed below, making political statements that would not always be reflected in the individual practices and negotiations of states in the following years. The declaration's significance is essentially located in the general process that transformed TRIPS into a new public health 'problem', to which the international community agreed to suggest some – partial – solutions. To that extent, it responded to some of the demands of the access to medicines campaign to transform the framework set up by TRIPS in a way that would limit the impact on access to health that the general public had now become aware of.

The declaration is therefore entangled in a broader movement that acknowledged the need for developing states to seize all the opportunities they had to use flexibilities and safeguards. States were encouraged by commentators of TRIPS to make use of parallel imports, not explicitly prohibited by TRIPS (Abbott, 1998; Correa, 1998; 2001). In this context, parallel imports refers to the doctrine of exhaustion of rights, upheld by the Doha Declaration and according to which a patent-holder loses some control over the distribution and marketing of its products once released into a market and becomes unable, for example, to prevent their entering into a new market, or their export by distributors. This is very relevant for access to medicines, as it means that if a drug company markets a drug for a low price in a low-income market (a practice that is relatively common), it cannot prevent its resale in higher-income markets. Consumers could therefore, in theory, obtain patented drugs for the cheapest price that the patent-holder had marketed them for, which can be crucial in relation to access to medication, by purchasing drugs that were originally sold in a foreign market before being imported and made available to consumers by a distributor (Heath, 1997; Balasubramaniam, 2002; Hammer 2002; Correa, 2003). The possibility for states to use compulsory licences was also reaffirmed many times, making these tools more directly associated with debates on public health than they had been when TRIPS was adopted. The material ability for the poorest states to do this was originally contested, as compulsory licences were first designed, in Article 31(f), as a tool to be used mainly for domestic purposes, limiting their relevance for states that had no generic industry. After extensive debates within and outside the WTO, an agreement was reached in August 2006 to authorize LDCs, under a long and cumbersome process, to get around this limitation. The workability of this technical process, in the context of countries with limited expertise and very small markets (creating few incentives for would-be exporters) is still highly questionable, as will become clearer throughout the following chapters. Additional flexibilities, such as the Bolar exemption, have also been recommended by commentators and policy advisors. Before any generic version of a drug is brought to the market, national regulations usually expect it to have been submitted to a number of tests and trials. Unless the law states otherwise (through what has become known as the Bolar exemption), these tests could potentially be in breach of patent-holders' rights. For countries wanting to ensure that tests could be carried out during the lifespan of a patent, in order for generics to be marketed as early as possible after a patent expired, the Bolar exemption is an important policy tool. Many of these recommendations, however, remain difficult to implement or use in local contexts with limited expertise and markets that are complicated by many other factors, as became evident in this research. In addition, and as has become more broadly documented, as pressure for implementation of the strongest standards of patent rights started growing, it appeared correspondingly unlikely that many countries would be politically able to make use of any of these options (Pretorius, 2002).[15]

Travelling IP

The textual blackboxing of TRIPS, and its resulting enrolment in global public health networks, is only the prelude to a very long series of travels. Marianne de Laet (2000) has explored the travels of patents and their transformation as they move across offices, moving from the US to Africa. The method I use in this book is comparable in its approach, although I am also interested in questioning the travel of patents and TRIPS outside of purposely designed IP offices. In these travels, once again, many different realities of TRIPS and of patents emerge.

The limited acknowledgment of these fluid and multidirectional movements in a large part of the literature is not without impact. Callon (2007) has written on the performativity of economics and his ideas are relevant to the performativity of law as a discipline, and of legal academia as well as practice. For Callon, discourses are performative in the sense that they participate in enacting the realities that they describe. The practice of legal discourses participate in giving legal objects their longevity and stability. In the early commentaries of TRIPS – and many have persisted since – the vision of TRIPS deployed was one in which TRIPS would necessarily hold a particular shape when travelling to remote places; somehow, TRIPS would have an 'impact' by being implemented, technical answers such as compulsory licences would be what developing states would need to concentrate on; in fact, categories such as 'developing' and 'developed' countries themselves became repeatedly performed in these discourses. Some connections became unquestioned (not necessarily 'unacknowledged', but often brushed aside), leading to a certain story of TRIPS and a certain reality of it. As some of the most established commentators also became advisors to the World Intellectual Property Organization or WHO, for example, this resulted in blurring the line between theory and practice and performing again this particular reality of TRIPS as being about a certain form of expertise rather than, for example, opening more questions about its multiple realities and the complexity and variability of local needs (Correa, 1998; 2000).

Alongside this widely performed story of TRIPS, however, its complexity plays out in the many networks to which it travels in its multiple forms. At one level, TRIPS can be conceptualized as essentially being a textual material destined to circulate; its creators expect it to be diffused and enforced in a

---

15 Further detail on these different safeguards can be found in the extensive legal analyses of TRIPS produced, for example, by Correa (1998; 2000).

way that results in the reshaping of many networks across the globe. In order to fulfil the expectation that it will act at a distance, it needs to transform other laws, other texts; other institutions; human behaviour; but also materials: some should disappear from the market, others made to appear only under specific conditions – such as compulsory licences. If following TRIPS as an object in this way, questions become: Does TRIPS actually do what it is expected to? Does it succeed in reshaping these networks in this way? How does it get transformed in the process? Does it remain the stable blackbox that is repeatedly performed in the discourses of its international observers? In other words, studying the deployment of TRIPS, and the deployment of IP in new localities, is partly about implementation. And here ANT seems to meet a traditional interest of socio-legal studies – how do laws turn from paper to action? But the story is also one about travels and translation that pays attention to the various processes through which TRIPS and IP are themselves reframed and reimagined by those that it meets – or doesn't meet. The role of connecting and intermediary materials in generating those multiple versions of IP and of their effects is crucial and the very nature of IP, for example, becomes contingent on local transport links, communication technologies, offices settings, or the blackboxing or lack thereof of governmental entities.

But when questioning the deployment of TRIPS, other aspects of its multiple realities must also be acknowledged. Following TRIPS in Djibouti or Ghana also involves questioning the role TRIPS has played in the local transformations triggered by the access to medicines campaign. In other words, the deployment of TRIPS is not only linked to its role as a textual legal blackbox, but also to its impact as a global public health actor. It is therefore also important to follow the traces it left as a core actor in the access to medicines campaign. The process at stake here is even more complex, and the links between global IP and the global framing of diseases, the reshaping of health priorities and the conflicting local and global stories of these all need to be considered to some extent when questioning the relationship between TRIPS and specific locales such as Ghana and Djibouti. Of course, the movement is reciprocal – diseases have the potential to radically reshape what TRIPS is, and in many contexts have done precisely this: the strength and action of TRIPS has been seriously challenged by the resistance opposed by certain key diseases, most significantly HIV/AIDS. The complexity of the deployment of IP goes even further than this, however, as the travels of TRIPS and of pharmaceutical patents do not necessarily fully overlap. Aside from their travels through patent offices, patents become inherently inscribed within the materials that they protect, travelling through markets and biomedical practices in influential ways. The complex relationship between patents and brands is at stake here, and a rich literature has specifically explored the influence of brands on the constitution of particular medicines as social tools (Greene, 2011b)[16]. Patents play an essential role in this shaping, by providing a monopoly on drugs that will shape patients' and health professionals' trust and fidelity. The workings of patents in practice, and the challenges that generic competitors face in practice, can therefore only be unpacked if paying close attention to the way in which the initial advantages granted through patents persist in the shaping of pharmaceutical practices, possibly beyond the life of a particular patent. Their role in social ordering is therefore similarly diffused through the various materials that they participate in constructing – from essential medicines lists to individual tablets. Evaluating the role of patents therefore requires a careful attention to different movements that animate the distribution of medicines in particular locales. Talking about TRIPS and access to medicines invites us to reflect on drugs/medicines as actors. In these various stories, the debate of TRIPS and access to medicines is not made of fixed objects, but only of fluid actor networks that are constantly being reshaped by new connections and disappearing links.

Conclusion

Overall, ANT invites us to rethink objects of inquiry as fluid actors that get transformed by their interactions and connections with others. This suggests a significant rethink of how transnational legal actors in particular, and legal actors in general, can be approached. Here I suggest that this calls for an analysis that explores the inscription of these actors within sets of identifiable movements or networks – from some that would traditionally be described as such (such as the access to medicines campaign networks) to others that are networks in the very localized sense of ANT (be they drugs or diseases). One of the challenges of this approach is to maintain its feasibility and balance the need for a readable narrative while seizing some of the complexity of each of these nodes. I propose doing it in the remainder of this book by focusing on specific issues, moments, or events that certainly do not provide a full story of the linkages between IP and health, even in the very locales that I have chosen, but start suggesting some of the ways in which effects can be approached. Here, my aim is both an exercise of methodological exploration and a substantive effort to enrich what we know of IP in Africa. I start by following, in the next chapter, the travels of TRIPS as a legal textual blackbox in the policy offices of Djibouti and Ghana.

---

16 For an analysis of a particular shaping of the patent/brand relationship in the Argentinian context, see Hayden (2011).

2
From Global Scripts to Local Translation

In this chapter, I consider one dimension of the translation of the Trade Related Aspects of Intellectual Property Rights (TRIPS) agreement, by following its translation as a set of prescriptions – as a set of official rules carried on paper, expected to have a predefined impact – in Djibouti and Ghana. I use the term prescription here with the meaning that is given to it within actor-network theory (ANT), when looking at technologies, to reflect the idea that any technology (including here legal technologies) comes with a script that carries, amongst other things, a series of expectations on its ability to generate actions from others (Akrich and Latour, 1992). I question here the impact that TRIPS as a set of rules is having on local legislation, and how the specific contexts of Djibouti and Ghana have responded to the expectations attached to TRIPS. In doing so, I therefore analyse what are commonly referred to as 'implementation' issues, and engage with the particularities of the networks at play, and in particular the links between the translation of intellectual property (IP) and local forms of expertise (Barrett, 2004). The nature of TRIPS as textual material is central to this analysis, and this chapter seeks to demonstrate the series of socio-technical translations that occur when the text of TRIPS and its embedded prescriptions interact with legal institutions in Djibouti and Ghana. This chapter constitutes only a prelude to unpacking the complexity of TRIPS, and of IP, in the rest of this study. But questioning this process of translation is also important for emphasizing the complexity of the process of translation from global law to local practices, systematically explored in the literature in this field. Importantly, the chapter also interrogates the travels of TRIPS into Djibouti and Ghana, by returning to their first entry points in the networks of IP – or what would become so under the influence of TRIPS. I am predominantly concerned here with exploring how those in charge of translating TRIPS initially responded to this new actor and, consequently, in the different realities adopted by TRIPS as it travelled to those two remote locations. Many other questions raised by the translation of rules into practice are explored in the next chapter, but these are best understood with a clear introduction to what implementing a complex legal text such as TRIPS in Djibouti and Ghana means in terms of process.

The two case studies are not directly comparable, and a comparison is not my aim here. Instead, I want to provide some insight into two parallel stories that took place in opposite corners of Africa, roughly around the same period of time, and that both speak to what TRIPS 'did' when travelling to those locales. The entanglement of local specificities, institutions and the historical constitutions of particular networks participates in shaping what remain very local answers to a travelling material. At the same time, some themes emerged in both cases that are more usefully discussed together. I start by describing aspects of the process of translation of TRIPS in the local IP networks of Djibouti, where the slow emergence of a very small network for IP was itself the result of having to implement rules on IP. I then turn to following the Ghanaian experience of TRIPS and the cynical perception of TRIPS as a new and unexpected burden on a legal domain only starting to fall into place. In both contexts, the issue of expertise and of the positionality of local actors towards this new transnational text is important, and I interrogate it, before concluding by summarizing the views of IP experts in Djibouti and Ghana to the project of globalizing IP. This chapter focuses on TRIPS within IP circles; in the next chapter, I turn to following the travels of TRIPS into the public health policy networks that it needs to mobilize in order to act at a distance.

Translating TRIPS in Djibouti

The story of the implementation of TRIPS in Djibouti is an interesting instance of the emergence of a new legal domain into a particular location. Prior to TRIPS, the history of IP in Djibouti, as an independent state, was almost non-existent – except for a few small steps that I summarize below. The translation of TRIPS, often told in very technical terms in the literature that explores its meaning for developing states, is in Djibouti the story of a very small network that very slowly tried to bring together the different threads of what makes IP a new domain in the country – law, institutions, expertise, staff. Here I briefly retell the story of the slow construction of a significant task – a task that, importantly, was the result of external demands rather than local needs. I start by turning to the situation of Djibouti in relation to IP before it adopted its first law on industrial property in 2009.

A brief history of IP in Djibouti

Since its independence Djibouti had had no system of patent protection in any form, no relevant legislation and, until TRIPS started being translated into national law, no institutional attachment for patents to be discussed. In other words, patents did not exist as legal or policy actors. The history of IP more generally was nearly non-existent, apart from one short-lived exception: in 1996 the Ministry of Culture proposed a law to protect artistic and literary creations, subsequently adopted by the Parliament.[1] Without a pre-existing IP institution, this proposal emerged independently from any talk on industrial protection or IP more generally, and was the proposal of one member of the ministry who thought this would be a 'useful step in the promotion of intellectual and creative activities in the country' (former member of the Ministry of Culture). This new law became an example of the fact that laws are not self-enacting, and that a text remains just this until it becomes part of a broader network that can empower it to bring effects. None of the institutions that the law suggested would be created were ever created, and as a result the law was never applied in any way. This was viewed as a fairly common occurrence in Djibouti, which is unsurprising in a context where institutional resources require prioritizing that spontaneous ideas or proposals from individual policy-makers may not take into consideration:

> This kind of things happens all the time – there are so many laws that have been adopted because of pressure, lobbying, or on the basis of external advice from organisations, for example. The Parliament passes the law, but then when it comes to applying it, no one knows what to do with it, and nobody is interested in it any more, or they realize we just don't have the means to apply it! (member of the Constitutional Court)

It is not necessary here to review in any detail the substance of this earlier law, but the contrasts between the formal legal process and the practice of law is illustrated by this, and the fact that this was the only attempt, before 2009, to bring IP regulations into Djibouti is illustrative of the country's very limited experience of IP. Until a new law was adopted in 2009, which I return to below, patents had not appeared even in this ephemeral form.

Progressively, however, IP started emerging beyond this example, if not in law, at least in some of the discourses relevant to Djibouti, and to which its policy-makers became occasionally exposed. An awareness of global negotiations in this area, and of activities undertaken in other African states, resulted in a progressive movement of interessement of Djiboutian actors into existing networks of IP, and in particular some attempts at joining IP organizations. These efforts reflect some of the ambivalence of Djibouti as a space, and its difficulty in defining how to locate itself in political spaces. In 1994,

---

1 Loi no 114/AN/96/3eme L relative à la protection du droit d'auteur.

and as TRIPS was being signed, Djibouti made its first attempt at joining an IP organization, and turned to the Organisation Africaine de la Proprieté Intellectuelle (OAPI), the first point of call for French speaking sub-Saharan African countries.[2] The process of accession was indeed initiated, in what was in its substance an attempt in Djibouti to start engaging with IP as a legal field and gather expertise, as well as developing tangible materials (texts and offices etc.) that would facilitate the process that TRIPS had started hinting at.[3] Soon, however, the OAPI ceased to be seen as the most appropriate source of expertise and resources for Djibouti. Although defining itself as 'Francophone Africa' had seemed appropriate, closer interactions with the OAPI saw the emergence of differences in culture, geography and economic and political traditions, and Djibouti turned to an alternative network for IP support:

> The Organisation covers in practice a very clearly defined geographical area – it mainly covers West Africa. Djibouti is located in a very different economical space, namely the Gulf. And in this area, countries have developed their laws completely independently, so we thought it would be more appropriate for us to work on an independent model, like our economic partners...(former member of the Ministry of Trade)

This ambivalence has important resonances with the postcolonial position of the country, still strongly linked to its French and francophone history, whilst turning to the Middle East in its new, growing relationships – with many investments stemming, for example, from Yemen or Saudi Arabia. In the field of IP, this meant a change of strategy, by which Djibouti had briefly dipped into a system that would have provided it with a certain form of expertise and legal models, before turning towards one in which the work to be done would essentially be carried out at the national level, independently.

In 2002, eight years after its encounter with the OAPI, Djibouti accessed the World Intellectual Property Organization (WIPO),[4] engaging with a new and different type of network of support and information. As a result, it ratified several legal documents in a relatively short period of time, in order to satisfy the conditions of accession to WIPO; the Paris Convention and the Berne Convention were therefore both also signed in 2002, enlisting a number of textual materials within the emerging network of Djiboutian IP.[5] It is telling of the superficiality of some of the processes at play here that for a long

---

2 For some background on the OAPI and its relation to TRIPS, see, for example, Matip (2008).
3 Loi no 63/AN/94/3eme L Portant Adhesion de la Republique de Djibouti à l'Accord de Bangui instituant l'OAPI, 26 November 1994.
4 Loi no 150/AN/02/4eme L Portant Adhesion de la Republique de Djibouti aux Conventions Internationales Relatives à la Propriété Intellectuelle 31 January 2004.
5 On WIPO, see, for example, May (2007).

time the website of WIPO indicated that Djibouti had an existing law on patents, when it in fact it never had. At one level, the process was significant: Djibouti moved from having had no engagement with IP, for almost 20 years and since its emergence as an independent state, to being member of WIPO, having one law of relevance (albeit non-applied), and having brought IP to the political table. At another level, the decisions taken had required only limited changes at the local level, mobilized very few actors in a minor way, and were unlikely to immediately place either constraints or entitlement on any of those involved. IP started emerging as a new actant in Djibouti but this emergence remained sketchy and limited.

TRIPS and local transformations

With the signing of TRIPS, Djibouti was therefore set a significant task. Not only did it need to create new legislation in a field where there was almost no pre-existing expertise, but it also needed to make some significant investments towards new institutions. As far as patents where concerned, the onus of this task was set primarily on the Ministry for Trade and Industry – the main focus of this section. Looking beyond the label, this originally meant that it was a task to be undertaken by one particular member of staff in that ministry, who had in fact very limited support because expertise was not spread around.

The deadline granted to Djibouti, as a least-developed country (LDC), to implement a new law on industrial property was extended over the years and was eventually set at 1 January 2013, with a possibility of delaying the creation of pharmaceutical patents until 2016 (Deere, 2010). Arguably, this is a significant period of time, but, in the case of a country like Djibouti with no pre-existing patent law or engagement with the specificities of pharmaceutical patents, the task required is also a major effort of policy-making, for a law that may not be of any immediate benefit to the country and in a context where all governmental resources are very limited. The technicality of the discussions surrounding the implications of TRIPS for developing countries, and for LDCs in particular, gives a sense of the challenges at play in this process in a country where no one has historically been trained in IP, because IP did not exist, but it also offers a striking contrast with the set of concerns that arise in this context, some of which I explore below. Beside these new rules, expectations of an effective system meant that the task would need to be accomplished more thoroughly than had been the case for the 1996 attempt at creating rights for authors. For the World Trade Organization (WTO), TRIPS needs to (or needs to make others) generate pharmaceutical patents as an active tool, produce written rules that should circulate back to the WTO, create new institutions that will ensure that all those that relate to TRIPS comply with its dispositions and, most importantly, generate some form of social mobilization – 'legal compliance'.

In 2004, when I paid my first visits to the office officially in charge of implementing TRIPS, the process of translation had already started, and the process of legal drafting continued until the law was finally adopted in 2009 – though the system is still not effective in practice, as I explain below. In 2004, the office dealing with TRIPS had not yet been labelled as being 'about' IP, and the directorship for industrial property within the Ministry of Trade was only created as part of the process of generating IP as a policy area, the domain and the title coproducing each other. The process at the time was carried out by one individual, deemed to be the only person in Djibouti to have some degree of expertise in IP. The process of adoption of the law was a mixture of attention to the textual translation of the TRIPS obligations and of inherent scepticism about the possible consequences of not following the process properly. In the process of drafting the law, the specific policy consequences raised, for example, by pharmaceutical patents were overshadowed by a focus on producing a text that could be returned to the WTO and be formally compliant with the obligations TRIPS had set. This focus on the text of the law as opposed to its policy implications is understandable if reflecting again on the processes at stake here, and on the general context of emergence of IP as something that did not exist yet as a policy field, and in fact only mainly existed as a text sent by the WTO. Interestingly, very few traces were left of the process, and policy documents and formal proposals or drafts to be circulated across the ministry were not available. Instead, for example, informants explained that most of the work was either their 'own drafts' or verbal discussions. Again, this particular approach is understandable given that only one person at a time was involved (the first individual mentioned, and later his deputy, who replaced him in this position and was formally made director of industrial property). The process of drafting the law was described by one of these two individuals directly involved as being 'very very slow, very long', and remained tainted by a faint scepticism about the actual implications that it might have:

> The way [TRIPS] works is that it doesn't change anything unless someone complains about what you are doing...we are so small that hopefully they won't complain! (member of the Ministry of Trade)

In 2009, the Parliament in Djibouti adopted, for the first time, a law on the protection of patents.[6] The text of the law drew inspiration from models suggested by WIPO and the laws of other states, as well as a general reflection on the specific needs of Djibouti. The text itself is carefully drafted and generally brings Djibouti into formal compliance with the demands of TRIPS – and

---

6 www.wipo.int/wipolex/en/text.jsp?file_id=216578.

my aim here is not that of a study in compliance. The safeguards provided for pharmaceutical patents in particular are not used to their full extent, as is commonly the case – and I return to this issue below when discussing the laws of Ghana. In particular, by adopting the law without isolating pharmaceuticals from other subjects of patentability, Djibouti did not make use of the extended deadline that the Doha Declaration granted to LDCs in relation to pharmaceuticals. Compulsory licences are integrated as a possible response to public health crises (Articles 61–6), as well as the French system of *ex officio* licences (Articles 67–76), whose compliance with TRIPS has been questioned (Pires de Carvalho, 2010). The Bolar exception, enabling tests and trials to be carried out on competing products before the expiration of a patent, is not integrated in the law, and not all flexibilities have been formally integrated yet, which is understandable given the task at hand and the limited amount of resources and staff working on this issue. Some of these may also not be of immediate relevance to Djibouti, and the Bolar exemption is, for example, not obviously useful at the moment given the absence of laboratories and local industry. Some of the limitations of the law are understandable given the context of policy-making and limited opportunities for discussions, exchange and reviewing, and also given the way expertise was only concentrated in the hands of very few. In addition, as is the case with the Ghanaian legal implementation process that I will detail below, the text of the law is a settlement that may be transformed and revised with subsequent amendments if weaknesses arise. However, the most significant challenge to the law at the moment is the potential to transform its creation on paper into an institutional actor.

Patent law, like any other regulation, is not self-enacting, however, and its ability to function is tightly dependent on institutional settings. For the law to have effects, a working patent office has to be created, and a complex system for checks and enforcements on the market and import system has to be deployed. In Djibouti, this entire institutional framework will need to be built and made to function in order for the law adopted in 2009 to be made effective. The country does not yet have governmental institutions in place for the licensing of drugs, and the import system, as I describe in Chapter 4, has very limited governmental influence. Even the creation of a patent office, the very first step in constituting a much more complex system, has been challenging. The 2009 law was followed almost immediately by a decree that creates a Patent Office in Djibouti, also adopted in 2009. In July 2011, a phone interview with one of the individuals in charge of IP started with the following statement:

> As it happens, I was just on the phone with our Minister! We have finally found a set of rooms in which we can set up the patent office... We have been waiting since 2009, but it is finally sorted. Now we just have to wait to find space for the staff who are

currently occupying those offices to be reallocated elsewhere! (IP policy-maker)

This is a good example of how day-to-day circumstances can come into conflict with the translation of law into practice. The drafting process of the law, the building of adequate expertise to enable a few in Djibouti to do so and the training of further personnel to become part of the patent office were all essential and difficult steps to put into place. Finding adequate buildings in which to establish these people, however, was a less foreseeable yet similarly tricky part of the process. The patent office was finally inaugurated in Djibouti in February 2012. At the date of writing, however, it was still not fully operational, staff were not fully yet trained, and its capacity to operate was therefore limited. Focusing on pharmaceutical patents, I question in the next chapter how some of the reactions of those involved in the procurement of pharmaceutical products to the idea of patents being created give an insight into some of the many issues that the practical operation of the patent office are likely to raise inside and outside of its walls.

TRIPS and Ghanaian IP

Turning to the translation of TRIPS as textual material in Ghana, the story is slightly different, and this in turn comes from a contrasting historical landscape for IP. In the era that directly followed decolonization, Ghana relied on the system that had been created during the colonial era. The first Ghanaian laws on IP were adopted in 1992, and Ghanaian IP therefore emerged very shortly before the adoption of TRIPS, creating difficulties in implementation:

> When I first took over we didn't have laws. We were using UK laws. That was before 1992. In 1992, we came up with our own law. We started using it in 1996, but that is when TRIPS came in. We were novices, and then they changed it. And we are not an LDC, so there are no flexibilities. (IP policy-maker)

A number of themes emerge from this quote, echoing some of the complexity of IP in Africa. Originated as a colonial product, IP was only owned by Ghana as a socio-political project for a very short period of time before global institutions and rules came to replace the former colonial system.[7] The ethical issues at stake here in the way the regulation of knowledge has been shaped by outside forces are clear. Arguably, IP has shifted from colonial origins to complex, neocolonial forms of influences in which local efforts to shape policies have been rendered difficult by global transformations.[8]

---

7 On the history of IP in Africa more generally, see, for example, Adewopo (2002).
8 See, for critical engagement with some of these issues, Drahos and Braithwaite (2002).

The implementation of TRIPS in Ghana is the result of a slow and tentative process, in ways that are not fundamentally dissimilar to the experience of Djibouti. Looking closely at the transformation of TRIPS into current laws on patents in Ghana highlights interesting aspects of TRIPS, and interesting aspects of the legal and political landscape of Ghana. TRIPS as a text was introduced in Ghana through the Attorney General's office, where most of the patent-related expertise is located. The prescription of TRIPS called for the existing text of the law to be replaced or revised.[9] If looking firstly at the changes made to the letter of the 1992 law when implementing TRIPS, several changes can be noted: the extension of the term of patents from 10 to 20 years (s. 12); the limits and boundaries set on insufficient local working as a justification for compulsory licensing (s. 14); and the removal of the ability of the Ghanaian government to temporarily lift patents on pharmaceuticals (Cohen et al, 2005). These are some of the key changes required by TRIPS, all potentially problematic in their own way if one is concerned with access to medicines. The general movement followed by the law is one of broadening significantly the influence of holders of pharmaceutical patents. The political economy underlying TRIPS is apparent in these changes, with the space created for patents expanding to the detriment of flexibilities for states.

Those changes also echo many of the transformations that developing state laws across the world underwent following the introduction of TRIPS (Correa, 2000). The flexibilities that TRIPS offers to states in relation to pharmaceutical patents have often been held to be underused in developing countries. The most commonly reported reason for this is pressure from developed states, including the US, to make developing countries comply more strongly with TRIPS than they actually have to – known as 'TRIPS-plus'. The story suggested in Ghana is different in its details, if not in its outcome. Ghana has made active use of some flexibilities: 'In 2006, the government used a compulsory licence for three drugs, so we are using some flexibilities.' (IP policy-maker). There, a local company was granted the right to produce antiretrovirals (ARVs) that were still under patents. Ghana did not face significant political opposition at the time, although interestingly, this compulsory licence was later made redundant by the regulations imposed by the Global Fund that now finances the procurement of ARVs in Ghana (I come back to this point in Chapter 6). Although compulsory licences have therefore been actively used by the government, other flexibilities have not been fully integrated into the new law. The reasons behind this lack of integration, however, are not so much direct pressure as the difficulties of fully

---

9   Ghana Patent Act 2003 (Act 657).

integrating local needs in a complex new legal system, difficulties shared here with Djibouti:

> For me, in terms of TRIPS, the first thing is that the laws are TRIPS compliant. But whether we have incorporated all the flexibilities that we could...the answer is yes and no. For example, we have compulsory licences, but there are other things we don't have...So in terms of flexibility, for example, we have no Bolar exception. So now we are incorporating this Bolar exception into the law. (IP policy-maker)

The lack of engagement with some of the possibilities and flexibilities introduced by TRIPS can be understood better if exploring the process of transformation of the 1992 Patent Law into a TRIPS compliant regime. It is useful to return here to the history of the implementation of TRIPS, which reflects some of the difficulties in assessing the meaning and impact of global pressures on developing states. As highlighted above, the adoption of TRIPS overlapped with the very first steps towards a Ghanaian IP system, and appeared just as the 1992 law was starting to be used. The description provided below of the timeframe of adoption of the different legal texts at stake is a striking account of some of the difficulties of those facing these transformations:

> So in 1996, we had to break this new system. I had just finished my masters in IP, and then I came back and this had been signed. And we were expected by 2000 to come up with new laws. And we knew it wasn't enough time. (IP policy-maker)

This quote is a clear illustration of the difficulties that those trying to engage with IP in Ghana would have faced at the time. The struggles of actors trying to establish a new system, and to see it made redundant by international decisions just at a time when it was about to fall into place, are illustrative of some of the contingencies that emerging legislative and policy systems have to face. This situation was created by the particular form of the political and expertise networks in Ghana, which are not necessarily overlapping – a situation which is not unique to Ghana:

> Basically some politicians went away, and they signed. They didn't know what they were doing. No one in Africa knew what they were doing. (IP policy-maker)

The same informant continued, describing the process of adoption of the new laws, and the response to this difficult political and policy situation, as follows:

> So the government hurried to pass the law, and you know, I was just fresh out of my masters, and I told them that we shouldn't let the laws go through because we haven't put all the flexibilities

[in place]. They said look at the process, how complicated it is already. Let's pass it like this, then we will make some changes later. And now we are in 2012, and still making these changes. It takes time, you have to consult, and sometimes what stakeholders want doesn't even conform with TRIPS. So we started the reforms in 2009, but now thankfully all amendments have been registered, there is a consensus, so we hope to be able to get this through Parliament. (IP policy-maker)

The pressures described here, which resulted in an underuse of some of the TRIPS flexibilities, are of a different nature from those relating to the forceful legislative and political TRIPS-plus pressures that led various developing states to go further than TRIPS required them to in their national legislation, but no less problematic.[10] The difficulties faced here are linked to the feasibilities and possibilities created by fast-moving networks and requirements in an environment where resources and expertise are limited. The pressures on the few charged with the significant task of implementing TRIPS meant that the process was inevitably rushed and incomplete, to the knowledge of those in charge who had to compromise between aspirations and feasibility. At the core of this debate are the interlinked issues of knowledge and expertise. These are relevant both to the developments in Djibouti and in Ghana, and of importance for all aspects of the stories of TRIPS and patents in these places. A careful engagement with the notion of expertise here, and the significant difficulties faced in creating and fostering 'experts' of the various key issues at stake, is essential.

Expertise and IP in Djibouti and Ghana

The fluidity of the notion of expertise, and the progressive enrolment of new actors in what have traditionally been defined as expert positions, have been explored in great depth in the work of Steven Epstein (1996) and Michel Callon et al. (2009), for example. Building on some of the core elements of ANT and post-ANT traditions, these works revisit how experts are constructed through processes of knowledge acquisition and social and political engagement. A mixture of individual connections, the gathering of materials, engagement with a particular form of discourse, are analysed as participating in the making and unmaking of technical expertise. The position of ANT on the concept of 'knowledge' is intimately related to this fluid approach to expertise. Bruno Latour has emphasized how knowledge had to be understood as a process rather than a defining concept, and engaged with in the progressive material construction of knowledge: 'becoming familiar with distant events requires...kings, offices, sailors,

---

10 On the issue of TRIPS-plus, see, for example, Gervais (2007) and Sell (2007).

timber, lateen rigs and trade' (Latour, 1987, p. 223). IP expertise and IP as a particular field of knowledge production – as well as knowledge protection – is tightly dependent on the material possibilities available to other networks. The produced nature of knowledge, and of expertise, also implies a close inter-relationship between the two. Processes of producing and redefining expertise, and networks of expertise, also impact on the very definition of what the object of knowledge is – so, defining how IP expertise is characterized also performs a particular definition of IP itself. In this coproduction of expertise and domain, legal fields are themselves transformed by the availability and nature of experts and expertise. The constitution of both knowledge and expertise through a series of codes, materials and discourses results in the shaping of domains and objects in different ways through different networks. The very nature of IP as a legal domain depends on the social situatedness of those who create its rules, implement its mechanisms, are expected to follow its requirements and experience their consequences.

The transformations experienced by IP as a field of expertise in the last 15 to 20 years, at least in particular settings, have been described amongst others by Stephen Hiltgartner (2009; see also Kapczynski, 2008). The movement of extension of expertise from a field of specialists to one where lay experts have an increasing role to play is particularly notable in issues relating to pharmaceutical patents. IP has progressively moved, in this area, from a technical domain to one of significant public concern and mobilization. In this sense, the example of TRIPS at the international level has shown how we have moved towards a model in which IP mobilizes publics. In turn, this new form of public participation in IP has produced new publics with their own form of knowledge and expertise about IP and what IP is, with groups such as Médecins sans Frontières having grown their own understanding of IP and how they interact with issues of more traditional concerns. Patient groups, in particular AIDS patients' groups, have developed a particular form of expertise and interest in the issue of IP. In this process, not only are publics transformed, but IP itself as a field, as a network, has become reshaped, translated into something very different: in our context, commonly portrayed as a barrier erected between patients and treatment, or patients and life. Moving to the localities of Djibouti and Ghana, however, the engagement with IP, expertise levels in this area and general public involvement in the field differed fundamentally from the global public engagement seen elsewhere.[11] Some of this implied that issues relating to access to health relocated IP within a much more fluid set of difficulties and hurdles, and I will explore this relocation when engaging

---

11 For a critical background on the concept of civil society in Africa, see Comaroff and Comarrof (1999).

specifically with access to treatment. However, the issues raised by expertise in Ghana and Djibouti, in relation to IP itself, are a useful point to emphasize. Expertise on IP was in both cases predominantly the domain of a few, with others having little engagement with the issue of pharmaceutical patents (and I will discuss some of the circulatory issues that this generated in local health networks in the next chapter).

The situation in Djibouti, as illustrated above, was a particularly striking example of how limited expertise can be in a specialist area such as IP in an LDC. In the course of the fieldwork, I only met two people who considered that they had specific expertise in IP, and the task of drafting new laws and creating institutions was contained between them, in turn, over the years of this research. One of these two experts summarized the situation in these terms:

> Well, our IP situation is 'very little, very bad'! There are very few people aware of it, and hardly anything is done about it. (member of the Ministry of Trade)

In Ghana, where IP has existed in some form, independently, for about 20 years, I expected to see a wider spread of actors with IP expertise. Institutionally, policy-makers involved with IP are located at the Attorney General's Chambers. When first contacts were made with the Chambers, I was directed towards the person who was described as 'the only person who will be able to give you information. And she will know everything. No one else will be able to help you, they don't really know.' (Member of the Attorney General's Chambers) Indeed this key person explained how being isolated in terms of having gained specific expertise impacted on their activity:

> What I do is interesting because we are understaffed. So I write the policy, I come up with the policy, then I implement it'. (IP policy-maker)

Efforts were being deployed to generate further expertise, and in particular grow the ability for 'users' of IP to play a more active role, either by applying for rights, or for granting these rights within the patent office. On the first issue, workshops and trainings were used to try, for example, to make inventors more able to use the possibilities that IP could offer to them:

> For patents, we go to research institutions, universities, etc... We explain that we are doing some reforms. I have been talking about compulsory licences, flexibilities etc... Today we are running a national workshop on patents, and raising awareness. We have 24 applicants, we will run a seminar and teach them how to draft patent applications. Then we have a competition and the winner will be sent to Korea. (IP policy-maker)

In relation to the patent office itself, expertise is generated through a mixture of training and direct external support:

> At the moment, the patent office only checks formalities. We also have agreements with WIPO and ARIPO [African Regional Intellectual Property Organisation] to assess novelty. Or we look as well at whether the patent is protected in other countries, and if so we ask to see their reports and here we can see all the details. We have an issue with expertise, and we are working on this. So at least I have some knowledge. And I also have one colleague who trained with the Swedish office and one with the Munich office. And in reality, a lot of it happens at ARIPO, before it gets to us. (IP policy-maker)

The dis-location of the IP network here is interesting, in several respects. Firstly, training is organized in part through a particular form of technology transfer, from Europe to Africa. Secondly, and maybe more interestingly, the practice of Ghanaian IP takes place, in part, outside of Ghana itself. Some of the evaluations and substantial judgments surrounding the granting of patents is done in regional rather than national offices, leaving the generation of patents as a largely exogenous process, responding to the limitations of local expertise, but also maintaining a certain form of decentralization of the network.

In this context, capacity-building, and in particular the role of WIPO, an organization which has capacity-building as one of its core aims, was extensively discussed, raising the strong ambivalence experienced by local policy-makers towards the institution (and I return to some of these issues more generally in Chapter 3). Although responses to WIPO in both countries showed that, indeed, it had played a part in shaping IP, WIPO's effects in growing expertise remained questionable. As phrased by an informant in Djibouti:

> The TRIPS agreement was a great opportunity for WIPO! Before, no one had ever heard of them in developing countries, now they are everywhere. They come and give presentations everywhere they can! (member of the Ministry of Trade)

The slight cynicism about the interests at stake here was followed through in further discussion about the role played by WIPO and how much support it actually had been. In Ghana, the history of WIPO's involvement was also interesting:

> Initially, we got drafts from WIPO, but we didn't adopt them. So they'd send you model drafts. But here, stakeholders decide, so we changed things, we didn't send it to WIPO, because there was no time. And later, I went back to the WIPO models and realized

that actually the gaps there were in our laws were the ones that
WIPO had warned us about. (IP policy-maker)

WIPO's approach is to provide models for IP laws that can be used when drafting national legislation. It is maybe not surprising that this approach is received with a certain degree of ambivalence by local actors. IP is a field highly permeated by the 'outside', and the entire domain remains received with a certain wariness and concern for local interests and opportunities. The standardization of models as an approach to capacity-building and technology transfer is certainly of concern to actors aware of some of the tensions at stake in this field. For those who are essentially working at developing a certain sense of ownership over IP as a domain, the need to have a home-grown IP system is essential – ownership over the growth of a new system for the allocation of property. Interestingly, Ghana's nascent networks of expertise, albeit limited in absolute terms, make it one of the leaders in the field of IP in its sub-region of West Africa (Deere, 2010), giving a useful perspective on the difficulties faced across West Africa more generally, and possibly across African LDCs:

Respondent: And then states have different levels of expertise too, so some of the LDCs have no expertise at all. We try to raise awareness there too, encourage them to do something.
Interviewer: And do you get a response?
Res: No, because no one is in charge. So no one is interested. They don't have the knowledge, or see why it is an issue. And that makes it difficult for a harmonized ECOWAS [Economic Community of West African States] market too. (IP policy-maker)

In a vicious cycle, IP in Africa finds itself limited by the sheer absence of expertise in this legal domain. The foreign origins of the concepts, systems and institutions, and of the regulatory map that has been drawn by TRIPS, makes it very difficult for local actors to become 'interested' (in the most usual sense of the term, but also in the ANT sense of 'interessement'). This is highly problematic in perpetuating mechanics of exclusion and domination that transcend IP networks at most of their levels and in many of their particular nodes.

As mentioned earlier, IP as a domain has been characterized in recent years as being increasingly permeated by public involvement and interest. In a context where IP is still nascent, and where expertise and interest amongst policy-makers is still very limited, it will come as no surprise that public involvement in relation to IP is very limited in Djibouti and Ghana – making, once again, IP very different as a domain from what it is in a Western location (in Chapter 3, I explore how this impacts on the deployment of IP legislation in practice). In terms of law-making, some efforts to involve publics were deployed in Ghana, a country with a strong tradition of public participation in policy-making, opening some possibilities for building some bridges between expert knowledge and lay expertise. For example, policy decisions involve some degree of consultation with relevant stakeholders – in accordance with common practice in Ghana:

> But here the stakeholders have to agree to the policy. So I give them options. And I show them best practice in developing and developed countries. For example, for trademarks, we signed the Singapore agreement. So they refer to taste marks, smell marks etc.…So I gave them the options, but they were like 'What? Who is going to taste? Who is going to smell?' (IP policy-maker)[12]

The specifics of global IP and local issues and practices come head to head here, in a way that the informant providing this quote thought was amusing, in spite of their acknowledgment of the seriousness of some of the underlying issues. New developments and emerging concepts can simply appear as inadequate and truly strange to local stakeholders. When there is an option to simply refuse to engage with them, as was the case here, it is likely to be just left aside.

> Again, when I explained sound marks, they were like 'How are you going to do that?' If it is something we can do, we will, but sometimes it just doesn't work. (IP policy-maker)

Overall, the networks of expertise that determine the development of IP laws in Ghana and Djibouti, and their current limitations, are essential to understanding the very nature of IP in both countries. Although direct comparisons are not the most useful way to approach such a project, some common elements can be identified across both case studies. In particular, the limited circles of expertise are obvious in both countries, where an exhaustive list of those with IP expertise could easily be drawn up. The scale of the contrast between those networks and European contexts, for example, remains striking: ultimately the core of the expertise remains essentially in the hands of very few actors and, both in Djibouti and Ghana, one individual actor appeared as having led most of the complex process of implementation of TRIPS.

---

[12] For the text of the Singapore Treaty on the Law of Trademarks, see www.wipo.int/treaties/en/ip/singapore/singapore_treaty.html. See also, for commentary, Dinwoodie and Dreyfuss (2009).

Questioning the 'TRIPS project'

The final issue I want to raise in this chapter relates to the views expressed by IP experts in Djibouti and Ghana about TRIPS as a project; specifically, I explore in this section what they saw as being the significance of the expansion of IP – in particular pharmaceutical patents – that TRIPS aims to generate.

Their views respond to a wide literature developed on TRIPS over the years in increasingly nuanced and subtle ways that seek to critique and engage with the effects of TRIPS on developing states (Sell, 2007; Deere, 2010; Shadlen et al., 2011). The findings from this research go in the direction of a cautious and conditional wariness of TRIPS, in Ghana and Djibouti, rather than outright opposition or challenge. Instead, the discourses of those engaging with the implementation of TRIPS project a general sense of scepticism over the potential benefits of the text in local networks, but also a general sense that its effects are actually likely to be quite limited, and therefore that its problematique may be different from what legal analyses of the text of TRIPS may suggest (e.g. Bass, 2002; Sun, 2004). This can be summarized as being linked both to an awareness of the many limitations that the transformation of law into practices can encounter, and to a general sense that IP is only a limited aspect of the broader issues of access to health, and a symptom rather than a cause of power imbalances.[13] Here, I introduce the perceptions of TRIPS as a project for those directly involved with its implementation. The responses in Djibouti and Ghana were more akin to a subtle cynicism towards the global project than to the open discontent that was visible elsewhere (including in high-profile instances such as the Pretoria trial that came to symbolize much of the TRIPS debate (Barnard, 2002; Sell, 2002a)).

A dominant theme in the discussion of what TRIPS signified for Djibouti and Ghana was the lack of usefulness that the text could have for local actors. Although they engaged with the theoretical benefits that IP could bring for development, and were aware of the global controversies surrounding TRIPS, those implementing IP in Djibouti, for example, also highlighted why the potential relevance of IP could only be a long-term one:

> In a context where all we have are industries just starting to emerge, some aspects of the text seem ill adapted. TRIPS is not flexible enough for developing states, and especially for least developed countries with a very small recent industry. (IP policy-maker)

---

13 The complexity of these links in general is well illustrated in Sell (2007).

This narrative highlighting the inadequacy of TRIPS to the current state of local industries, and therefore to local possibilities, also appeared in Ghana when discussing the possibilities of benefitting from pharmaceutical patents specifically:

Int: How likely do you think it is for any of these to file patent applications in the near future?
Res: That is a long way. A long way. What we are trying to do is to get our herbal medicines but you know in patents, traditional knowledge is an exception. Until that has changed, what we have required our researchers to do is to see how they can move the traditional knowledge to become a scientific knowledge so that the patent issue is dealt with. But it would take us a while. (National Drug Programme worker)

The issue of the transformation of knowledge from 'traditional' to 'scientific' is at the very core of some of the criticisms made of IP in general, and the issue of the valorization of knowledge only as far as it falls into particular networks of scientific and technological production is problematic (Dutfield and Posay, 1996; Hayden, 2003). The role of patents in generating and maintaining flows of power and influence that results in reinforcing the position of some at the expense of others is therefore a common criticism. If taking the example of pharmaceutical patents only, the physical production of materials able to fall within the remit of TRIPS is dependent on levels of approved expertise, scientific tools and IT technologies that are simply not available in localities like Djibouti and Ghana.

The active opposition to TRIPS that has been illustrated by global movements, or movements in other localities, was nonetheless mostly absent in both contexts. Instead, a certain scepticism and cynicism was often expressed towards the phenomenon at play here:

> You know, prior to TRIPS, we were not protecting patents, but instead the pharmaceutical industry were using trademarks, trade secrets, other things. The big firms used other tools to go around it...So patents, ok, if they want, let them call it whatever, incentive, whatever. For me what matters are also the killer diseases in Africa that no one is interested in. (IP policy-maker)

Much can be unpacked from this quote. Most striking to me is the general sense of frustration expressed by someone who has worked for many years at trying to engage with some of the problems shared across Africa and has seen TRIPS emerge as another symbolic tool in broader patterns of pressure and dominance. Here, the idea is that the power and influence that emerge from the global industry's position and practices pre-existed patents. Trademarks – IP rights that protect distinctive signs and symbols associated with particular companies – and the broader establishment of brands and manufacturers that they entail, enabled some producers to establish their influence independently from patents, for example (a point I return to in Chapter 5). The new legal entitlements created by patents become only significant in stabilizing practices that would have found a way of emerging in any case, and, indeed, did so in the past, in the view of this informant. Patents become a tool to perpetuate relationships, but not the cause of significant transformations in the networks. A certain feeling of disempowerment is also underlying this quote; options remain in terms of making adjustments, or responding to an emerging legal tool and legal framework, but, nonetheless, little can be done to engage with the broader challenges of TRIPS:

> We can do nothing apart from taking advantage of the provisions they have made under TRIPS and so the issue of breaking the law does not arise because we have already agreed as a country that we will be compliant... (IP policy-maker)

Overall TRIPS appeared essentially as an actor of very limited benefits and as the symptom of the more general patterns of disempowerment that have animated specific areas relevant to IP in the past, the relationships between African locales and the global pharmaceutical industry being an example.

Conclusion

The process of implementing TRIPS in both Ghana and Djibouti demonstrates some of the problematic movements that occur when IP travels to specific locales in Africa. The translation of a technical textual material designed in one corner of the globe into networks that had little influence on its design, and little to gain from its creation, raises practical and political issues. Although the forms of legal engagement prior to TRIPS were different in the contexts of Djibouti and Ghana, the ownership of IP as a local institution was similarly limited. The processes through which a new TRIPS-compliant law needed to emerge in Ghana and Djibouti differed, with Ghana being expected to transform texts that were already there, and Djibouti having to generate these texts for the first time. Similarly, 'intellectual property' as a domain existed in Ghana, even if it was still nascent, but some institutions, written laws and expertise could already be found. Nonetheless, the active role of any IP tool was still very limited, and any law that had emerged in Ghana had not had time to generate new impact or practices when TRIPS came into play. In both contexts, a significant legal apparatus with important consequences for what constitutes valuable knowledge, but also what constitutes legally valid entities such as particular drugs, was distributed to new actors with limited experience to translate it into the legal system. Their quiet scepticism of the benefits that may be derived from this text, and their general sense of disempowerment over the process, has much to say about the position of African locales in the design of valid or validated systems of knowledge across the globe. The processes of implementation were deployed in ways that can be described as highly localized and 'micro' in their appearance – in both cases, the text of the law was predominantly the work of an individual, the only genuine IP expert in the country. The process of adopting the law was also, in both cases, a very slow process, in which the law emerged as inherently incomplete. The ability of using the flexibilities offered by TRIPS, in turn, was highly constrained by time, and by lack of expertise. Although external pressures not to use the flexibilities were not reported in either cases, material impossibility prevented both IP offices from genuinely doing so, giving to the problems of flexibilities a very different form from that reported elsewhere. At the same time, the lack of significant concern over the impact that TRIPS may have on access to medicines in each context has much to say both about perceptions of what TRIPS may actually change in practice and about the current patterns of power and circulation that affect the public health networks of both Djibouti and Ghana. I turn to the former in Chapter 3.

3
From IP to Public Health in Djibouti and Ghana

The legal implementation of the Trade Related Aspects of Intellectual Property Rights (TRIPS) agreement (and the challenges it raised in terms of expertise and process of translation) is only a small aspect of what needs to be looked at in order to understand the effects of TRIPS and of patents as a source of formal regulation in Djibouti and Ghana. If understanding legal regulations as part of broader processes of social ordering, and as having ordering as one of the very aims of legal regulations, the next level of inquiry should question how TRIPS has transformed or is transforming local relationships and how pharmaceutical patents influence behaviour and practices. The significance of TRIPS on healthcare in specific localities is dependent on its ability, and of the ability of intellectual property (IP) regulations more broadly, to shape specific networks; in particular, the effect of pharmaceutical patents in general is codependent on their ability to ensure that drugs in breach of international standards of patents remain excluded from the territory concerned. And this implies that those importing drugs are aware of the rules and made to obey them. In order to understand the potential and actual effect of rules relating to pharmaceutical patents on social ordering in Ghana and Djibouti, it is thus essential to move away from the networks of IP *stricto sensu* and explore how TRIPS affects practices and behaviour in other offices. In both case studies, the picture emerging from this further investigation is one in which the limits and weaknesses of IP as a set of legal prescriptions are apparent and are a constitutive part of the system.

This chapter is divided into two parts and looks at some of the networked mechanics that affect the travels of both TRIPS and pharmaceutical patents in Djibouti and in Ghana. The focus and the set of issues that arise in both cases differ slightly and correspond to the various moments at which the processes at stake became visible. As explained in the previous chapter, the legal field of IP is newer in Djibouti than it is in Ghana, and institutions have not emerged yet in Djibouti in the way they have in Ghana, in response to IP as well as other issues. Both stories, however, illustrate the contrasts that are experienced between global discourses on IP and local responses; between official and non-official; between theory and practice. Through these two stories, I try to recapture some of the order and disorder in which pharmaceutical patents, and TRIPS as a set of rules and prescriptions, become entangled. Investigating the role of TRIPS in both Ghana and Djibouti, outside of the dedicated circles where it was implemented, was often a difficult process of chasing absences. Methodologically, it required some careful balancing between opening discussions with actors within, for example, the public health field, and avoiding performing the importance of TRIPS within circles where it may not have been relevant. In other words, it necessitated asking actors their opinions on and experiences of patents without framing interviews as being inherently 'about patents' in order to avoid an artificial emphasis on what may, for informants, not have been a crucially important affair.

Mainly, this chapter is a brief story of patents and TRIPS as elusive regulatory tools outside of their point of entry – a story that creates a significant contrast with the popular engagement with IP seen in other locations. The narrative here will be complemented by the analysis provided in the following chapters that go on to demonstrate how IP and patents play a significant role in shaping movements and practices in both countries, through routes that are not those officially set within the countries, but in fact result from mechanisms, including market mechanisms and (post)colonial sets of relationships that link Djibouti and Ghana to other localities. But here I focus on the self-defined 'legal route', or the traditional implementation route, followed by IP when entering both Djibouti and Ghana.

The travels of patents and TRIPS as regulatory scripts in Djibouti and Ghana

When discussing the potential impact of IP on healthcare in Djibouti and Ghana, or more broadly what stricter rules on IP and the introduction of patents may mean in each country, all public health actors I met emphasized that it did not and would not significantly matter to their practice. The potential importance of patents was often dismissed with a laugh, a smile, or other indications that the question was somehow misconstrued, and far removed from what was actually happening in the local public health field. For example, in Djibouti, it was explained to me that:

> This will not affect us in any way. For at least one good reason: international law doesn't mean anything here, and nobody will change the way they work because of it. It is utopic to think it will have any effect, no one will be interested here. (member of the Ministry of Health)

> As far as my job here is concerned, TRIPS is not gonna change anything. I can't see anyone being interested here, and I really can't imagine it changing anything. (private pharmacist)

Similarly, in Ghana, a pharmacist who had also previously worked for the Food and Drugs Board (FDB) explained:

> I can say with all certainty here it doesn't work. It doesn't work. It only works when a complaint is made to the Food and Drugs Board and they follow up on specific issues. Maybe somebody has been getting a product in Ghana and that still has a patent... But I think that sometimes the government overrules them because it's about the life of your citizens... It's not something that is really really implemented.

These statements contrast with the progressive mobilization of lay experts on IP in different fora (Barnard, 2002; Sell, 2002a), which may not be fully surprising in a context where the day-to-day urgencies public health actors deal with rarely involve the form of technical specificities of IP. Looking more closely at the processes at play here provides, nonetheless, a useful insight into the actual and potential workings of patents in both Djibouti and Ghana.

When talking to those very actors on whom the workings of patents depend – those who buy drugs, choose drugs, distribute drugs – in Djibouti and Ghana, it seemed that the patents may simply be irrelevant to most of those they are supposed to mobilize. Some of the comments brought back questions that related more broadly to understandings of law itself, and its own significance – law in general, and international law in particular. The ambiguities and ambivalences of local actors towards the influence of law in reshaping local orderings appeared throughout this research, in different forms. For those aware of the requirements of TRIPS, these statements took an informed format. In Ghana, as an example, some of the nuances of how to play with the law were explained in an interesting way: 'because we have to be compliant we cannot break the laws and so we have to go round the law' (National Drug Programme worker).

This particular perspective on the law, and its indeterminate role as a social actor, permeated many of the interviews carried out in the course of this research, and is an important background to rethinking why the translation of IP from written law to law in action was neither a simple nor a certain process in either Djibouti or Ghana. In a useful summary of some of the difficulties in defining the legal/illegal boundary, a Ghanaian wholesaler characterized some import practices breaching the terms of licensing regulations – that I come back to below – as: 'It's illegal, but it is allowed... Or at least it happens.' I will return in the concluding chapter to the questions this study raises in terms of how to approach the law, and of the meaning of ANT and post-ANT approaches for understanding the legal, but these questionmarks about the direct relevance of the letter of the law to permeating policy institutions across governments are important here as background to the difficulties for IP to circulate across new policy areas.

When trying to understand further the reasons why IP as a written set of rules did not seem to mobilize actors in a traditional, implementation format, other issues need to be considered, and specific factors exist that explain further the distance and potential discrepancy between the translation of TRIPS into a material set of written rules in both countries and its enrolment as a fully social actor in political networks. For most actors interviewed in this case study, and in particular in the public health field, TRIPS and patents were a 'non-social issue'. They did not see how it could affect them; they believed that it would not become any more than a set of rules excluded from active networks. Again, the issue of expertise is relevant here. Although debates on IP and access to medication have grown in many different networks, knowledge of these within public health networks was very limited in Djibouti – and to a lesser extent in Ghana. On several occasions, informants in Djibouti acknowledged TRIPS as something they knew about, but when asked further questions about it they seemed unsure about its substance. This was particularly explicit in one interview script:

> Of course I know what TRIPS is!... can you remind me again, what does it say exactly? (member of the Ministry of Health)

But the lack of expertise on IP was also referred to by most public health actors:

> I don't know much about this whole issue – only what I have read in the press. (member of the Ministry of Health)

> The problem here is that no one has any kind of expertise here. There are a few pharmacists, but they won't understand what it is about. TRIPS, everyone talks about it but no one knows what it is about, so it just won't change anything! (member of the Ministry of Health)

Most public health informants also mentioned having received only very little official information about IP, or surprisingly sometimes about other aspects of IP than pharmaceutical patents:

> I am not interested in patent law, and I know hardly anything about it – I have followed some training a while ago, but it had to do with software and issues like that, not with drugs... (member of the Ministry of Health)

Similarly, in Ghana, part of the difficulties in translating patents into effective tools that regulate imports and marketing relate to the diffusion of expertise and information across networks, and beyond the small circle of IP:

> For sure, it is about educating policy-makers. The ministry of health, trade, customs, need to understand the rules. If there are any problems at customs, custom staff need to understand.
>
> And at the moment, they don't really understand. There is no real continuity in the chain. We need more workshops, more awareness. (IP policy-maker)

The workings and processes behind the lack of interessement of some crucial actors in issues surrounding pharmaceutical patents differ slightly in the contexts of Djibouti and Ghana. In the following sections, I question in turn some of the connections and lack thereof that explain the discrepancy between the letter of the law and its seizing by those who are supposed to be influenced by it. In Djibouti (as covered in the previous chapter), IP is still at a very nascent stage. The relevant regulations have only just been introduced on paper, and the institutions that they will depend on have only just been created. It is therefore to be expected that only a limited degree of mobilization has occurred in relation to TRIPS beyond its specific entry point in the country. Nonetheless, the global debates that have surrounded TRIPS in the past 15 years, and the significant concerns that have been raised by access to medication, project a certain expectation that those involved in access to healthcare in a least-developed country would have to a degree been mobilized by these issues. The situation in Djibouti is interesting both for what it tells us about the challenges of interessement in IP, but also for what the circumstances there highlight about the broken nature of the networks that TRIPS and patents are most dependent on – which may or not become transformed in the longer term. In Ghana on the other hand, national laws already existed that have been transformed following TRIPS, but which have had institutional support for several years. The lack of interessement of public health actors in patents therefore holds a different type of significance. I start by presenting some of the interesting elements that Djibouti raises in relation to the response of public health actors to the emergence of pharmaceutical patents.

Circulating in Djibouti

The first point to raise at the outset, and that I will come back to when discussing more closely public health and access to medicines, is that the importance that patents may have in Djibouti was inherently limited by the fact that the drugs that patients depended on tended to be in the public domain. This made the issue of patents on drugs in Djibouti – and Ghana, to a different extent – one that ran beyond, and was different in nature from, the issue of access to 'modern' drugs. Consequently, the case of AIDS, which has been used as symbolic of the problems of IP, appears as being in fact a peculiar one.[1] I will explain in Chapter 4 that the links between medicines and patents are more complex than the straightforward assumption that out-of-patent drugs are not in any way affected by patents anymore,[2] but, as a starting point, it is useful to acknowledge that the indifference of public health actors stems in part from their self-distancing from discourses on access to 'modern drugs':

> The drugs we need are very basic medication, they're not under patents anymore. (member of the Ministry of Health)
>
> If you look at the health situation here, most problems could be solved without access to 'modern drugs'. What we really need is paracetamol, aspirin, a few antibiotics, some antiseptic and some anti-diarrheic. All of these are in the public domain anyways, and don't cost anything! Our real concern is first: how to get those to the population? We are really far from there, so modern drugs will probably not be a concern for a very long time. (member of the Ministry of Health)

Nonetheless, the lack of mobilization of public health actors for IP and patents can be seen as having deeper roots in the governmental structures of the country.

The traces left by TRIPS in the public health networks of Djibouti when this research was carried out were very limited. In particular, actors all emphasized that they had received little information about the substance of TRIPS. Whilst one could question whether this could be simply explained by the fact that the main period of this fieldwork was carried out when TRIPS was just starting to be implemented, it is worth bearing in mind that the World Health Organization (WHO), World Intellectual Property Organization (WIPO) and the World Trade Organization (WTO) all started the process of capacity-building several years prior to this research. In fact, mobilization is important not only as an outcome of legal implementation, but also in order to enrich the process of local translation of the law.

TRIPS as a textual material was present in at least one form in public health networks in 2004 – it was in the Djibouti Ministry of Health, in a report

---

[1] I return to the links between IP and AIDS treatment in Chapter 6, but their problematique was highlighted in a wide-range of papers, for example, Lamptey (2003) and Dolmo (2001).

[2] An assumption that has been used extensively by the pharmaceutical industry to try to argue that the issue of access has nothing to do with pharmaceutical patents (e.g. Attaran and Gillepsie, 2001) – an assumption challenged since then by many others (Sell, 2007).

published by the WTO and the WHO on TRIPS and public health (WTO/WHO, 2002a). But this was passive material, sitting at the corner of a desk, and not discussed by the official sitting at this same desk until I mentioned it and it was brushed aside as something that 'was sent to us'. I return to this example below. Overall, TRIPS as a set of prescriptions appears largely weak outside the particular office where it is being implemented. The impact of this lack of mobilization is double: on the one hand, if TRIPS only mobilizes actors in one particular office, it is unlikely to be followed with practical effects; on the other hand, if TRIPS has not been integrated within the health sector, it might mean that there will not be any coordinated action in response to the impact of TRIPS on public health. Ideally, in order to develop a public health-oriented approach to pharmaceutical patents regulation, public health actors should also have been involved in the debates before the law was adopted and, indeed, fed into policy-making. This was done to a limited extent at later stages of the drafting of the law, but the lack of initial interest kept this participation to a minimum. This indifference is also particularly interesting for its obvious contrast with the significant mobilization that the debate on IP and health has generated in other contexts, as has been well documented, for example, in the context of South Africa (Heywood, 2009; Muriu, 2009). Part of the significance of this study is, I hope, to return to the global South some of its inherent diversity and complexity.

In this section, I question how the circulation of IP as a legal domain, and of TRIPS as a particular international agreement, is influenced by the specific shape of policy networks in Djibouti. In particular, the section considers to what extent the production of a defined 'pharmaceutical patents network' is hampered by the lack of connections between different, isolated parts of this possible – yet so far imaginary – network. I focus here on the story of the circulation of TRIPS in Djibouti, and of its limitations, and link in particular the difficulties of circulation of TRIPS and the difficulties I had, as a researcher, in circulating across policy fields when carrying out this fieldwork – both of these aspects of the research as a process in generating findings being symbolic of the disconnectedness within policy networks.

On governments as 'punctualized' units

A significant part of the legal literature on the impact of TRIPS on 'developing countries' tends to discuss how 'countries', 'states' and 'governments' react to the text (e.g. Scherer and Watal, 2002; Zainol et al., 2011). The notion of stability behind the term government is one that is often assumed – and in some cases, indeed, the coherent action of governments and the stable connections that hold them can justify their terminological punctualization.

Andrew Barry, amongst others, has questioned the reductionist nature that the notion government can often have:

> If we consider complexity as an index of irreducibility, then one of the intended and imagined effects of governments has been to reduce complexity and to produce a unified and economic order, an order that can be summed up. The very popularity of the idea of 'the state', conceived as a functional and indivisible unit, attests of the prevalence of this view. (Barry, 2002)

Rather than being stable blackboxes, the networks surrounding IP in Djibouti – and to a different extent in Ghana – were disjointed and fragile. This section introduces some of the manifestations of this fragility and its implications for TRIPS and its circulation. In so doing, it presents some of the reasons why TRIPS as prescription is not constructed as having effects outside of the specific office where it is being implemented. It suggests that one of the key features of the environment in which patents are expected to grow in Djibouti is the absence of a coherent governmental network where IP can be enrolled; it explores how the shape of institutional connections can participate in understanding the action – or absence of action – of IP as prescriptive rules in Djibouti. When looking at pharmaceutical patents in Djibouti, many of the people who could be expected to work together on this issue, or would need to work together for patents to produce effects, were in fact in complete isolation from one another.

This section revisits the possibility of TRIPS and patents producing any effects within questions raised by the punctualization of policy networks in Djibouti – and highlights the fragility of constituted networks that is hidden behind terms such as 'governments' or 'international organizations'. It highlights how the difficulties met when trying to circulate between actors from different 'fields' for the purpose of this research soon illustrated the lack of connections between different networks and provided essential elements for trying to understand why TRIPS was deprived of agency outside its 'official' implementation setting.

Moving across policy networks

Fieldwork is illuminating in many ways, and sometimes the process of it says as much about the topic being investigated as the substantial findings from interviews – merging the different threads of ethnographic work to produce patterns of interest to the researcher. The investigation of the policy networks of Djibouti in relation to patents and healthcare was one of those instances where process and findings become entangled, and for this reason the following section retraces some of this journey.

Chronologically, this empirical research started with interviewing actors in the public health field. Connections were made very quickly, and informants knew each other enough to introduce me to whomever they thought might be a relevant contact. Although actors from different institutions – hospitals, Ministry of Health, WHO – were not always sure of what each other's job exactly was, they were generally able to name some people they thought were informed about specific questions and to explain roughly where they worked and what their responsibilities were vaguely about. As mentioned before, actors in the public health sector were mainly unaware of the current steps of implementation of TRIPS, or of what TRIPS might mean for them – or rather they all agreed that TRIPS would mean nothing to them when discussing its official implementation. Although this was a rather surprising start compared to the findings I was expecting to make, and the background information I had collected on public health actors' reactions to TRIPS (e.g. Nogueira, 2002; Sell, 2002; Third World Network, 2004), their lack of information became more understandable when I looked at the way in which they related to those officially in charge of implementing TRIPS in the Ministry of Trade. When following the course of this fieldwork, it became an increasingly clear element that TRIPS as official written prescription was perhaps not entering the public health network because there was no channel for it to circulate from the Ministry of Trade, where it had arrived in its written form, to the health sector.

After having met most of the actors I wanted to talk to in the public health sector, the next logical step was to try to meet their 'contacts' in the trade and industry field. The ease with which each informant had been able to introduce me to relevant colleagues made me – wrongly – assume that meeting someone in the trade-related field would be as simple. I truly expected that people creating rules on pharmaceutical imports for the Ministry of Health could introduce me to someone they knew working on import rules more generally. Considering that the President of the Chambre du Commerce is also a pharmacist, I believed that the relations between the two sectors must surely be somehow facilitated? At least he would certainly know who was working on trade and industry issues? I assumed that it was probably all going to be straightforward. Surprisingly, it was not the case. When asked to what extent they worked with other ministries, or actors from different fields, informants in the public health sector were all rather unsure: 'I think the minister here sometimes works with the Ministry of Finance to try to get some tax limitations for pharmaceuticals...But it is really punctual action...' (member of the Ministry of Health). Overall, it was impossible to find anyone in the Ministry of Health who could name anyone in the Ministry of Trade or the Chambre du Commerce – and after a few days of searching, my sampling specifications had become very loose! It was finally through personal relations only, by asking different people until someone mentioned a name, that I could find a way to meet someone from the Ministry of Trade. As had been the case with the health sector, once I had met with one person things progressed quickly again, and that person was able to put me in touch with a number of other relevant informants. Although this does not call for as much attention, since it does not touch as closely on the issue of pharmaceutical patents, it is worth mentioning that this difficulty of circulating from one field to another, from one building to another in some cases, was also felt in other circumstances. The emergent pharmaceutical industry could only be accessed by almost randomly meeting someone who was directly involved in it, while the Ministry of Trade and Industry, the Chambre du Commerce et de l'Industrie and the Ministry of Health had all been ruled out as potential sources of information and contact. No one truly seemed to know what was happening to this industry or who was involved in the project. I also visited the National Research Institute of Djibouti only to find that none of the researchers had received information on IP from anyone, in spite of their interest in the issue, and did not know anyone in any other governmental agency who could provide them with information.

From the very first stages of this research, it therefore appeared that the issue of the limited action of TRIPS as prescription could not be isolated from understanding the lack of stability of policy-related networks in the country. It was not only TRIPS that was not circulating or mobilizing, it was much more than this – it was most actors. The question of networking and punctualization in governmental action raised elsewhere, including within developed states (Barry, 2001; 2002) appeared clearly in this particular case study. It is crucial in an area where coordinated action from different fields is necessary not only to create a specific regulation, but also to build a specific tool as a policy issue. These overall findings on the weakness of relations across fields in Djibouti can seem even more surprising given the size of the country (highlighting the contrasts between topological closeness and relations in a networked space (Law, 1999b)) and the small number of actors actually involved in any form of governmental institution, but are illustrative of difficulties in diffusion of information across institutions that were explored, for example, by Everett Rogers (1995). It is also most surprising because actors who did not relate in any way at work, despite their interests having a common ground, would often know each other on a social level – they just did not have any work-related information on each other. For example, many actors went to the same school, studied in France in the same town where a strong Djiboutian community is established, and were often relatives or family friends. Personal networks seem never ending, but professional ones much weaker. The lack of interaction between actors did not stop them from manifesting some curiosity and interest as to what each other was doing, or where expertise and information was located. It was thus often the case that when discussing patent issues with actors from either public health or trade and industry, informants seemed truly interested in working with the other sets of actors, but completely unsure about how to go about it. Informants from each field thus asked me if I could let them know who would be an approachable actor in the other field, and explained that they wanted to get information or raise awareness – depending on whether health or trade was concerned – but did not know where to start from or who would be receptive. This illustrates some of the risks of performing the very network one tries to investigate.

Several key questions need to be addressed here: How does this lack of connections between actors and fields relate to the difficulties for TRIPS as prescription to move beyond the associations generated in the Ministry of Trade? Is it because actors do not relate that TRIPS does not generate action? Or should TRIPS itself generate this new set of connections?

International organizations and the circulation of TRIPS

When investigating the integration of TRIPS as a set of rules in the health system of Djibouti, the question of the role of international organizations was raised. In particular, such organizations are often presented and understood as creating a link between TRIPS and actors across 'governments' – when starting this research, it was assumed that this would include public health actors. While TRIPS originated from the WTO – at least the finalized, 'printed and stamped' version of TRIPS – WIPO is expected to offer advice and guidance to states when implementing it. The WHO has also participated in the debate on the impact of TRIPS. However, the specific role of international organizations in local contexts is important to interrogate and, in this case study, this manifested itself as part of the story to be told on the circulation of TRIPS[3].

Few international organizations have a local office in Djibouti. Most carry information to relevant people locally through 'visiting advisors' or posted documents. The WHO is the only relevant institution to have a local office. Its representative mentioned being frequently in touch with the regional office, and many documents produced by the central office were also available in the small library of the WHO office. Whether this should be understood as an appropriate diffusion of information from the central office to representatives in Djibouti is, of course, contingent on the Djibouti representatives reading these documents. However, it is also important to ask whether the WHO plays any role in making TRIPS an issue for public health actors: 'We are in charge of organizing meetings on TRIPS and other issues, and we work with WIPO on this, for example', commented a representative of the WHO. But for actors in the Ministry of Health: 'The WHO has never talked to me about

---

[3] The impact of some of these programmes, and the importance of problematizing some of the relationships created, are explored further by Christopher May (2004).

anything like that. We sometimes work with them on specific projects, but we don't see them very much...' So the office of the WHO based in Djibouti may well have organized meetings on TRIPS, but has not gained successes in mobilizing other public health actors in Djibouti. Nevertheless, the WHO still had some links to the Ministry of Health, at least through the unread report sitting on a desk (mentioned above). The contrast between intermediaries and mediators put forward by Latour could not be more striking than when thinking back about this particular trace of TRIPS. For Latour, while intermediaries transport others without modifications, mediators participate directly to stimulate change and cause movement (2005). In this case, while such reports may be expected to act on others, this specific one appeared to have transported ideas and advice to Djibouti in a way that would have little impact on further network transformations.

When discussing them, informants presented rather strong and passionate views on the role of visiting advisors and insisted that they could not be perceived as 'appropriate sources of information'. They expressed the view that none of the advice provided could be considered as tailored to the needs of the country, and that it was therefore of no use to anyone in Djibouti. Examples of this were widely quoted:

> Recently, in the Ministry of Finance, an international advisor came to help them change the tax system. You have to know that in the Ministry of Finance, in particular, people are all very qualified! They all have at least four years of university in France behind them! Well, this advisor came, and tried to explain to them that we should introduce VAT in Djibouti...If you know even a bit the system in Djibouti, it is obvious that it's impossible to introduce VAT here at the moment! Businessmen don't even have an accountant, and don't actually hold anything like a real accountancy book! Everybody tried telling him, and they are all qualified, and they all know the place, but he didn't listen to anyone...Instead of giving us appropriate advice on what we could actually do, he held onto his idea that we should introduce VAT, and wrote a very complete report, but perfectly useless for us!' (solicitor)

This idea that international advisors not only had little knowledge of the local needs but also very little respect for the opinion of local actors, or for the local specificities of the country, was put forward many times, by people from different backgrounds and working in different institutions:

> International advisors are really funny...they come here, stay here for a while, come to lots of cocktails, and meetings...the rest of the day, you hardly see them. We don't actually know what

they do...and then after a few days or a few weeks, they go back home, and they send a report which is meant to be adapted to the specificities of the country...that's why they come, after all, to look around, talk to people, find out what our needs are, and then give us advice on this basis...well, you just can't imagine how many times I received a report with in its introduction: 'Djibouti – Capitale: Dakar or Nouakchott or something else'...They just take a report they had prepared for another country, and put 'Djibouti' in there...but what worked in Cambodia might not work here...It's a bit discouraging!' (member of the Ministry of Trade)

The role of the WTO as an institution is also of relevance here. It is through the WTO that TRIPS as written law officially originated and it is also the WTO that should ultimately evaluate behavioural compliance with TRIPS as prescription. It is an integral part of TRIPS, as much as TRIPS itself only exists through the WTO. Djibouti has a representative in the WTO central offices in Geneva. However, he does not deal with TRIPS. The only way in which the WTO communicates about TRIPS with actors in Djibouti is through the reports it sends and through occasional contacts it makes in the country. When asking someone in the Ministry of Trade if they were made aware of changes 'regularly' by the WTO, they replied with a laugh: 'Regularly...no! but sometimes! Once in a while! But things change so quickly that by the time we have been informed and decided to react others have already moved on!' (member of the Ministry of Trade) Thus, when looking at the WTO, it therefore also appeared that connections were weak or missing.

As a whole, when observing more closely the role of international organizations in Djibouti, they appeared as rather fragile networks. While the involvement of the WTO, WIPO and WHO can be found through the many reports they have published linking TRIPS and public health (e.g. WHO/WTO, 2002), and while 'governments' and 'countries' are widely described as being influenced by the new set of rules created by TRIPS, the connections followed here all appeared to be coming to a complete stop at some point, and the circulation of TRIPS as written prescription, the necessary movement that makes social associations remain *active*, could not be retraced further than a range of punctual and limited associations. However, if wanting to look for further explanations of the weak circulation of materials and information in Djibouti, a few other elements could be put forward. It appears that TRIPS entered the Ministry of Trade, but did not truly move out of it. It is also in the WHO, in the form of many reports travelling from the central office and through the awareness of the main representative. It was in the Ministry of Health, in the form of a report on a desk. The user of the desk, in turn, was never truly interested in the document, or not enough for it to be circulated to others. The difficulties of things travelling within the Ministry of Health are instead dependent on a number of breaks and disconnections within the ministry itself. The structure of the ministry is one in which French cooperants operate alongside Djiboutian officials, with varying degrees of expertise – in terms of specific policy issues but also in terms of knowledge that is specific to Djibouti – and an allocation of duties and responsibilities that are frequently questioned. The ambivalence of the state structures and relationships with the former colonial power are still very visible in some of the governmental institutions, where cooperants operate in posts that have a significant degree of training and knowledge transfer, sometimes with resistance from government officials who may be hierarchically above them yet be openly considered by those below as being less qualified. Tensions and dead-ends are easily generated and can riddle institutions. In addition, in institutions that are small and have no obvious procedures in place for circulating or sharing information, any exchange is the result of individual initiative and, therefore, inherently unpredictable. In the current example, a report about TRIPS somehow travelled onto a desk in the Ministry of Health but was never read, enrolled, or circulated anywhere else.

Overall, TRIPS and pharmaceutical patents in Djibouti are hard to locate within the public health policy networks of the country. This is codependent on the truncated form of the relevant networks – creating obstacles to the circulation of IP – but also symptomatic of the failure of TRIPS and international organizations to create links that they have been associated with.

I now turn to the travels of IP within Ghana and illustrate some other issues of disconnections and discrepancies. Here, the story is focused on the circulation of patents as a tool that is meant to be already active and has, indeed, been integrated in national law for several years. The lack of effect of patents was highlighted in ways that are not radically different from those of Djibouti, but the processes that led to their transformation and disactivation are of a different nature.

From books to action: enrolling patents in the public health networks of Ghana

The travels of TRIPS and patents in Ghana and the obstacles and challenges they meet are constituted in a different set of 'moments'. In Djibouti, IP is still nascent and, as a result, the circulation of IP is essentially, for the moment, about the circulation of TRIPS, and of IP as a domain, and about possibilities rather than past experiences. Essentially, the problematization of TRIPS as a public health problem did not occur in the public health spheres of Djibouti. In Ghana, pharmaceutical patents have existed in national laws for many years and, as a result, this section follows more closely the travels of patents from law to action in the pharmaceutical markets in which they are expected to be acting. I hope that the case studies of both countries can partly respond to each other and that the problems experienced in Ghana can at least give a sense of some of the further questions that may arise when Djibouti, given its current situation, tries to implement pharmaceutical patents in practice.

The travels of patents in Ghana from the IP sphere to a public health sphere are facilitated by the existence of a policy interface, where the two domains officially meet. Two distinct organizations, the Pharmacy Council and the FDB have duties and activities that are supposed to engage with pharmaceutical patents in some ways. Therefore, the ruptures that were apparent in Djibouti are less obvious in Ghana, and there is a space for pharmaceutical patents to travel to. Nonetheless, the impact of patents, as official legal tools in Ghana, on behaviour and social networks remains challenged by other forms of disjunctions. In this section, I question how far patents that have been recognized by Ghanaian law and the Ghanaian patent office succeed in travelling through their official channels. In other words, how much impact does patent protection have on the networks that it is supposed to regulate?

As had been the case in Djibouti, one of the first findings that emerged from this research was that there was a significant difference between patents being created on paper and their impact in practice. As explained in Chapter 2, the patent office of Ghana provides a site in which the law can be turned into specific patents – something that in Djibouti is still a challenge in itself. The networks that patents are then supposed to follow, to be translated from being a textual statement to being an influential intermediary in public health networks, are officially well defined. However, their effectiveness was challenged by the public health actors that are expected to respond to it, as I have illustrated earlier. A closer look at the networks surrounding the import and marketing of drugs, and the series of authorization, duties and constraints that operate, provides a story of the complexity of attaching practical consequences to a tool such as pharmaceutical patents in the context of Ghana. The deployment of patents in Ghana needs to be understood within the process of registration of drugs that grants pharmaceuticals the legal status that they need in order to be officially brought onto the market.

Registering drugs in Ghana

Drugs in Ghana all need to be registered by the FDB before they can be imported or marketed. Officially, the registration process and the FDB are therefore obligatory passage points for all drugs that will enter Ghana and ultimately reach patients. The registration process involves, officially again, a process of verification of the patent status of each product, and the travels of patents are therefore dependent on the practice and deployment of the registration process.[4] In reality however – and understandably so in a context were resources are scarce and health and safety is the most central concern and expertise on IP is limited – little attention is given to patents. The first level of discrepancy between the letter of patents and their enrolment in routines and practices therefore appears at this level, most apparent in this excerpt from an interview with a member of the FDB:

Interviewer: What about patents? Do you deal with that side of things?
Respondent: No, for now, no.
Int: So that is not part of the registration?
Res: No. There are many legalities to do with patents... For us that is an issue between Mr A and Mr B... what we are more concerned about is who is a legitimate agent and has registered and is responsible for the distribution of the product.

The fact that the registration process does not put a heavy onus on checking for patents certainly raises issues about their implementation in practice in excluding from the Ghanaian market drugs that are infringing patents. A thorough registration process, to which the question of patents is attached on paper and that requests that information on patents are provided with the registration document, could nonetheless be sufficient to deter those who are infringing patents to try to apply to register their products. Similarly, if the issue was simply one of adjusting the process of registration to include a more thorough attention to patents, the travelling ability of patents could be transformed quite rapidly. In order to better understand how deeply rooted are some of the challenges of ensuring that IP can travel into public health networks, however, it is interesting to look more closely at the general discrepancies between the process that officially needs to be followed by those wishing to market drugs in Ghana and the actual practice surrounding registration, import and marketing. Here, the extent of the difficulties of translating rules on the books into rules in action is particularly visible, and the entanglement of patents within those fluid and uncertain networks helps in understanding the difficulties that they meet in practice in following the path that has been officially drawn for them. In the next sections, I review some of the most interesting aspects of the registration process for medicines in theory and in practice in Ghana, in order to demonstrate some of the patterns of the systems of which patents are supposed to be part.

---

4 www.fdbghana.gov.gh/pdf/downloads/guidelines%20-drugs/ALLOPATHIC%20DRUGS%20REGISTRATION.pdf.

Official stories of registration

Officially, the FDB, and the registration process for drugs, is an obligatory passage point for every medicine that will enter the local market.[5] A drug only becomes an entity that can be legally traded, distributed to and used by patients, if approved by these offices and through a dedicated process:

> Res: That is the law that says that any products, medicines, whatever under Food and Drug Board jurisdiction. If it passes through our set-up here then it has to get registered.
> Int: Every single drug...
> Res: Every single medicine, basically, has to get registered in Ghana before it can go to the markets. (member of the FDB)

The registration process aims to evaluate any potential risks associated with the drug and provide a centralized control over what should be allowed to circulate. When entering Ghana for the first time, a drug is translated into a complex dossier that will form the basis of whether or not the medicinal (simplified?) version of the drug is allowed to enter the market. The history of the drug, where it has been produced, what it contains, the environment in which it was made, the ability of its makers to fit the profile of a reliable company, are all criteria that will help shape a drug into one that is deemed acceptable for the Ghanaian market. The processes of exclusion that are at play here are not exceptional, and the filtering is a well-established tool to maintain standards, with a variety of socio-political implications (e.g. Abraham, 1995). Interestingly, the process is not in itself the answer to issues of counterfeiting that pervade the Ghanaian market (that I will come back to in Chapter 5). Here, I am interested essentially in the translation of medicines into an application for registration, before being transformed again into a marketable product:

> A whole history, yes. That comes in the form of a dossier. The company's drug samples. The samples are taken to the Food and Drugs Board laboratories. They also do an analysis to ascertain whether what they are telling us is true or not. The dossiers sometimes contain information to say if it's a new chemical entity, whether you have done clinical trials and studies and a whole lot of things. They can be compared with the original...in terms of side effects and everything. We look at all these things. There is a committee looking at dossiers. And then if your dossiers meet our regulatory requirements and your samples pass all the tests,

---

5 A term developed by Michel Callon (1986a) to capture nodes of a network through which all connections circulate repeatedly and 'inevitably'.

the manufacturing of them has to be verified. They have to be audited. If it's local we do [it] and if it's outside the country we travel and go and do it...The dossiers, the history we will look at that and samples for analysis...' (member of the FDB)

The various processes of evaluation of what makes a drug 'acceptable' therefore reflect on the drug as more than a tablet – questioning the modes of production that have created it, and understanding the product in its continuity rather than its individuality (which potentially has significant political implications that I return to in Chapter 6). It is also a process that is possible and feasible only because of the availability in Ghana of experts and laboratories able to test the sample of each of these drugs – something that is not yet available in the context of many other African states, including Djibouti.

Enforcement

The registration process is only the first step of a more general process of inclusion/exclusion of particular drugs. In order to ensure that only drugs that have been registered, and therefore have complied with particular standards of acceptability, are marketed, several levels of monitoring and enforcement are deployed. In this process, two distinct categories of drugs at least are being targeted: those that may represent a risk that would have made them unfit for the registration process; but also drugs that may be valid by all other means but have not been submitted to this process of approval (and I will return to these distinctions in Chapter 5).

The process of registration involves various strategies of checks and enforcement and associates the FDB with custom officers in the first instance. Officially, the process is therefore organized around what appears as a coherent network in which the first point of check to ensure that all drugs have gone through the appropriate process are the physical points of entry for the drugs; this is therefore also an essential aspect that patents should, in theory, be travelling through:

> We have representation at the ports. We have an office at the international airport and we have an office at Tenmar, a big one. When they come, they come to customs to do their part. And then we also take over to do the inspections to ensure that we do random sampling to ensure that the products really conform. Then, aside from this kind of activity, we have other activities like post-market surveillance. (member of the FDB)

This is delegated to the Pharmacy Council. Again, the institutional setting in Ghana is well articulated, and, while the FDB is in charge of processing registrations and issuing licences to medicines before they are imported or marketed, the Pharmacy Council ensures, as part of its duty, that the activity of pharmacy practice is regulated, that all medicines sold in pharmacies have been registered. Drugs that have escaped the official process and made it through customs without being seized and removed will therefore need to go through the additional hurdle of avoiding market surveillance by the Pharmacy Council:

> The Food and Drugs Board deals with manufacturing. If you want to sell drugs in Ghana they must be licensed. If you want to bring any product into the country it has to be licensed. While they do that, they provide us with a list of all the products that are licensed. We then take it from there.' (member of the Pharmacy Council)

The penalties associated with law infringement here have also become significant, and the possibility that these penalties act as a deterrent is certainly important in theory.

> There used to be a fine complementing our law when [people who infringe the law] are found guilty in the law courts. It used to be 50 Ghanaian cedis. Recently we sent a petition to Parliament and through executive instruments we have had an approval for the fine. Now you have to pay a minimum of 2000 dollars. (member of the Pharmacy Council)

In principle, the drug market in Ghana is therefore organized around a thorough system of checks and controls. Consequently, there is at least a system through which patents have the possibility of travelling, which did not appear to be the case (yet?) in Djibouti. However, once again, investigating the same networks beyond this official surface illustrates the fluidity of the process in practice, and how different the networks in which pharmaceutical regulations, including patents, look on a day-to-day basis. Next, my main focus is on illustrating how difficult it is for the rules on which patents are dependent to be translated into practice.

Licensing, registration and the translation of projected networks into daily practices

I focus on five key moments where the unified network presented by the FDB is challenged: its ability to exercise long-distance control on the vast spaces through which drugs travel; its ability to 'interest' loose parts of the networks that it aims to create; the risk of individual parts reopening negotiations that the FDB had aimed to settle; the challenges to post-market surveillance; and the weaknesses of enforcement networks.

Long-distance control

The networks of registration and regulation of medicines are dependent on the ability for governmental agencies to control at a distance the entry and circulation of drugs in Ghana. This in turn is dependent on an ability to rely on the material control of borders. The geographical position of Ghana, and the many entry points for drugs into the country, associated with the limited resources of customs offices, means that it remains relatively easy for certain medicines to escape regulatory control. In the words of one member of the FDB:

> We also found out that some products were also filtering through our approvals into the market. From the border areas. Border areas through the eastern corridor and the western corridors and then from the northern areas. We've also gone a bit further to establish office posts at those border areas to work hand in hand with customs.

The smuggling of drugs by land through the porous boundaries of the region is a significant problem in Ghana, and one that creates the largest part of the counterfeit medicines market (that I will come back to in Chapter 5). Here, I am interested predominantly in focusing specifically on following the official trail of the import of medicines and questioning whether the projection of the registration process that emerges from the FDB's procedures is reflected in practices.

Interessement

When talking to wholesalers and pharmacists, the challenges to the efforts of the FDB to control at a distance the drugs that circulate, or attempt to circulate, in Ghana were even more deeply rooted in an issue of interessement. Even drugs that circulate through the legitimate networks of regulated customs commonly escaped the networks of registration and control. Although registration was presented by the FDB as an obligatory process on which the entire framework of control of medicines is dependent, practitioners of the system highlighted that in fact the entire network was commonly avoided. Indeed, they argued that many of the drugs that are on the market have never been registered – in particular many branded medicines that have been on the market for many years. More than an explicit strategy of resistance to the system that has been established by the government, or pro-active avoidance strategy, this was presented mostly as something that had 'never really happened' – importers failed to be 'interested' (in the sense proposed by Michel Callon (1986a)) by the registration network developed by the FDB:

Res: Most of them are not registered.
Int: Why is that?
Res: Because nobody bothered. If you are able to get something free, why would you register it?

Int: So nobody checks?
Res: They check, but you have to pay. (private wholesaler)

This links to the next element that makes the network of registration and control much looser than projected by the FDB: the possibility for individual actors to separate from the network and engage in individual negotiations.

Individual negotiations

The issue of payment and corruption was woven through many of the discussions we had about the practical enforcement of this registration. The question of corruption is one that arises commonly in law and development literature, and in particular in policy literature that revolves around the idiom of the promotion of the rule of law (Davies and Trebilcock, 2008). Here I suggest reading this issue in symmetrical terms, and propose that payments to customs officers can be understood as part of a broader process of negotiations through which drugs are imported into Ghana. The registration and licensing system designed by the FDB therefore becomes one avenue that importers can choose, rather than the obligatory passage point that the FDB projects. The negotiative aspect of the process of import and the transition of drugs through customs can be illustrated further by looking closely at interactions at play here.

At one level, inspections were presented as inevitable and a process through which every drug would, indeed, need to go. The systematic checking and emptying of containers relied upon by the FDB was, indeed, reported to happen by importers. However, the networks then become more fluid than the FDB and their written regulations may project. If drugs that have not been registered are identified, negotiations (as opposed to enforcement and penalties) are open in which importers and customs officers come to an agreement about how the absence of registration can be addressed:

Res: When I was there last time, before Christmas, it was like hell over there...First of all they have to empty the whole container...They empty the container and they inspect the container. Sometimes they target, but it's, you know, every container is emptied if it's drugs. If it's like a container full of tvs they know it's full of that. What is there to inspect? If it's a container full of mixed or 30 or 100 products, different products then you will have to inspect it.
Int: They check everything?
Res: Yes. That is when you are like, 'I ordered for this but you know the suppliers...They send whatever they have. It's not my fault.'...And then you...you can import anything...(private wholesaler)

In these series of negotiations, the role of the registration process becomes transformed. Its value is not as much in ensuring compliance or avoiding fines per se as it is about gaining some credibility in the discussions that ensue. The position of a particular importer is dependent on its relationship with the registration process, and its punctual enrolment into it. However, the position of a particular drug is not necessarily dependent on its own individual enrolment in this same network:

> It's easier for you to import anything if you register some products, if you know what I mean. Even the top people haven't registered a lot of products...I mean, they have registered a lot of products, but sometimes what they have registered doesn't make sense. If you look on the Food and Drugs Board...They registered products from G D Cooper. G D Cooper doesn't have any products. They don't have any products. They are wholesalers. They are distributors...(private wholesaler)

In these negotiations, the process of registration is constantly reinvented and transformed by its practitioners; the projected actor-world (Callon, 1986b) on which the FDB relies, expecting compliance with a stable, defined system, is itself rewriting the very nature of the licensing and registration process. Its stability is challenged and it becomes enrolled by its users as commonly as it enrols them. Rather than being a stable obligatory passage point for all drugs, as in the imaginary projection of the FDB, it is turned into a tool amongst others that can be deployed to bring medicines into the country. Alternatives exist, in the form of one-off payments, bargaining and negotiation with customs officers, that the registration process influences and is linked to. The decision to register or not to register particular products is one based on business decisions and transactions rather than being the direct effect of governmental regulations in the way envisaged by the government.

The fragile practice of post-market surveillance

The same ruptures in the chain that translates rules on paper into practice can be traced to the practice of post-market surveillance, which is restricted by a context where resources are scarce. Again, the translation of institutional labelling into specifics is important here. Although the Pharmacy Council is a significant governmental actor in the translation of rules relating to pharmacies into practice, post-market surveillance is in fact delegated to a handful of individuals. As an example, only two officers are in charge of post-market surveillance in the Greater Accra region and its population of around 3 million inhabitants. In the words of one of its members:

> Res: And then there is us and the institutions who also have difficulties, because we are [supposed] to be monitoring the system. If you take the whole of Greater Accra it is quite densely populated...There are only two

officers. That is when they [the officers] review the monitoring... We have over 1000 pharmacies in Accra and over 1000 licensed chemical shops.
Int: So two people...
Res: Exactly. You want to be monitoring and visiting them to see whether they are doing the right thing and it's not easy... Manpower in terms of organization is the problem. There are no resources to [do so]... We receive some support from the government. We also generate some funds internally. They are not enough to meet our needs. (member of the Pharmacy Council)

Here, the process of punctualization associated with institutional creation can hide some of the practical specificities of the networks that they refer to – and sometimes of the very restricted networks, in their size and their potentiality to act. Here the Pharmacy Council, in the context of post-market surveillance and the enforcement of a detailed system of regulation, turns into a handful of individuals. Their ability to control at a distance the diffuse network that they are expected to follow is inevitably limited.

Penalties, enforcement and the further ruptures of networks of control

The system of registration is ultimately dependent on the ability of those who identify the breach of specific rules to take sanctions. The most serious breaches identified by the Pharmacy Council officers need to seek the involvement of the police to ensure that sanctions and penalties are followed through. This next node in the chain that the FDB has projected creates further difficulties and another place where theory and practice differ widely:

[L]aw enforcement is also a problem... If you look at the act... it's treated as a criminal offence. So we get them and then we hand them over to the police to carry on their prosecution. Often it doesn't go through us as you would expect. You hand them over to the police and nothing happens... (member of the Pharmacy Council)

Here the negotiative rather than definitive nature of the process is probably relevant again. Overall, the chain followed by medicines to enter through the most legitimate channels is characterized by its fluidity and by a series of discrepancies.

Where do those discontinued networks leave patents?

It is in this context of permanent shifts in interessement/disinteressement and efforts to enable the travels of regulatory demands that the potential for pharmaceutical patents to travel within Ghana needs to be understood – at least the possibility of travelling through the expected, 'regulatory' route. In the network of import and marketing of medicines, patents disappear from sight at both ends. At the level of import and registration, they are not the primary concern of the FDB, for whom health and safety is, understandably, the main focus. At the other end of the chain, the Pharmacy Council does not engage with patents any more specifically than the FDB did:

Res: Yes. Patents, I will not be able to give you much. We don't deal with the registration. The Food and Drugs Board will be able to give you much more information on that.
Int: Part of the registration looks for the patents and you work from the list?
Res: Exactly. If it is registered and then we accept it. (member of the Pharmacy Council)

Overall, the role of patents outside of IP circles is again rather weak and uncertain. The possibility of individual patent-holders trying to enforce their rights when particular instances of breach are identified remains open, but, in their day-to-day deployment, pharmaceutical patents remain far removed from the key concerns of those within public health circles who have a role to play in making them effective. Politically, and practically, this is something that is very difficult to object to – in a context where health and safety is the prime concern, and facilitating access is crucial, those who have an oversight of the practice of import and distribution have other more pressing issues to respond to. What is most interesting about this context, however, is to question the issue of implementation, of what it means to 'implement TRIPS', or create IP, in the context of sub-Saharan Africa. In the case of Ghana, although the rules have been carefully created and expertise is progressively growing in the field of IP, it remains a specialized issue that few engage with in the day-to-day practice of health. Again, my concern here is with implementation, and I will demonstrate in the following chapters how patents have acquired their own means of acting, indirectly and often aside of official regulation, and how their enrolment into markets that cross legal divides make them determinant factors in deciding which drugs will in fact reach patients.

Conclusion

The analysis of how actors within the public health sector responded to questions relating to patents and TRIPS in this research demonstrated some of the discrepancies between the theory and the practice of new legal tools – expectations that law may modify behaviour, and the fact that it simply does not always happen in practice. This of course relates more broadly to questionings known in the socio-legal field as the contrast between 'law on paper' and 'law in action' (Pound, 1910; Nelken, 1987). However, these notions are not necessarily sufficient to seizing fully the mechanisms that enable regulatory tools to order society, sometimes in ways that are more complex and unexpected than their implementation *strico sensu* may suggest. Here, a closer look at the networks through which patents would need to circulate in order to have an effect as official regulatory tools highlighted sets of ruptures and the instability of connections that are often assumed to be stable in terms such as 'systems', 'government', or 'organization'. By looking more closely into particular connections, their weakness and the avoidance of their performance by many actors appeared as essential elements in understanding how TRIPS in its written/ official pharmaceutical patent dimension stopped its circulation and social integration.

The public health networks in Ghana and Djibouti responded in different ways to patents and TRIPS, and a strict comparison is not particularly useful here. Nonetheless, in both cases, rules that were essentially brought in as the result of external pressures and demands become transformed into something fundamentally different, and here less influential, under local pressures. In Djibouti, a key element was the absence of punctualization of the 'government' in responding to TRIPS, and the difference between the segmented networks in Djibouti and the organized response reported in other contexts (e.g. Muriu, 2009). In Ghana, overlaps between the demands of IP and of public health exist in some specific institutions (FDB, customs, Pharmacy Council). However, the processes that these institutions are expected to follow, or set up to follow, are constantly transformed as a result of limited resources and an ultimate lack of interessement into the issue of IP.

Neither of these stories, however, gives a complete view of what pharmaceutical patents or TRIPS mean in Djibouti and Ghana, or what they do in each place. In fact, the question of implementation that I have explored only covers one particular dimension of TRIPS and has only considered pharmaceutical patents as far as they relate to their official creation. Although these might be the most widely acknowledged roles and dimensions of both objects that have been looked at, they remain only a limited part of what makes the story of TRIPS and pharmaceutical patents in Djibouti and Ghana. The next chapters will demonstrate why, in spite of the lack of mobilization caused by pharmaceutical patents in the public health networks of Djibouti and Ghana, both instruments managed to develop other ways to acquire social agency – and social agency in the public health field more specifically. Although defining them as actors in 'a legal way' (Latour, 2005, p. 239) in each country remains too broad and therefore uncertain, their social action through living and dynamic connections needs to be fully understood in order to explain what both tools mean for society in Djibouti and Ghana.

4
Pharmaceutical Patents as Silent Regulatory Tools: Escaping Branded Drugs in Djibouti

In this chapter, I question the links between the existence (or absence) of pharmaceutical patents in written national law and the role of pharmaceutical patents in ordering the local pharmaceutical market of Djibouti. I explain why the set of regulatory forces that shape the market cannot be deduced fully from the absence of intellectual property (IP) in the legal landscape of Djibouti until very recently, and why the absence of engagement of public health actors with patents cannot be interpreted as meaning that they are fully irrelevant to the way in which the market for drugs is shaped. I argue throughout that patents in Djibouti have in fact always been highly influential and can be conceptualized as silent regulatory tools with fluid jurisdictional boundaries. In this analysis, I position my understanding of regulation at the crossroads between actor-network theory's (ANT) approach to analysing processes of social ordering (Latour, 2005; 2010) and recent approaches in regulation theory that have emphasized the increasingly fluid and decentred nature of regulatory forces (Black, 2001; 2002; Scott, 2004). The discreet but influential modes of action of patents in Djibouti invite one to reflect carefully on the role that patents may play in public health systems aside from their official role, and what this may mean for the ways in which the markets of states that do not or did not protect pharmaceutical patents may have been shaped.

Although pharmaceutical patents have still never been officially granted on any drugs in Djibouti, interestingly, its pharmaceutical market is characterized by a vast predominance of innovator brands. In the time-span over which this research took place, their relative influence diminished slightly, as the market was partly transformed. Nonetheless, changes affected only a relatively contained part of the pharmaceutical market, with its remainder built essentially around branded/patented medicines. In this chapter, I explore the constitution of the Djiboutian market for drugs and the regulatory roles that patents managed to play in it, in spite of their lack of official existence. I start by describing in depth the market as it stood in 2004, when this research was started. I then turn to more recent developments and explore how, alongside this persistent and dominant market, a new system emerged in which generic medicines became available to the poorest patients. Throughout, I discuss how the action of patents as unexpected and discreet regulatory tools was generated and facilitated by a number of contingent situations. I argue that the role of patents in ordering the market in a way that almost systematically excluded generic medicines for many years, and still only allows them in under specific conditions, is best understood as the cogenerated effects of complex webs of practices in which industries, doctors, pharmacists and medicines fall into repeated patterns. First, I briefly introduce the context of public health in Djibouti, which is essential to understanding the analysis I provide.

Accessing healthcare in Djibouti

As might be anticipated from the economic situation of Djibouti as a least-developed country (LDC), access to healthcare is difficult for many people and diseases are widespread in the country. The limited amount of official data available, and the significant variety that exists in data provided by global organizations, makes any statistical estimate very difficult. As in many African states, tuberculosis (TB), malaria and AIDS feature amongst the health concerns. TB is uncontroversially considered a major problem, both by global organizations and actors in Djibouti – and Djibouti frequently ranks amongst the states with the highest rates of TB in the world. The extent of the malaria and AIDS crises are both subject to more contestation. Although both feature amongst the key concerns of global organizations involved in Djibouti, actors on the ground have questioned whether they were of immediate urgency. (I come back in Chapter 6 to the controversies surrounding AIDS, in its prevalence and relative urgency in Djibouti, but the narratives of malaria are similarly contested.) Whilst, according to global institutions, malaria is an important concern in Djibouti, with the World Bank stating, for example, that 'since 1988, malaria is steadily increasing and reaching areas where it was unknown before' (World Bank, 2003), this contrasts with statements from doctors in Djibouti, one of whom stating, for example, that 'there was lots of malaria 20 years ago, but in the last couple of years that I've been here I have only seen very few cases. It's not really a problem at the moment.' (medical doctor) The difficulty of gathering reliable statistics in a country where many people will simply not be enrolled in health facilities, and not necessarily be tested for particular diseases, is acute in the context of Djibouti. Many of the health concerns experienced, however, are linked more generally to the stark poverty of the country. Malnutrition, respiratory and diarrhoeal diseases and maternal death were described as constituting a significant part of the day-to-day experiences of health professionals and of patients.

As can also be expected by the economic situation of Djibouti, access to healthcare is often problematic.[1] Hospitals in Djibouti tend to be the first point of access to healthcare for patients. In contrast with what is the case in many countries, private doctors are the exception rather than the rule and patients will visit hospitals for most consultations. Standards in the hospital system of the country vary widely, making 'health for all' an unlikely project at the moment. The public hospitals are generally considered to be of a poor standard, and the only alternatives that exist, the French military hospital (Hôpital Bouffard) and the semi-public structure for local workers (Organisme de Protection Sociale (OPS)), are favoured by patients whenever possible:

> Patients will basically first try to get into Bouffard. If they can't, they'll try to get into the OPS. And if they can't be accepted in either, their only option will be to go into Peltier. (member of the Ministry of Health)

The issues faced by the public sector are best illustrated by the difficulties experienced by the main hospital – Hôpital Peltier. Largely supported by a variety of programmes of aid and cooperation, the governance of the hospital has caused uncertainty and discontinuity:

> There is very little coordination between anyone's action or approach here – donations come from here and there, different countries send a bit of money, a few staff, but nothing seems coherent. (medical doctor)

Specialisms are not all always represented and depend on the ordering of the network at a particular moment in time. The equipment and facilities of the hospital also improve and fall into disrepair quickly, depending on the availability of particular funding. New buildings are regularly added, while others are poorly maintained. New equipment is regularly donated. For example, a new x-ray machine was received during my fieldwork in 2004. However, without any radiologist in the hospital at the time, it was very likely that no one would be able to use or maintain the machine and many wondered why so much money had been put into something that would be of very little use: 'What are they going to do with it now? It all looks great, and we can say that

---

[1] For an analysis of the ethical dilemmas of access to medication, underpinning most of the following discussions, see Pogge (2008).

we have a highly modern device – but then how to use it? How to maintain it? In a year it will probably be completely out of order…' (member of the Ministry of Health) Smaller public hospitals exist outside of Djibouti town and in its different districts, but are in very poor condition and significantly understaffed, as are the few specialist clinics – obstetrics, TB and AIDS.

Alongside the public sector, the semi-public OPS provides free health services to private employees in Djibouti. It is based on a health insurance system paid through contributions by private employers. Most of the people treated there have low incomes – many employed as maids or private guards, for example – and would not be able otherwise to access health treatments. 'We mainly treat people with little resources, people employed privately as maids for French people here, and their families.' (medical doctor) The standard of services is believed to be better than in the public hospitals, although it still operates with very limited resources.

Finally, and as is the case in many former French colonies, Djibouti has a French military hospital – CHA Bouffard – administered by the central health administration of the army, staffed exclusively with French medical staff. Access to the hospital is administered both by formal and informal rules. Officially, the hospital is open to French military staff and their families, as well as members of the Djiboutian army and their families, and a number of contractors – such as German soldiers based in the region, or most other employees from military boats using the port. In addition, local people can access the hospital according to rules which seem more based on customs or habits than on written regulation. Over the years practices regulating access to the hospital have become more restrictive, creating various conflicts between doctors wanting to see patients who were not on the priority list and the hospital management. Personal connections with doctors are often the answer to who may ultimately gain access. Apart from these controversies, the hospital is a well-run structure, of high quality even by European standards, and with most medical specialities represented. Many patients who can access the hospital are exempted from payments although most medication is bought from private pharmacies once the patient gets out of hospital. In terms of facilities, tests or drugs available within the hospital, the structure also follows French standards and does not encounter any specific difficulties.

As is the case in many areas in Djibouti, figures and statistics are difficult to provide, but the fact that access to treatment is problematic for wide sections of the population is unquestioned:

> When you look at the 'number of beds per inhabitants', which is one thing the WHO, for example, always looks at when estimating the state of public health services in a country, it all seems quite good. But then when you get there and ask to actually look

at the beds, it's another issue...some of them are simply not there. And many are there, but hardly look like a bed anymore! (former World Health Organization (WHO) representative)

The system of distribution of medicines is mostly dependent on private pharmacies: specifically four private pharmacies, all in Djibouti town, run by two private pharmacists, with one holding shares in all of them. The private pharmacists also provide most of the medicines for the public sector and are the main importers of drugs in Djibouti. Some drugs can also be obtained through the pharmacy of the OPS, for its patients. Finally, since 2006, a parallel system of import and distribution of selected generic medicines has been implemented, offering the first generalized opportunity for the poorest parts of the population to access medicines. I return to this below.

Although traditional medicine is often considered an important element in countries where access to 'modern' drugs is limited, reliance upon it is not significant in Djibouti. For informants in this research, it only played a limited part in the health sector as a whole and, indeed, I rarely observed traditional remedies being displayed anywhere in the course of this research. Informants attributed this in part to the fact that there were only restricted 'natural resources' in the country, and in part to the fact that people in town had become used to relying on modern drugs, even if the degradation of the public hospital had now changed this. Traditional remedies were said to play a more significant part in the most rural areas of the country, but were not widespread in the way that they are, for example, in Ghana (as I explain in Chapter 5). Similarly, counterfeit medicines only started being a concern recently, a point I return to below.

Silent regulations and materials

It is against this background that the role of patents in Djibouti is deployed. As explored earlier, patents have been heavily theorized from a variety of perspectives. Here, I wish to focus more specifically on the materiality of patents, which is particularly important to an ANT study. On the one hand, this materiality can be found in the documents and texts that surround patents and are in many ways their official expression. At the same time, patents become embedded very intimately into the very 'inventions' that they reward; in the case under scrutiny, patents become an inherent part of the drug for which they provide exclusive rights to their inventor. In fact, when considering more closely both patents and drugs from a public health perspective, it becomes clear that the object of study becomes a unique but complex hybrid. Once a patent has been granted, a new hybrid is created, made up of both the complexity of the pharmaceutical patent and of the drug. This complex object is a material that will be distributed to patients, but whose cost, value, accessibility, marketing, packaging, naming and many other of its dimensions will be defined by the fact that it 'contains' a patent. The difference between this drug and its 'generic' version is exclusively located in the fact that one carries a patent and the other one does not; the material may look the same, but is a radically different public health actor. The hybrids we are looking at are very different in nature, even though the chemical entities are similar. The implications of this for this research, or for research on pharmaceutical patents in general, are important. They imply that, if wanting to reflect on the role and action of patents, and if wanting to understand if and where patents can be 'found' in Djibouti, their material presence within drugs should not be neglected.[2] In simple terms, looking for the impact of patents also implies looking for the presence and role of patented medicines – the 'legal' object is also a material one.

This material occurrence of patents appeared, in Djibouti, in stark contradiction to the findings that emerged from following the role of patents as official regulatory tools. Indeed, when talking about the role of patents through official 'legal' channels, all actors interviewed, as explained before, dismissed pharmaceutical patents as something that were of no social relevance to them. They stated many times that patents were not part of any action in the country and were almost invisible apart from reports emanating from institutions external to the country and from the basic expertise of a few officials. When explaining this, one of my informants vehemently stated his own lack of interest in the concept of patents in these terms: 'Patents, no patents....all the same here!' (private pharmacist) Although this statement was made essentially to express an indifference towards the content of written law, based on the perception that introducing patents would not influence individual behaviour, it later appeared than in fact 'not having' patents did not make the ordering of the pharmaceutical market in Djibouti appear any different to that of countries that 'had' patents. The official absence of patents from written law in Djibouti did not make patents/drugs any less present in the pharmaceutical market of the country.

When investigating the pharmaceutical market of Djibouti in 2004, the inherent presence of patents became a clear characteristic of the network. Although patents were not present in words or opinions, they were embedded in the range of medicines that were selected on medical prescriptions, within doctors' and pharmacists' strategies and patients requirements. If pharmaceutical patents are understood as more than their written/official dimension, if the hybrids that patented medicines represent are understood as keeping

---

2 For other explorations of the regulatory role of materials, see Hermer and Hunt (1996), Hunt (1996), Lessig (1999) and Lippert (2009).

patents alive, patents were certainly a crucial part of the pharmaceutical network of Djibouti. In the dominant part of the market, built around the four private pharmacies, generics were almost systematically excluded. The statements below were made by the private pharmacists:

> In Djibouti we don't like or the doctors don't prescribe generic products yet so in the Republic of Djibouti we essentially don't use generics.
>
> I own two pharmacies. One has about 90% of foreign customers, the other 100% locals. But the drugs are the same in both – no generics.

Although every actor in charge of importing drugs affirmed that patents did not play a role in their decision-making about which drug to import and from where, generic drugs struggled to enter the country – and mostly failed to do so. In the largest of the pharmacies, a drawer marked 'generics' contained a few boxes. In the time spent in the pharmacy, either as a pure observer or as a patient, I never saw this drawer accessed – I only observed what was inside when I asked one of the staff members specifically to open it. Outside of this particular drawer, and with the very few exceptions of some 'branded generics', most drugs sold were the originally patented version of a given product. The same was true in the different hospitals – with the exception of the OPS, as explained below. Most pharmacists and doctors interviewed similarly confirmed that they did not deal with generics. Finally, doctors' prescriptions observed at private pharmacies similarly contained lists of branded medications only. Although patents were officially 'non-existent' and 'irrelevant' for policy-makers, it was particularly difficult, outside of the exception that will be presented below, to find any drug in the country that was not a patented drug or the branded version of a drug which was originally its patented version – that was not one of those *hybrids* mentioned above.

The only exception to the vast predominance of branded medicines in Djibouti was found in the pharmacy of the OPS. Doctors and pharmacists in this hospital all affirmed that 'we use almost exclusively generic medicines', as reflected in their lists of medication and a brief look at their stocks demonstrated. The two pharmacists estimated that about 75 per cent of the drugs used in the hospital were generics. However, a closer look at the range of generics imported in the OPS highlighted once again more similarities than discrepancies with what could be found in Europe, for example. As is well known, the term generic refers to two fundamentally different situations: one in which these are new versions of a drug still under patent; the other where they are a new version of a drug whose patent has officially expired (and this second type of generics is those that can be found even in countries where patents are part of the written legal landscape).[3] The generics imported by the OPS only belong to this second category. In this respect, the generic drugs found in the OPS were not any different from what one would expect to find in a country where patents are officially part of written national law. All the generic drugs used in the hospital were also commercialized in generic versions in France or the UK. In other words, none of the drugs used in the OPS and found on the lists of generic imports would have been infringing patents in Europe. The drugs network created in the supposed (official) 'absence' of pharmaceutical patents was not looking any different from the situation in states in which patents officially exist. In contrast, generics of drugs still under patent elsewhere, including antiretrovirals, were not imported. Therefore, even within the network where generics managed to be imported, they remained limited to those that are 'patent-compatible'. Drugs in which patents are embedded were still chosen over other versions in cases where patents were still officially valid in other countries. Other generics were still prevented from entering this secondary, more open, pharmaceutical market. Therefore, in Djibouti, in 2004, there was no drug – or at least no drug which I came across during my research – that would infringe patents if it were sold, for example, in Europe. Even drugs for which generic versions were legally sold in Europe only appeared as 'generics' in the OPS; and in the OPS, only drugs that were out of patent in Europe appeared as generics. In practice, the limits placed on the entry of generics into the market of Djibouti appear even tighter than those experienced by European markets. In fact, in Europe some drugs at least, once their patent has 'officially' run out, start appearing in new generic versions in most pharmacies – new drugs *without* patents. But in Djibouti, outside the OPS, patents socially exist independently from any written rule and any official, written, temporal limit. Patents are not only what gives drugs market exclusivity for several years, but they determine which drug will or will not enter the territory with no pre-established time limit.

The situation in Djibouti, in terms of medication and the de facto limits of a 'generics market', complexifies the narrative provided by commentators and non-governmental organizations of the links between patents and access to drugs in developing states. For example, according to an Oxfam report: 'These longer patent periods will delay the availability of the low-cost generic equivalents that traditionally supply developing-country needs; only the expensive, patented version of a new medicine will be available.' (Oxfam International, 2001, p. 6) The general assumption that generics would be widespread in

---

3 For a critical exploration of those various generics as techno-legal constructs, see, for example, Hayden (2007).

markets that are not regulated by patents is not unique to this statement and, when referred to, the high reliance on branded medicines is often left unexplored by commentators (e.g. Watal, 2000; Sun, 2004). Here, instead, the market appears to have become ordered by practice, and barriers to generics have emerged in ways that are not foreseen by the law. However, the situation of Djibouti is by no means unique, and getting generics into poor countries can in fact be a difficult process. Examples from other African countries have been found, although their significance has never been conceptualized (Direction de la Pharmacie et des Laboratoires du Tchad, 2004).

The de facto ordering of the pharmaceutical market, by patents, and around patents, suggests an interesting version of the classic 'gap' issue, widely explored in socio-legal studies (Pound, 1910; Nelken, 1987). Here, a particular set of socio-legal objects appeared to have agency *without* being rooted in written rules, giving the gap between law in the books and law in action a new and unusual shape (Cloatre, 2008). Somehow, through means and connections that I return to below, patents had become a part of the system, which were never truly bypassed by importers, patients or doctors. The jurisdictional boundaries of patents, as emerged in places other than Djibouti, and in France in particular, became so blurry as to make these tools travel to Djibouti, through the brands and medicines in which they are inherently entangled, to find effects in this distant market (Cloatre and Dingwall, forthcoming). Here, both legal boundaries and the nature of global/local networks are brought into question, as both seem to become more complex. The public health implications of this are important. The effect of the repeated exclusion of generics from a significant part of the Djiboutian market means that access to medication has traditionally been very problematic for the poor, and those that did not benefit from the OPS could often simply not buy the drugs that they would have needed. I will come back to some of these issues when discussing the transformation that occurred in more recent years, linked to the Trade Related Aspects of Intellectual Property Rights (TRIPS) agreement. The problem exposed, however, also highlights some more conceptual themes. Patents had become silent regulatory tools; embedded in materials, they shaped and influenced connections and relationships without ever being acknowledged or granted official status. Their very nature becomes difficult to seize. Whilst they may be defined as 'legal' objects, their modes of action in this context have little to do with legal mechanisms. They pertain more closely to material relationships – bringing us close to ANT's view that relationships and connections are all material in some way. More precisely, this example brings the existence of a definable 'legal space' into question; the modes of connections identified here and below are not by nature very different from others. In order to understand these modes of action better, I turn to analysing how patents were made to be effective and how they became such a dominant aspect of the local pharmaceutical market.

Making connections: how patents travel to Djibouti

This section presents some of the key connections that explain how patents find a way of acting in Djibouti, although they have not been officially created by written law in the country. It focuses on some specific connections within the import system, and within the medical field more generally, that help to explain why a country with no official system of pharmaceutical patents had for a long time a pharmaceutical market almost exclusively based on branded medication, fully in compliance with the strongest patent systems worldwide and in which patents were, in fact, more extensively embedded than in many countries where they are an official legal instrument. Throughout, patents are conceptualized as silent regulatory tools, acting through material connections rather than official texts, and travelling across fluid jurisdictional boundaries. To retrace and explore the routes through which patents manage to travel to Djibouti and order the local market, I start by describing the various ways in which medicines enter Djibouti.

Importing drugs in Djibouti

In 2004, the import system for pharmaceuticals in Djibouti was made up of four different routes: a dominant system centred on private pharmacists; and three complementary routes – one for drugs imported by the OPS, one for the French hospital, and the system of the Pharmappro that essentially dealt with donations.

Predominantly, pharmaceutical imports and distribution were managed by private pharmacists – they bought and selected medicines directly from producers and dealt with them all the way to patient distribution and distribution to public sector hospitals. This last aspect is quite peculiar and is symbolic of the dominant role played by these private actors in the public system. Although some of the donations managed by the Pharmappro were distributed to public hospitals, this remained marginal compared to the bulk of drugs that had to be bought from private pharmacists; as explained by a member of the Ministry of Health: 'At the moment, public hospitals get a bit from the Pharmappro and a lot from private pharmacists.' Official data on the topic is limited and it is therefore impossible to provide specific numerical data as to the actual share of the import system occupied by private pharmacists, but this was estimated as at least two-thirds of the market. The situation was summarized as follows by a member of the Ministry of Health:

> At the moment, the import and distribution system in Djibouti is almost exclusively private – and almost exclusively based on

branded medication. Private pharmacists buy very few generics, and sell their drugs for a very high price.

Overall, private pharmacists were the most influential actors in the import system of Djibouti in 2004. When talking about private pharmacists with any governmental actor interviewed, one of the key elements they emphasized was the complete lack of power the government had over what pharmacists chose to import. This meant that controls exercised by the governmental inspectors on the quality of drugs were very limited. This also meant, most importantly for the purpose of this chapter, that the government did not have any influence on issues such as prices and procurement of drugs, cost efficiency, or selection of drugs (including generics v branded). For informants in the Ministry of Health, this sometimes meant that the private interests of pharmacists were privileged over the public interest pursued by official government policies. Any changes to the import system proposed centrally could be stopped by private pharmacists:

> The private pharmacists have a lot of power here – and especially one of them. He was clearly not happy with the changes we are trying to make, and blocked any attempt to move forward we have made so far. And it's no surprise that things were held for so long by the Chambre du Commerce... (member of the Centre d'Achat des Medicaments et Matériel Essentiels (CAMME))

This informant implied that the fact that the director of the Chambre du Commerce is one of the two private pharmacists described above meant that it was even more unlikely that any regulations on imports in the pharmaceutical field that would limit pharmacists' independence could ever be implemented. Private pharmacists act mainly independently from the government, with limited control and limited interactions with national health policies. As private businesspeople, they remain motivated by what will be most convenient, practical, or financially rewarding, rather than by governmental policies.

Alongside private pharmacists, and as mentioned above, some drugs entered the country directly through the OPS (and these were then exclusively distributed to patients of the OPS). The OPS has developed its own policy in relation to both import and distribution of medication to patients, based largely on generics. It operates independently from the health policy network. This was presented as potentially damaging by one key actor in the Ministry of Health: 'We have some issues of coordination with the OPS in relation to pharmaceuticals'. The OPS imported drugs fully independently from private pharmacists. All generics were provided by the (Dutch) IDA Foundation, with additional supplies provided by a French wholesaler:

> About 75 per cent of our drugs are generics, and all of these come from IDA – we send them two orders a year, and drugs come either

> by plane or by boat, which is of course cheaper but much slower. And then we have about 25 per cent of branded medication, when these particular drugs don't exist as generics on IDA's list. In this case we buy from the CERP in Rouen. (OPS pharmacist)

Alongside private pharmacies and the OPS, a few other drugs entered Djibouti either through the French hospital – for in-patient treatment and through the centralized provider for the French army (Faure, 1999) – or, more interestingly here, through international donations. Traditionally, donations have been centralized in a specific institution, the Pharmappro, before being distributed to public hospitals:

> Until recently, the only public system of imports was the Pharmappro. But it had a very very limited budget, and it was almost exclusively living from donations. But it was kind of 'DIY' – bits and pieces brought together. (member of the CAMME)

This system had already largely crumbled in 2004 – excluding the building itself, some exceptional donations and remaining stocks. The relevance of this example lies maybe more firmly in its progressive disappearance than in what was its temporary stabilization. The Pharmappro was created as a structure through which international donations – from France essentially, but also Yemen, Egypt or India, for example – could be received, managed and distributed in public hospitals. The system was considered beneficial for a while, until France started limiting its donations. The remaining 'gifts' from countries then became criticized by people in charge of dealing with the stocks. One of the reasons for this was that doubts emerged on the quality of the drugs given – no test could be carried out locally as Djibouti does not have any laboratory in which this could be done, and there was not always any guarantee from donor governments that tests had been carried out at home. The main reason, however, was that the donations were very often completely inappropriate to the needs and facilities of the country. For example, when visiting the buildings of the Pharmappro, the pharmacist in charge showed me a number of ophthalmologic materials that could not be used in any of the public hospitals since none of them had an ophthalmologist, or anyone qualified to use these materials. In addition, a donation from India had just been obtained by the President and was being distributed to representatives of different public hospitals, but most of the drugs were unsuitable for the needs of the country, for example, because they targeted diseases almost non-existent in Djibouti, or because they needed to be used in combination with products or materials unavailable in the country, or administered by a specialized doctor that the country did not have. Overall, most of the people present seemed reluctant to take any of the boxes with them, but had to in order to make sure that political sensibilities would not be hurt by refusing a donation obtained by the President himself. As a whole, the Pharmappro's efficiency diminished over the years, with changes in the flows of medication, themselves entangled in wider political and practical changes.

An interesting factor in each of these networks of import is the lack of control by the government over what drugs are imported and distributed in Djibouti. I return in the final section of this chapter to the emergence of the first central system of procurement since 2004, and its progressive enrolment of new generic drugs for the poor.

Patents and the routine ordering of the market

Complex sets of connections have allowed patented drugs to become omnipresent in Djibouti and stabilized enough to exclude any generic version of patented drugs – and exclude *any* generic in a predominant part of the market. In this section, I explore how patents come to be determinant in the process of ordering of the Djiboutian market, and how, reciprocally, generic medicines come to be systematically excluded from this market. Whilst the processes are partly linked to the proactive and deliberate influence of the pharmaceutical industry ('Big Pharma'), I argue that this influence alone is not sufficient to explain the shape of the Djiboutian market. Instead, attention to the practices and routines of those who import drugs in Djibouti illustrate a mixed web of heterogeneous connections and contingencies that lend to patents their influence over the market and stabilize the role of some drugs (innovators) over others (generics). Those connections themselves are significantly maintained and facilitated by the particular shape of the links between France and Djibouti, bearing the marks of their (post)colonial relationships.

PRIVATE MARKETS AND THE REPEATED EXCLUSION OF GENERIC MEDICINES

First, stable and repeatedly performed connections entangle pharmacists and patents/drugs hybrids. This link is stabilized by a range of practical and commercial connections that have to do with information and advertising, shipping conditions, importers' habits and trust. They also have to do with doctors' habits and patients' expectations. I question these connections, before turning to how the limited market of generic drugs of the OPS is regulated, and why it is limited to out-of-patent medications – thereby restraining the potential exception set by generic medicines to the role of patents in Djibouti.

ACTING AT A DISTANCE THROUGH ADVERTISING, INFORMATION AND OTHER 'THINGS'

When discussing with private pharmacists why they only imported branded medication, they suggested various factors. The first was that they in fact 'worked' only with a few companies, mainly large multinational companies, and bought their drugs essentially from branches based in France. Smaller generic producers were not generally used as sources of medication, and a large set of drugs was therefore already excluded by the strong links between large multinational companies and Djibouti. When asking for explanations as to why the range of exporters was so limited and why private pharmacists were so close to large multinational companies, they gave several reasons. First mentioned was the unequal circulation of information between various drug producers and pharmacists based in Djibouti. Put simply, pharmacists in Djibouti imported and distributed drugs they knew about. Only drugs that had been brought to their knowledge would enter the country – and the quasi-monopoly of the two private pharmacists may have made it rather unnecessary for them to go out of their way to find out about new products. When asked how they found out about particular drugs, or how they chose which drugs to import, private pharmacists listed spontaneously the range of strategies used by large pharmaceutical producers to advertise their products – and the proactive strategies used by Big Pharma have been well documented (e.g. Ecks and Basu, 2009). Much of this advertising is done through the provision of materials, from leaflets to pens or notepads, which have been proven to influence the prescribing and procuring attitude of health professionals.[4] Pharmaceutical companies also travel to Djibouti through the regular visits paid by their representatives to pharmacists and doctors in Djibouti, and the French pharmaceutical company Sanofi has a permanent local representative in charge of organizing monthly meetings with health professionals where specific products are be displayed – not necessarily *new* products, but, from what was observed during the meetings I attended, some of their well-known products and original brands. In addition to this, one of the two private pharmacists explained that he attends the Pharmagora meetings held in Paris every year. Instead of this being presented as an opportunity to broaden the networks with which he typically liaised, he presented this, however, as mainly being an opportunity of maintaining contacts with companies that had been in touch through the profusion of materials that they send over. Each of these strategies is summarized in the following quotation:

> There are two important ways to find out about drugs – the first one is to attend those big meetings held in France once, sometimes twice, a year. The other is through the permanent or non-permanent representatives of companies who come to Djibouti. (private pharmacist)

---

4 This has led to the prohibition of this practice in the UK, for example, Association of the British Pharmaceutical Industry (2012).

This enrolment of pharmacists in strong connections with large French-based companies runs even further in one case. One of the private pharmacists in Djibouti mentioned that he owned an advertising company through which he promoted the medication of some of these French-based companies:

> I own an advertising company for pharmaceuticals...basically I hire people to go and introduce new drugs to doctors. (private pharmacist)

The information he provided was rather vague, and the conversation we had about this could not move into more detail. However, this is an interesting and highly symbolic element which illustrates the entanglement between those who produce innovator drugs and those who distribute them in the largest part of the Djiboutian market. Although the proactive influence of the pharmaceutical industry that has been reported elsewhere, and its co-related ability to act at a distance, is visible here, the repeated influence of patents on the market is also linked to many other factors that make this action particularly successful and unchallenged.

Reliability and the persistence of the 'tried and tested'

Although the strong links between private pharmacists and multinationals in terms of advertising do not necessarily mean that generic companies could not find a way to reach Djibouti (and given the size of the market of Djibouti, they may in fact not have been interested), importers explained that they chose to import drugs from large companies based in France for several additional reasons. These had to do with the practicalities of importing drugs in Djibouti. Shipping drugs, or any other product from outside the region to Djibouti can be particularly lengthy. As an illustration, there are three scheduled flights a week from Paris to Djibouti and the only other flights are to destinations in the sub-region in East Africa and the Gulf. Shipping products regularly from India, for example, would therefore involve logistics possibly quite different from those of shipping products from France, especially in cases where they may be needed urgently. As a result, importers tend to privilege well-established routes and providers and, once convinced that the medication they ordered will reach them as planned, they explained that they tended to remain with the same provider. As phrased by one of the pharmacists: 'At least we know it works!' The inherent concern with reliability, and the impact that this has on maintaining the pre-existing arrangements and closing down the possibility for new strategies, is closely linked to the more general economic and practical difficulties faced by Djibouti – and some of these concerns were shared by pharmacists of the OPS as I explain below. The comments of importers in Djibouti on the difficulties they encounter when dealing with any 'new' provider, for practical reasons, and on the fact that shipping any product without delay through new routes is particularly difficult, also puts the debates about compulsory licences and their relevance to small markets in LDCs into some context. The solutions offered by the World Trade Organization to enable countries like Djibouti to issue compulsory licences to generic providers abroad are likely to require a degree of innovation and testing that are not in line with current practices and the framing of risk and possibilities.

The importance of advertising and shipping issues explains why large companies are privileged over smaller generic producers by pharmacists in Djibouti, and also explains the exclusion of some producers, in some localities, from the networks of import. However, it does not fully explain the omnipresence of innovator brands on pharmacy shelves. The fact that even 'branded generics' are very rarely found in Djibouti is not explained by this link between private importers and a few large companies – as these commonly produce their own branded generics. In order to understand this second set of exclusions, and gain a better overview of the processes of ordering at play here, I turn to the practice of prescribing in Djibouti and the role of doctors in stabilizing the connections between patients, diseases and patented drugs.

Doctors, patients and patented drugs

Doctors in Djibouti tend to prescribe branded medicines rather than generics and prescriptions will therefore, as a result, come to embed a specific branded medication.[5] This is not an unusual phenomenon, and is linked to training and habits. Many doctors in Djibouti are French, or trained in France, and the tendency of French doctors to prescribe branded drugs has been documented elsewhere (Kapferer, 1997; Larrieu and Houin, 2001). Doctors explained this as deeply rooted in long-standing habits:

> That's what we've been taught at uni, and maybe for younger doctors it is different, but if I need to prescribe Prozac or Primperan I can't tell you the generic name, and I don't have time to go and look it up. (medical doctor)

Brand fidelity as a phenomenon amongst health professionals has been well documented and is the effect of brands as well as patents (Greene, 2011b). Nonetheless, the specific advantage that patents grant to drugs by making them the first name patients and providers become familiar with, over many years, is one of the most determinant factors in making a particular name the one that will be most commonly used to refer to a drug. In France, where

---

5 For an analysis of the links between doctors, the pharmaceutical industry and health policy, see, for example, Das and Jeffery (2009).

pharmacists are legally allowed and actively encouraged to replace any prescribed medicine by its patented version, this does not necessarily have implications. In Djibouti, however, this entanglement of a particular brand within a prescription is more problematic, as pharmacists rarely seek to overrule the suggestion made by doctors and are not particularly incentivized to do so. They also suggested that, even if they tried to propose alternatives, patients would not accept generics – or replacement of drugs by any equivalent medicine, for that matter:

> Patients don't want generics. They want what's written on the paper. (private pharmacist)

Here, it is important to keep in mind the mixed positionality and interests of the customer base of pharmacists. As far as the many French patients of the pharmacies are concerned, most of them would not be interested in buying cheaper versions since they would be fully refunded by the Securité Sociale on their health expenses. As far as Djiboutians are concerned, the difference in income between a relatively rich part of the population and extremely poor sections means that those who could afford drugs of any kind would often be relatively wealthy. Those patients, once they had managed to access a doctor they trusted, would be unwilling to see their prescription 'overruled' by pharmacists or pharmacy staff and would not want anything other than the specific drug that had been prescribed. The poorest patients, on the other hand, would simply be priced out of what was available in the private pharmacies. Of course, the issues here are interrelated, and one also wonders how frequently pharmacists have tried to substitute brands with generics, given their reluctance to import any, but it is fair to assume that these different factors all co-contributed to the situation. Overall, it appeared clear that the relations between doctors, patients and drugs were set in such a way, and stabilized in such a fashion, that generic medicines were almost necessarily excluded from the network in which private pharmacists were involved.

As a whole, the near omnipresence of innovator brands in the private section of the pharmaceutical market of Djibouti is an interesting example of the way in which repeated patterns of behaviour, habits and social, economic and historical connections can allow regulatory tools to act in spaces where they have no official existence. Here, patents granted in France on some medicines have participated in making them the first choice of prescribers who travelled, or travelled back, to Djibouti. The privileged position, geographical and historical, of some producers has also made them the preferred choice of those who import drugs for the private market, with very limited control or influence from the government. Big Pharma is, as a result, highly influential in Djibouti, but its influence cannot be explained only by the aggressive marketing strategies that Big Pharma is known to use across the world. Instead, these are made particularly successful by the possibility that routines can be maintained in a context where little can be done by a disempowered policy network to change them. Although the actions of the industry can explain how some drugs are given an advantage, they are not sufficient to explain how the original advantage given to some remains repeated and uncontested. I now turn briefly to exploring the processes of inclusion and exclusion of generics in the secondary market built by the OPS.

Inclusion and exclusion of generics in the pharmacy of the OPS

Alongside the private import system, some generics managed to become enrolled into the Djiboutian health system, within the OPS. However, even there, those drugs were only the ones that were out of patent in Europe. To that extent, although pharmaceutical patents might not appear as a central actor for most of the imports carried out in this network, they remain embedded in at least some of the drugs bought and distributed by the OPS. I briefly explain why – in spite of the attempts made in the OPS to keep the price of drugs as low as possible through generic medicines – it in fact only imports generic versions of drugs that are out of patent in other countries.

Primarily, drugs imported by the OPS were provided by IDA, a Dutch nonprofit organization that provides affordable drugs to poor countries and as a result essentially distributes cheap generic medicines. The lists of medicines IDA provides is based on the WHO essential medicines list (EML), which is itself considered as made up of around 90 per cent of out-of-patent medicines (Laing et al., 2003). Therefore, the pool of medicines that the OPS relied upon was primarily made of out-of-patent products. Briefly, the links between EML and patents deserve to be explained and interrogated here, and the EML is a key actor in the discourses and the practice of access to medicines that is only occasionally unpacked. It is nonetheless an interesting site of entanglement between patents, drugs and diseases. It provides the basis for most national EMLs, including those of Ghana and Djibouti. The first EML was written by the WHO in 1975, and since then has been transformed yearly to take on board advances in medicines and the changes in needs of populations. A common argument to the fact that patents only have limited effects on access to medicines is to insist that most of the drugs on the EML are out-of-patents (Attaran, 2004; Noehrenberg, 2006). However, a closer look at the process of the enlisting of drugs within the EML demonstrates that it is inherently more difficult for patented than non-patented drugs to be enlisted within the list. This is due to the fact that 'cost' and 'affordability' are important criteria in deciding which drugs should be prioritized on the list (t'Hoen, 2010). As a consequence, patented medicines will only usually be included on the list if no alternative treatment exists, and patents therefore determine the ease with which treatment will be labelled as 'essential'. In many ways, the drafting of the EML can be seen as a clear example of 'impure science' (Epstein, 1996), in which the scientific conclusions of what the most 'important' medicines may be is heavily influenced by political and socio-legal issues and practices.[6] In addition, unavoidably, the larger picture of patents and global health is also of relevance here: the lack of innovation in pharmaceutical research that targets diseases essentially prominent in the South is a well-known problem, with diseases like malaria or dengue fever being associated with preventive or curative treatments that remain inadequate in various respects. Again, a critical view on the links between patents, drugs and diseases within the EML would highlight that the absence of patented drugs also reflects the absence of innovation in relation to killer diseases in the South.

As well as the fact that drugs obtained by the OPS were essentially from a pool of out-of-patent medicines, the origin of those medicines, and their transit through Europe, means that they were also caught up in regulatory networks that recognized and enforced patent rights. Again, the reasons why only one provider was used are a mixture of needs and practicalities. The list of medicines provided by IDA was deemed generally sufficient to the needs of the OPS, and it was also an easy and well-established point of entry for medicines:

> We have worked with IDA for six years, we know them. We have had so many problems before that, now that at least we know it works, we decided to stay with them. (OPS pharmacist)

In a similar way to private pharmacists, OPS staff then explained that practical transport issues were essential to be taken into consideration, as it could be complicated to import drugs in a reliable way in Djibouti.

One notable exception to this route for procuring medicines, when starting this fieldwork in 2004, was the import of anitretrovirals (ARVs). These had traditionally been provided by pharmaceutical companies themselves, and therefore the main set of essential drugs that were still under patents were provided by the patent-holders. Interestingly, in 2004 when starting this fieldwork, IDA was starting to procure generic ARVs. This was done at the time through a system that was partly independent from the main list of medicines IDA procured with which the OPS pharmacists had worked so far. In 2004, this system had only just been put into place, and the immediate reaction of the OPS pharmacists to it was one of general wariness towards this novelty. In particular, although this was underway and already advertised in different countries, the pharmacists of the OPS emphasized that they

---

6 For an in-depth problematization of the EML, see also Greene (2011a).

still regarded this as speculative and not something they would consider straightaway as they had only been given limited information on the matter. Moreover, they had not yet received lists of price or specific explanation on the steps of how to participate in this new system:

> It is all very new, and therefore very complicated, so at the moment we are buying branded antiretroviral and we will probably do that for a while still. (OPS pharmacist)

The high levels of uncertainty that have traditionally riddled systems of import in Djibouti understandably made its main actors wary of novelty. As a consequence, the possibility of moving aside from the mainstream and most established networks of import, and of breaching the repeated patterns of supply, appears difficult to achieve in Djibouti. This in turn makes the ability of new providers and generic providers to enter the system, even the more open network of the OPS, very problematic. Routines, habits and repetitive practices inherently maintain the predominance of certain suppliers over others, even in contexts where pharmacists are actively seeking the most affordable medicines.

The emergence of new networks of generics

Against this background in which generic drugs were repeatedly excluded from entire sections of the market, and generic versions of drugs still under patent were excluded from the entire market of Djibouti, a new system of central procurement of affordable drugs has slowly emerged since 2004. Interestingly, this new system also provides a historical snapshot, as it developed during the course of this research and was only just falling into place when my fieldwork started. The project is also interesting for what it says of the global movements that have emerged since the adoption of TRIPS (and I return to questioning it from this perspective in Chapter 6).

In 2002, the World Bank financed a new project in Djibouti that proposed the creation of a new system of import and distribution of affordable essential medicines (World Bank, 2002). This was built around a central system of procurement – the first of its kind in Djibouti – and a system of 'pharmacies communautaires' in the most deprived parts of the country and, in particular, in the districts where access to any kind of medicines had been very difficult so far, outside of the (deprived) local hospitals. The medicines would be primarily subsidized by the funding allocated and patients would only pay a very small contribution. The procurement is managed by a specially created institution, the CAMME. Against the background of the pre-existing pharmaceutical market, this new system offered an opportunity to provide medicines in a new and more systematic way to the poorest sections of the population, and therefore to alleviate the weaknesses of the private system that dominates the market:

> The aim of this programme is to start facilitating access to medicines in the whole country. This will be achieved by introducing generics – which would be very cheap, and therefore accessible. We also need to create a new system of distribution – basically we have been given money by the World Bank to develop these structures and finance the first order of medication. (member of the CAMME)

Drugs are procured by the CAMME through international and restricted bids, officially seeking to identify the most competitive providers. Because of the limited facilities available in Djibouti to test medicines, companies are only eligible if they are authorized to sell the drug concerned in their own country – and only if this country has the institutions necessary to carry out drug testing. The selection of drugs is still so far limited to a few essential drugs, with a focus on simple medical conditions that do not necessitate a diagnosis or immediate attention from a doctor – mainly, paracetamol, aspirin, anti-diarrhoeal drugs and a few antibiotics. The 12 purpose-built community pharmacies then provide the drugs without patients needing a prescription, and on the advice of the pharmacy staff.

The system has met practical difficulties that are germane to many of the problems faced by other public health institutions in Djibouti, were already emerging in 2004 as the system was just being built, and have not been fully resolved since: amongst these, the problematic management of limited resources ('It has just started, and already we don't really know where the money is going...' (member of the Ministry of Health)); issues of expertise ('We had a training session for the new staff – but it was a one day course!' (member of the CAMME)); and, in spite of the original aim to keep costs as low as possible, the high level of 'complementary costs' ('the inspectors have a van to go around pharmacies every day... the claims for money for fuel keep increasing all the time' (member of the Ministry of Health)). The system is also limited in its ambition and targets exclusively a few conditions for which the healthcare management can be delegated to staff that do not have extensive medical training. It certainly does not solve the difficulties that many of the poor, especially in remote areas, are still facing, but alleviates some of the immediate concerns. In terms of the pharmaceutical market, the system is also interesting and has generated some significant changes in the availability of generics – albeit predominantly in this specific, parallel market. In doing so, the project has limited the predominance of branded medicines as a whole, and therefore slightly shifted the extent of the entanglement of patents within Djibouti and the ability of the pharmaceutical industry to act at a distance. However, it is important to remember that the CAMME and the pharmacies communautaires are not a replacement for the private system that long pre-existed them. In fact, they are predominantly directed at people who were de facto excluded from much of this system, either by being priced out, or by being unable to access the existing pharmacies, all located in Djibouti town – a long journey away from some rural areas, in spite of the relatively short distances, due to the state of the roads. While the pharmacies communautaires have therefore created new opportunities to access generic medicines, those are essentially in the form of a new market that was added to the pre-existing one, rather than being a radical transformation of what was already in place. The market served by private pharmacists has not significantly changed in itself, as was indeed predicted by the person in charge of launching the CAMME:

> Private pharmacists expressed some concerns at first, but when you look into it, we really won't deal with the same share of the population. Our aim is mainly to supply those who don't buy anything at the moment. Those who buy from private pharmacies now will certainly keep doing the same.

Interestingly, however, the possibility of more substantially revising the market of Djibouti was initially considered and rejected because of the political difficulties met in doing so – highlighting again the relative influence of the private pharmacists: 'The original plan was that it would supply every drug in the country, like it is the case in other countries. But obviously, private pharmacists did not agree to that.' (member of the CAMME) The impact of the new enrolment of generics has nonetheless had some external repercussions. In particular, the progressive entry of generic medicines and the broadening of the spaces in which medicines are distributed has also become associated with the slow appearance of counterfeit drugs – actors so far surprisingly absent from the very tight Djiboutian market, as previously mentioned. Participants to this research therefore quickly pointed out what they saw as a side effect of this liberalization. I explore in much greater detail the shifts between generics and counterfeits in Chapter 5, but a few points are useful here. Until recently, and contrary to what is the case in many African countries, including Ghana, counterfeit medicines were not a concern in Djibouti. In the very narrow market described above, medicines were sold exclusively in the few official outlets, and these were selling a narrow range of branded medication, as I have explained. As the market opened and medicines started entering, in new forms, and as 'health' started appearing as a broader market, more actors got involved in obtaining and distributing medicines, without holding any required qualifications and without having any possibility of checking or knowing the quality of the medicines they were offering. As an interviewee put it:

> Now you can buy medicines in cornershops; not on the streets yet, as we see in other places, but in many grocery stores. And of course these are often counterfeit, entering from Somalia. It is a real problem here now. So you know, liberalization...it has its downsides too! (member of the Ministry of Trade)

The changes experienced in the Djiboutian market are therefore multidirectional, and 'messy' in their constitution. Alongside a dominant market in which innovator brands prevail and large multinational companies are highly effective at acting at a distance, a lesser system of distribution to the poor has emerged in which cheap generic medicines are playing a significant part. This system is restricted in its capability for expansion and very narrow in nature – focused on some drugs only, selected within the limits of a system with little local capacity for testing and assessment, difficult transport links and a small market that is not necessarily attractive to all suppliers.

The most interesting aspect of the project, however, becomes apparent on reflection of how the transformations of the market occur in parallel to the implementation of TRIPS. When considering the aim of the proponents of TRIPS and its creators, what transpires is the fact that TRIPS was mainly directed at 'reinforcing' pharmaceutical patents – at making them available in more places, for longer, on a wider range of inventions. This is very clear when looking at the role of the pharmaceutical industry in the pre-TRIPS era (Sell, 2003), and it can be interpreted as meaning that patents should and will probably be more active, more important, more relevant after TRIPS becomes active in specific networks than before. Interestingly, the changes that have taken place in Djibouti following this new international project seem to be having the opposite effect. Whilst so far pharmaceutical patents were de facto inherently part of most drugs imported into the country, their share in the market is now becoming more limited. While pharmaceutical patents were central to all imports apart from those of the OPS, the CAMME is now creating a parallel system of imports from which patents are for the moment largely excluded as potential determinants. The impact of patents on the country is therefore becoming more socially restricted, at the same time as patents are being officially introduced in written law. I come back to these issues when exploring further the various movements that surround TRIPS and access to medicines in Chapter 6.

Conclusion

The relation between the absence of national written law on pharmaceutical patents and the embedment of pharmaceutical patents in the dominant market of Djibouti raises important issues about the role and modes of action of patents as socio-techno-legal objects. Overall, patents appeared in Djibouti as a complex set of connections that became enrolled repeatedly in much of the health system. Some of this was undoubtedly linked to the ability of the global pharmaceutical industry to act at a distance, in ways facilitated in Djibouti by the close links that are still maintained between Djibouti and France as the former colonial power. However, the repetitive enrolment of patents is also, after a certain point, largely dependent on the practices and habits of individuals. The strength of the industry, as a result, becomes permanently reinforced without the need for further intervention or aggressive marketing – making its influence even more difficult to address directly. Patents are not the only factor that cause some drugs to be privileged over others, but, nonetheless, by providing particular drugs with the possibility of becoming part of those systems, and doing so largely uncontested, they are an essential element of the production of localized power. Throughout this process, the artificiality of the potential divide between 'social', 'legal' and 'technical' appears very clearly, as these connections emerge as blurred, uncertain and in constant flux. While for Bruno Latour legal objects act in a 'legal way' (2005), the very definition of these ways is problematic, and they can in no case be predefined or split from other practices and strategies.

As a whole, the embedment of patents in most drugs sold in Djibouti is the result of complex sets of codependent relationships. The weakness of shipping networks, of material connections between Djibouti and other places where drugs are being produced, the unreliability of many systems of transport, the crumbling system of international donations, the absence of local labs where drugs could be tested, are all examples of some of these connections, and more specifically of limited networks, less extended and less stable than found in other locations. Next to these somewhat restrained networks, several stable systems have developed. The first one is built around two private pharmacists and their shops, obligatory points of passage (Callon 1986) for most drugs entering Djibouti, which are entangled in sets of strong and well-run connections that are expected to remain stable and are not foreseen as likely to crumble. This set of stable connections has involved actor networks of which patents are an inherent part and have been reshaped in such a way that patents have become materialized and present through most drugs in the country. Bypassing their non-existence in written national law in Djibouti, this tool, which officially emerged on paper in other countries, supposedly for other countries, has become centrally realized through the connections lived and relived by private importers in Djibouti. Patents have not even been fully bypassed by the OPS, although it has created its own stable network, of which generics are an official part, and in which a different set of actors is therefore present that could be expected to exclude pharmaceutical patents. In particular, when dealing with drugs under patent, the OPS uses the patented version. Alongside this system, the emergence of generic medicines outside of the OPS, and in pharmacies available to those who are not employed and living in Djibouti town, is confined to a particular parallel system and does not significantly affect the largest part of the market, in spite of significant financial support from global institutions. In turn, the opening of new spaces and the enrolment of more varied products have also created opportunities for illegitimate networks of medicinal distribution to emerge. I return to the complexity of some of these issues in Chapter 6.

5
Ghana, Pharmaceutical Patents and the Ambivalence of Generic Medicines

The pharmaceutical market of Ghana highlights further aspects of the complexity of the relationship between access to medicines and pharmaceutical patents. In this chapter, I attempt to unpack the actions of pharmaceutical patents in Ghana, starting from the point of view of the pharmaceutical market and health system, rather than from the letter of the law. I focus here on the main system of distribution of medicines, to the exclusion of the distribution of antiretrovirals (ARVs). This is because this particular system is organized alongside an alternative model that does not directly link to the rest of the market in terms of procurement, or in terms of distribution (and I turn to exploring it specifically in the next chapter). Here, I therefore focus on other medicines, many of which are out of patent, but that nonetheless, as was the case in Djibouti, remain entangled in networks that emerge through and around patents. In contrast to happenings in Djibouti, however, the Ghanaian government has actively tried to facilitate the enrolment of generic medicines in its healthcare networks, and by comparison tried to avoid seeing innovator brands dominate a market in which access for the poor is still difficult. These efforts are challenged time and again, however, by practices, habits, discourses and attitudes that repeatedly resist generic medicines. In this chapter, I explore those efforts and the continued processes of inclusion/exclusion that are at play in the Ghanaian health system and question the various possibilities and limitations that are created and encountered when trying to bring good quality and cost-effective drugs to patients in Ghana. The story told here is one of constant tension between the need to keep prices under control and to promote the most fundamental instrument for doing so (generic medicines) and the difficulties encountered by these generic medicines in stabilizing their role beyond policy documents and government offices. Generics become an essential yet fragile object of public health. The chapter can be read as echoing some of the issues seen in Djibouti: for example, the struggle of generic medicines to become established and stable actors and the strength used by patented drugs to oppose their enrolment and stabilization. Throughout, I deliberately avoid reducing the strength of patented/branded drugs to merely the expression of the power of multinational companies. Instead, I hope that exploring the various ways in which branded drugs are stabilized will contribute to explaining how this power is constituted through a set of localized practices and heterogeneous connections and disconnections.

I start this chapter with some context on the challenges of bringing medicines, and in particular 'modern' medicines, as opposed to traditional remedies, to the poor in Ghana. In particular, the difficulties in enrolling sections of the population into the modern healthcare system are discussed. I then turn to reviewing the strategies deployed by the government to try to build a system of import and distribution in which generics are central actors, before analysing the persistent challenges to these efforts, with a particular emphasis on the interface between generics and the counterfeits market.

Networks of healthcare and the challenges of enrolling patients

Before looking at drugs and their distribution in Ghana, it is useful to briefly define the health burdens that the country faces. As in many sub-Saharan African countries, public health problems in Ghana are a mixture of the well-known global diseases (tuberculosis (TB), Malaria, AIDS) and other chronic or acute conditions that are not specific to developing countries, and may seem benign in other contexts. Those may nonetheless be significant killer diseases in countries in which getting basic healthcare to patients can still be a challenge. Interviews we carried out with medical professionals in Ghana echoed the policy documents that summarize the health situation:

> It all depends on age group. Typically across the board you have infectious diseases. You are looking at things like malaria. That is a very big problem. For kids it's all respiratory infections. You are looking at gastrointestinal infections, diarrhoea, post-diarrhoea and vomiting and things like that. You have UTIs as urinary tract infections. And then obviously as you get to the older age group you have lifestyle problems like diabetes, heart problems, hypertension...things like malignancies, cancers, breast cancer, prostate cancer, they are there as well...We've kind of covered the things that can be preventable by vaccination, so you don't really see too much of polio, you hardly see that. I don't think I've ever seen a polio case. Maybe one. (medical doctor)

Those conditions are usually treated with medicines that are out of patent, although some combination drugs, in particular for the treatment of malaria and TB are still relatively new and expensive.

I start an exploration of the issue of 'access' by setting up some of the context in which patients obtain – or don't obtain – 'drugs' in Ghana. Here, I am essentially concerned with modern medicines, as opposed to traditional medicines. Nonetheless, access to healthcare is commonly negotiated by patterns of shifts between modern and traditional. Those shifts and the context of the coexistence of multiple networks for healthcare bear the remnants of colonial tensions and contestations that make any inquiry in this area exemplary of some of the politics of modern science and modern medicines. Because of the tight inter-relationship between modern and traditional healthcare in Ghana, I also introduce briefly the role of traditional medicine in the negotiation of access to treatment. Overall, I explore here the processes of enrolling patients into a healthcare system in which they can access modern medicines and the various strains experienced in those processes, including the shifts between modern and traditional healthcare.

Navigating through the health pyramid

As is the case in Djibouti, family doctors are not a significant part of the health system in Ghana and enrolment in the health system is negotiated primarily around chemical outlets and hospitals. As a first step, many patients wanting to enter the modern healthcare system in Ghana will turn to a chemical outlet – either a pharmacy, manned by a qualified pharmacist, or one of the 'chemical sellers' that are spread across the country. I will come back to this distinction and its significance, but as a brief introductory note, chemical sellers are small outlets that are licensed to sell exclusively over-the-counter medication, are not staffed by a pharmacist, and were introduced as a response to the insufficient presence of pharmacies in some parts of the country (especially rural areas):

> In our system, that is how it works. The first point of call for a lot of people is either pharmacy or the chemical shop. You may have to wait for hours to see the doctor. A lot of people find it more comfortable going to the pharmacy before going to the hospital. (medical doctor)

The reliance on pharmacists or chemical sellers as first point of call comes with a number of difficulties, some of which I return to later in this chapter:

> Some drugs you can get off the counter. I think, these days, people are being discouraged from doing that, especially when it comes down to antibiotics and anti-malarials and things like that, if you

are resistant. Some pharmacies will still dispense I guess... (medical doctor)

When pharmacists or chemical sellers cannot solve a particular health problem, patients will turn to hospitals, ranging from small local hospitals to the larger regional ones. Simple conditions will be treated at the first point of contact and more complicated ones will be referred to specialists:

> Typically with the big hospitals they get referrals. But for the common illnesses like malaria and diarrhoea and vomiting and things like that, sometimes the patients will access the health facility that's closest to them. If it's bigger than the health facility can handle they will refer. So, yes, there is a certain pyramid of points where people seek medical attention and sometimes it depends on the doctor. If you are confident enough to handle and feel very comfortable with the case well, good. If you aren't, onwards and upwards. (medical doctor)

This system is not necessarily respected to the letter by patients, who will commonly misapprehend which hospital to approach first and how:

> So, you are not just supposed to walk into the hospital and say, 'I have this problem', you should be referred. You should have a referral. People still come in. You get people who want to meet for an 8am appointment. They arrive like 2am and they spread out their mats and they align them and they want to be the first in the queue when the clinic is open. There are lots of people... (medical doctor)

The process of accessing a hospital is a complex and uncertain one, and can be a discouraging and off-putting experience. The challenges are played out at several levels. First, the practicalities of accessing the hospital as a site can be difficult in the most rural areas, for people who often have limited means of transport. Once the site has been reached, seeing a doctor can again be a lengthy process, in hospitals that are often understaffed and overburdened, with insufficient resources:

> If you go to the hospitals it is not pleasant. We have problems with manpower. Doctors and professionals are all running away, because they are not being paid well. We have a problem there as well... (medical doctor)

In smaller units and rural areas, these difficulties are amplified, and the possibility of good quality healthcare is even more limited:

> Sometimes they are also mismanaged in the smaller health care facilities in the villages that are quite deprived of equipment and

> facilities. Sometimes it's really difficult to get stuff like insulin in, like, the village hospital. They may not have a doctor but a medical assistant who is overburdened and doesn't really have the experience, the background, to be able to handle some of the things he's faced with. By the time you finally decide you are going to refer this person and the people actually agree to be referred it's almost the end. (medical doctor)

The process of access to health becomes defined by its exclusionary nature, either direct, because the possibility of access does not exist for a particular patient, or indirect, because some patients will choose not to turn to a hospital system with which they have become disheartened. The following quote summarizes some of the processes that are at play here:

> Again even the facility, access to the facility…there are some places that you can easily get access to the health facilities when you are sick. There are some places where it is very difficult getting access. You can see the facility alright but it takes a longer time for you to access it. Sometimes it will take you almost close to three to four months before you can see a doctor. It is serious. So, you come there and there are some people who would tell you that they don't want to come to Ridge Hospital because this is the situation. So, there are some people who have taken the decision that once I'm sick, I will not go there. I will either go to the herbal clinics, go to the pharmacist…That is why we have a lot of preventable deaths in the country. So people are sick and they don't know. Even when they are sick they tell you everything is going to be okay with faith it would be okay. (member of the Coalition for Health)

The system therefore becomes one where patients negotiate across the various sites that are available to them, which will vary greatly depending on what they can afford; the pharmacy or chemical outlets, the traditional healers that I return to below, or private clinics for the wealthier sections of the population:

> They go to a private hospital because the queues are shorter. If they have the funds, yes. So they go there or they go to the pharmacy. You go to the pharmacist and see a whole bunch of things and he gives you things. Some of the pharmacists also want a prescription for certain medication and others don't. (medical doctor)

Patients being driven away from hospitals and therefore not attending early enough to their health concerns is a significant problem, and a symptom of the indirect processes of exclusion that are at play when a system cannot attend to its patients in a reliable way. The exclusionary nature of the system also means that the treatment of some conditions is simply not possible in the current context, in particular when these conditions have not been enrolled in any of the global funding that is being directed at healthcare in Ghana (and to which I return in Chapter 6). Medical professionals expressed much sadness and discouragement about the daily limitations as to what they could offer or what they could not offer to their patients and this seizes some of the realities of healthcare in Africa:

> Chronic diseases sometimes require things like transplants, which we don't do. So, the chronic kidney disease, they are quite young. It's pretty sad, because you can always tell the natural process of this, this person is going to have kidney failure in the short term without dialysis; the diuretics are not going to work after a while; medication is not going to work after a while; the kidneys are going to shut down if there is no dialysis and there is no transplant... Dialysis is like, what, three times a week. And each session is very expensive. There is no equivalent programme funding. (medical doctor)

Fatalism understandably spreads across the networks of healthcare, navigating between patients and medical professionals aware of the inherent limitations of a system for which resources are limited and treatment is often not provided on time:

> I'm sure if you go to the websites there would be something about the delays. They are the three 'D'[s]. There is a delay in deciding that you need care. There is a delay in getting access to the healthcare in terms of transporting yourself. There is the delay in actually getting the healthcare when you get to the healthcare facility to seeing the doctor. It's three 'D'. There is a fourth one people created... The D block in Kumasi? We have different departments sort of organized into blocks... And the D block is medicine. They kind of say that D block is where people go to die. Sometimes they do come pretty late. (medical doctor)

In a vicious cycle, the limitations of the healthcare system repeat themselves – patients, aware of the limitations of the system, often delay entering it until it is too late. When they do access it, the limits placed on treatment and advice are such that the system will often not enable them to travel fast enough to a node of the network in which they may access sufficient care.

Traditional medicine as an alternative medical knowledge system

The context of the interessement of patients into the state-based healthcare system also needs to be understood in relation to traditional medicine, which is very important in Ghana, and its role in filling the gaps left by modern medicine and hospitals. Given the limitations of the modern healthcare system, patients commonly navigate across traditional and modern medicines, and traditional remedies are significant players in the health system.[1] For the health professionals we interviewed, the significant reliance on traditional medicine was largely linked to a lack of education and an attachment to local cultures:

> It's the lack of education of most of the people who are sick. Before they even admit they are sick it takes a while and I think it's lack of the proper information and enlightenment, because they tend to ignore the illness for a while and then when they realize they have to deal with it then they opt for more traditional means of dealing with the illness before they come to the hospital – it is usually the last resort, because most of them are quite uneducated. I'm talking like basic education. I don't know if it's the same thing, here it's a little bit different because in Kumasi people are proud of their roots. Refuse to speak English and their attitude is a little bit different. (medical doctor)

However, these views do not fully seem to grasp the political nature of the rejection of a modern healthcare system that has been highlighted by many commentators (Cunningham and Andrews, 1997), nor the inherent interdependency between the limits of modern healthcare as it is currently deployed in Ghana and the attachment to its alternatives. The critical commentaries made on the conflict of knowledge systems and processes of contestation surrounding traditional medicine are of relevance here. Western medicine has commonly been understood as one of the agents of imperialism in Africa, and the challenges of its dominance by traditional medicine have been reframed as a political process of contestation. In this research I interviewed healthcare professionals within the modern or 'Western' healthcare system, as the essential focus of this research was on the market in modern medicines.[2] Nonetheless, the discourses that emerge within the modern healthcare system around traditional medicine are best understood with an awareness of the broader political and postcolonial contexts in which the practice of medicine is deployed in Africa (Vaughan, 1991; Fassin, 1992). The processes at stake in selecting a particular healthcare network are at the same time practical, cultural and political decisions that are codependent on a range of factors, such as availability and patients' experiences. The systems are

---

[1] On dual healing systems more generally, see, for example, Press (1969) and Romanucci Schwarts (1969).
[2] For a more in-depth study of the role of traditional medicine in Ghana, see Bierlich (2007).

therefore entangled in a constant movement of interessement and disinteressement, attempts at inclusion by the state and resistance or quiet contestation by sections of the public.

Traditional healing has also developed as a significant market, with its own practices for marketing and advertising:

> They have like billboards in the hospitals...There is a course of study in the university. But traditional in terms of the needs of doctors with their chickens and their skulls. They are quite open about it. You see these [sic] traditional healer and he's got these masks and things on his face and he's got like billboards advertising 'this is where my shrine is and come see me and I will solve all your problems from dissolving your fibroids to curing the environment', that sort of thing. People do patronize them a lot. They spend a lot of money that they don't have. (medical doctor)

The processes of entanglement are exercised both by each medical system towards patients but also by the state's attempts to institutionalize the exercise of traditional medicine, resulting in making it more akin in its format to that of modern medicine. Courses for traditional healers are now offered by one of the main schools of pharmacy in Ghana, and traditional medicine has become increasingly regulated by institutions that oversee the pharmaceutical market more generally. The spaces occupied by traditional and modern medicines also overlap frequently, and the boundaries between both systems are sometimes blurry; for example, some private pharmacists sell traditional medicines alongside modern drugs.[3] Similarly, self-medication and practices within the home will frequently associate traditional and modern treatments. However, the links between the traditional and modern sections of the health system are also dependent on subtle shifts between opportunities and individual choices:

> A lot of people don't take the prescribed medications. When you go to the remote areas, some people don't have access to health facilities. So you get some of these people who when they are sick, go to the herbal. Medications that they know work for generations. And people buy them because over a period of time they know there are medications which work for them. So people like these would not go to the hospital to look for the possible cause of the pains. (member of the Coalition for Health)

---

3 Marsland (2007) explores the constitution of modern/traditional hybridity in the context of Southern Tanzania, highlighting in further depth the mechanisms at play here.

A fundamental issue of trust is also underlying the above quote, and more explicitly referred to by a young doctor as follows:

> They are maybe not trusting the modern system. I don't trust it because my grandfather's brother's uncles, sisters, nephews went there and this is what happened and all of them went there and this is what happened. It's also a lot of ignorance on so many levels.

Throughout these statements, the tensions between knowledge systems and their cultural embedding are very clear. The dominant narrative, of truth and scientific 'accuracy' of one system over the other, pushing traditional medicine to the boundaries of the acceptable in improving the health of the population, is also very apparent. The position of traditional medicine in Ghana, however, raises complex and multidimensional tensions that cannot be fully seized by simply denying the potential value of traditional practices to health. Science and technology studies and studies in the history of medicine have provided alternative accounts of the development of Western medicine across Africa and re-emphasized how it inherently embedded particular political and cultural values. In Ghana, a concern of the government has been to try to regain control of the practice of traditional medicine and institutionalize it in order to ensure that each of its practitioners would be trained according to centralized procedures and that herbal medicines would all have to be registered with the Food and Drugs Board, for example. Inevitably, this increased institutionalization and growing governmental control also has a hand in reshaping the very nature of traditional medicine and rewriting its politics as a knowledge system. The nature of the tensions and movements between what we tend to define as the modern and the traditional is similarly modified throughout this process. Various processes of 'modernization' and constructing dichotomies are at play here, echoing the questions raised by Latour about the artificiality of these categories and their political and practical repercussions. In addition, the reliance on the traditional system, and the choice of using it over or in addition to modern healthcare, also flows from the inherent limitations of what hospitals can offer patients. In other words, the interessement of patients into modern hospitals is negotiated in a context where an alternative exists that will become more or less attractive depending on what modern healthcare has to offer.

Enrolling generics in the healthcare system

It is in this general context of access to healthcare that the issue of access to medicines needs to be questioned. In Ghana, the government has introduced a number of different strategies to ensure that those who have chosen to be enrolled into modern medicine can have access to affordable drugs. The role of patents within this context is important, as the process of ensuring affordability also involves a constant process of negotiation between several types of medicines – patented/branded/generics/branded generics – all constituted categories of variable cost and of quality that may or may not be equivalent.

The example of Djibouti has shown that the influence of patents in healthcare systems and practices can be subtle and discreet, and not necessarily directly connected to official regulations. Specifically, challenging the prevalence of innovator brands, and of medicines produced in particular places, is difficult. In Djibouti, the government has not managed to do so in the private pharmaceutical market. In Ghana, the government has, for several years, been more proactive in developing specific strategies for enrolling generic medicines into the health system in an effort to manage limited health resources. I focus on three strategies to achieve this enrolment – each of which was notably absent, by contrast, in Djibouti, creating a situation of high dependence on branded products. First, a degree of control over the procurement of medicines in the public healthcare system has been developed, giving the government some control over the price and quality of drugs entering public hospitals. Second, a National Health Insurance Scheme was introduced by the former government. Finally, prescribing practices are being targeted by the adoption of the universal nomenclature system by medical professionals. I will review briefly these different strategies and highlight some of the difficulties they are encountering, before interrogating, in the next section, the persistent resistance exercised against generic medicines.

National drugs policy and the central procurement of the public sector

The first aspect of governmental strategy to increase the use of generics has been focused on the public sector, and on a central procurement system for the public sector. In other words, the government has tried to establish some control over the medicines that come into public hospitals and to ensure that these are of good quality and obtainable at a price that is as low as possible. As was the case with the import system for medicines explained above, the procurement system for public hospitals was described both through an official and 'unofficial' narrative – both of which I introduce here.

Officially, the system is organized through detailed regulations related to the quality of providers and through a careful system of bidding and selection, aiming overall at procuring the most affordable quality medicines that are available:

> You know we have a procurement law. And so everything must go through first and foremost what we call pre-qualification of the suppliers and that you are trying to assure quality. And then

> when the bids are tendered in, whoever wins the bid brings samples of the product and it is evaluated by the Food and Drugs Board and a team of evaluators and so that is how the role of government is [involved] in it. (representative of the National Drugs Programme)

The first step in the process of procurement is the enrolment of suppliers that are considered to be reliable. Drugs produced by these providers may then become enrolled into hospitals, subject to further procedures. Importantly, the ability to test medicines is a central feature of the procurement system; this scientific or technical ability allows for a broader range of medicines to be imported into the country. As much as a process of exclusion, the ability to test for drugs actually becomes a process of inclusion. It is worth noting that the possibility of running such a system is dependent on the presence of a degree of local expertise and material enablement. The absence of such a facility in Djibouti, for example, is a constraint on possibilities of breaking an overreliance on multinational producers. The ability to unpack the drugs, physically as well as metaphorically, is essential here to allow a broad range of sources to be accepted in the pharmaceutical system. Generics will more easily enter, originating from a variety of sources, if their quality can be assessed. This is then translated at the level of each hospital, where registered providers are able to offer products that have been tested and approved:

> At the end of the year, the pharmacy department has done their forecasting, identified what they will need to buy, and then when it is done they give a notice to the public for tender. So we give a list of drugs the hospital needs, and this is done in each hospital, centrally for the hospital. Then the providers will give their best prices and we will choose. We look at the accreditation of suppliers, that they have been checked by the Food and Drugs Board, and also that some of the samples for the drugs have been tested. And that is very important because we can be confident that those suppliers will provide good quality medicine. (representative of the National Drugs Programme)

Again, the network here is more fragile and contested in practice than may appear from this description, and permeated with more micro-level negotiations than is officially the case. This discussion with a wholesaler illustrates the movements of individual negotiation that in practice influence how particular providers may see their products selected by the committee:

Res: The thing is the competition is so big for the public sector. Say you are the procurement officer. I want to register or draw a contract to supply you...but you know, I have to give you $500 for lunch...and you

keep going, then you have to give $1000. The highest bidder gets the contract...that is what happens. And in Ghana, anything you do, you have to give something. You don't do that, you don't get anything.
Int: So officially how do public hospitals buy?
Res: You have to be a registered supplier. So once you are on the list, your name is with procurement department, then if they need something, they call you.
Int: So how do you get registered?
Res: You just go and fill in a form. Then they call all of us to come and they tell us everything they need. Then if you can supply it, the politics start again...the lunches and the...let me give you an example: I went there the other day, and I heard them talking to someone about tilapia [a type of fish], so on my way back I am like ok, I told my wife to send the driver to bring tilapia...it's the little things, you just have to do. Every time you go, you have to 'this is for your lunch, this is for petrol, this is for the weekend, have a drink'...

The central procurement system is therefore one over which the government tries to have some control, with limited success and with some resistance at the most micro-levels. The relative ability of individual negotiators to secure their share of the public market is nonetheless as determinant as the price and quality of a medicine to their ultimate entering of particular hospital networks. The drugs that are selected are therefore not necessarily only those that are most affordable, but also those that are associated with individuals, companies, or material connections that are most appealing to individual decision-makers.

National Health Insurance

The second key aspect of the governmental efforts towards affordability of medicines was the creation of a National Health Insurance Scheme (NHIS) in 2003. The scheme has become highly politicized in its nature, being one of the key promises made by the government of President Kuofor, and it has become the focus of much political contestation by the current government ever since. Here, I focus essentially on the workings of the scheme and its relationship to the stabilization of generics as actors in the public health system, but it is important to keep in mind the broader Ghanaian and African politics that animate such wide-scale programmes.

The scheme is open to all patients in Ghana and is paid for through direct contributions, calculated with reference to patients' incomes and some governmental funding. Patients who have subscribed to the NHIS can obtain free treatment and free medicines, in accordance with the rules of the scheme.

Overall, the system aims at broadening access to medicines, in particular for the poorest:

> In the public sector some patients may be under health insurance, there is a health insurance scheme, the NHIS and some people are on it and some people aren't and they have to pay up front. The people on the NHIS are covered by the health insurance to a large extent. Sometimes they have certain medications that they have to provide themselves. (medical doctor)

Public hospitals are all registered with the scheme, and some private pharmacies are, but not all. As is common with public insurances, the system sets maximum limits on which medication will be paid for and how much the insurance will pay for specific medication, and this is based on generic prices, whenever possible. Processes of inclusion/exclusion are therefore at play in the deployment of the scheme in terms of medicines and limited to particular spaces – registered pharmacies or public hospitals:

> Not all medications are covered by the health insurance. So even if you have health insurance, you might have to pay for some of these ones. Of course, if you have the money then it's up to you where you get the drugs. (medical doctor)
>
> The health insurance reimbursement will not reimburse anything that is beyond a certain price. So that is what we think we can use to get people to come to do the right thing. (member of the National Drugs Programme)

Directly, the NHIS is therefore instrumental in facilitating access to healthcare for the poor and is a tool for controlling expenses for the government. Indirectly, the system also participates in a more general trend towards 'normalizing' the use of generic medicines in general practice and embedding them in the routines of both patients and doctors. Although it has contributed to significant improvements in access to healthcare for the poor, the system has also started encountering various issues in recent years that have brought its viability into question. The main issues encountered are resources and management, which have progressively resulted in a restriction of the scope of conditions, treatment and situations that are covered by the insurance:

> Not everything is covered by the national health insurance. Even when you are admitted, I mean, they had to take some things off, because they saw it was putting a lot of strain on the insurance scheme. Even for inpatients who have to be admitted for over two weeks...after that you are kind of on your own. Those who can't afford surgery to correct fractures, for instance. They have to be

> there for at least six weeks. We have them, like, two weeks and then after that you are on your own. (medical doctor)

As a result, users report an increased lack of reliability in the system. This has led to some opting out of the system, in particular many private pharmacies, resulting in the narrowing down of a network that was conceived of as a generalizable system:

> There are a lot of challenges working with the NHIS, payments are difficult and it is not good for business. But there are private insurances on the market, and those ones I take. They pay you. 30 days, they pay you. But the government...six months and they don't pay you. (private pharmacist)

In addition, the NHIS is radically different depending on where individual patients live, and across institutions and locality. Its very nature is contested as it, and as patients, travel across the country:

> Sometimes it depends on what area of the country you are working at [sic]. I used to be in a regional hospital and you can get things done much quicker. Some hospitals lose a lot of money, because...they probably don't get payments from the NHIS regularly, so because of that it's difficult for them to offer the whole package of services that maybe someone else could access. The NHIS...it's different in different areas of the country. Some places are able to, as soon as maybe you have a patient come, you offer treatment up front. You claim whatever you've spent on that patient later on. Some facilities are able to get the monies quicker. So, obviously, if that happens then there is incentive for you to offer the service more readily. If there is a very big time lapse between when you are offered the service and then when you get your money back then that discourages you in some ways. Maybe sometimes you say, 'Well, for this particular service you do have to pay up front.' Sometimes even people who are on health insurance, sometimes it's a hassle to get a treatment on health insurance. You might just pay up front, because it's faster. Sometimes you sort of go through a long process and you need to have documents signed and you just can't be bothered and say 'Well, I'm going to pay for it.' (medical doctor)

This understanding of the NHIS as progressively showing weaknesses and creating uncertainty and inequality was common in Ghana, and is illustrative of the broader difficulties of financing healthcare in sub-Saharan Africa. Importantly here, this first attempt was inscribed in a broader strategy of the state to control and limit the cost of healthcare, for patients, but also inevitably for the state. However, the difficulties in keeping control of individual events in the procurement process are also illustrative of the problems that are experienced when trying to keep track of a system supposed to run across a significant range of localized institutions. Efforts to act at a distance by a government that is not always unified in its institutional setting, nor materially able to reach remote locations, is difficult and uncertain.

Challenging powerful names

A third strategy deployed by the government in trying to generalize the use of generics, and therefore limit the role of branded medicines and the influence of global pharmaceutical companies in the country, is to encourage the use of non-proprietary names in medical prescriptions. The role of brands in stabilizing relationships between patented drugs and patients and patented drugs and doctors was very apparent in Djibouti, where the power of the name itself could contribute to raising prices and perpetuating the action of patents beyond their 'official term'. In order to avoid this sort of effect, those within the Ministry of Health in Ghana have endeavoured to encourage more use of the non-proprietary names of medicines, for patients as well as health practitioners – or rather, firstly for health professionals, and as a consequence for patients:

> First of all, you have to also remember that as a country we have subscribed to the generic policy that for us we will list our medicines in their generic forms or call it in [sic] the international non-proprietary name (INN) so that if given the choice, we can go for a generic that is of good quality, rather than going for an innovator. But if we do not have a choice between a generic and an innovator, we may just have to go for the innovator. (representative of the National Drugs Programme)

Again, the practical implementation of this scheme has been shown to have serious limitations, and I return to these in the next section. Nonetheless, the purpose of this strategy is to blur some of the differences between 'patented' and 'generic' drugs; these differences subsist while the patent on a drug is running, and any alternative needs to be produced either through a particular licensing system, or in breach of intellectual property (IP) rights. The patented medicines come to be known, on the other hand, through a general nomenclature, and when other versions of the same drugs are produced post-patent, they will be more likely to be known and named in the same way (Greene, 2011b). The message sent to professionals, and most importantly to patients, is that these drugs are 'the same', since they carry the same name. Very importantly, patents do not become embedded in the essential translatory instruments that are medical prescriptions. When the proposal for treatment provided by a doctor to their patient is materialized in a prescription, the medicine that is suggested and embedded is not a 'patent/drug', but a chemical entity that is mainly detached from any legal implications. Patents may have an impact on the number of alternatives for such a drug, but are essentially absent from the prescription. The impact of patents, in this way, comes to be entangled in a different set of networks, in which producers, patent officers and importers may play a central role, but in which patients are less likely to be driven by the request for a specific medicine.

Overall, the government's actions aim to keep the cost of medicines as low as possible, in an effort to increase access to drugs. If reflecting by comparison on the phenomena at play in Djibouti, where little governmental control is exercised, most of the actions described above are aimed at ensuring that patents do not run beyond the power that has been granted to them by the legal system, seeking to avoid the very situation that has dominated the Djiboutian market so far. The efforts of the government aim at ensuring that medicines that 'used to be patented' and those that have never been so are offered similar opportunities to circulate across the networks. Such strategies, and the broadened use of generics, have adopted various forms in different contexts, but have at times led to a substantial decrease in the prices of medicines (Hayden, 2011). In Ghana, however, in practice, generics have remained a difficult actor to enrol in the local health networks, and I now turn to the various aspects of the resistance that they meet.

Fluid labels and the shifts of generic medicines

In this section, I look at the challenges that efforts to stabilize generic medicines within the Ghanaian networks are meeting. My focus here is on the medicines themselves and their progressive enrolment in and exclusion from particular networks. I start by looking at the difficulties met by generics, before turning to some of the elements that explain why their entry and stabilization remains difficult, in spite of the general agreement by policy-makers that they are an essential tool for access to affordable healthcare. I then turn specifically to the issue of categorization, shifts and legal labelling and question how the significant counterfeit market in Ghana impacts on the possibilities for drugs other than innovator brands to be enrolled into the health system.

In spite of the significant efforts of the government to generalize the use of generics, non-branded medicines still struggle to be enrolled into the pharmaceutical market of Ghana. This is the case both in the public and private sectors, although their interdependency is significant as doctors prescribing in hospitals will affect the choices of patients in private pharmacies.

In the private sector, the enthusiasm for generics of the early 1990s has not allowed them to become fully stabilized into the main market and, instead, many of them have become pushed to its edge. In the remaining market for generics, the space occupied by the cheapest generics has progressively been replaced by upper-end products:

> In those early days, the market was dominated by Indian products. But now we are beginning to see people demanding UK generics, which is going very strong. So a lot of UK generics are in the system especially in the private sector. (private pharmacist)

Similarly, the generalized use of generics that is sought by the government of Ghana in the public sector has not been achieved in the way expected; this has been a concern for the government, and the basis of various investigations that fed back into the strategies described in the above section. In particular, the level of prescribing of generic medicines, as opposed to brands, is still relatively low and, according to governmental quantitative studies, only about half the medicines prescribed in hospitals are prescribed under their generic name (Ghana Ministry of Health, 2008). In the course of this research, the difficulties in generalizing the use of generic medicines in the public sector was similarly reported:

Int: So, now I will be assuming that to a large extent our hospitals would then be using the quality generics?
Res: They are supposed to but we are also mindful of the fact that our borders are not too strong and therefore a lot of medicines come through the borders and also the fact that our post-market surveillance is a bit weak, we are not able to pick some of these substandard generics that come through... But to say that the hospitals depend on generics, we have done a lot of studies and we know that generic use in the hospitals are [sic] very low. (representative of the National Drugs Programme)

The causes of this difficulty in enrolling generics are multiple, and here I come back to some of these. Fundamentally, I argue that the difficulty in enrolling generics into the public health system comes from their inherently fluid nature as entities and the shifts of their meaning across the global networks of pharmaceutical production and use. Several factors have been highlighted by previous research in Ghana to explain the tendency of doctors to continue prescribing branded medicines in spite of being encouraged to change their practice towards generic prescribing. Some of these are very similar to the situation described in the case of Djibouti. In particular, doctors' habits, familiarity with a particular name and time pressures result in the repetitive prescribing of names, or labels, that immediately come to mind.[4] The relationship between patents and labels, entangled in a way that enables labels to establish themselves in routines in a way that others cannot, results in patented drugs' ability to mobilize remaining stronger than that of generics, beyond the expiring of the patent itself. But, as was the case in Djibouti, the stability of innovator brands also needs to be understood in relation to the broader networks to which they belong, and in which they need to travel. In Ghana, their role, and the enrolment of generics, is significantly shaped by discourses on counterfeit drugs in the local market, which I focus on in some detail below. First, I discuss briefly the fluidity of generic medicines, which is central to understanding their inherent fragility in the health system.

Fluid nature of generics

Generic medicines are by nature fluid actors, navigating between their different 'others' – branded medicines on the one hand, counterfeit on the other – and navigating across networks that reshape their meaning – from competitors, to affordable medicines, to fragile drugs that struggle to be accepted. In addition, they are complex techno-regulatory hybrids, constituted through heterogeneous networks mixing scientific processes and regulatory acceptance (Carpenter and Tobbell, 2011). For the Ghanaian government, they are first and foremost tools for the management of limited resources that can guarantee a higher level of access for more patients:

> Generics are cost containment tools. When we talk about generics, especially quality generics, I will qualify. Quality generics are cost containment tools because when we did some study on pricing in this country, I am sure I can share that also with you, and you will see the difference between innovator brands and other generics and that tells you that, as a developing country, we do not have a choice but to go with the generic policy whereby if you have a choice between a quality generic and an innovator, because of cost issues, you will want to go for quality generics. So the generic policy is a government policy to contain cost. (representative of the National Drugs Programme)

For patients, the nature of generics can switch, between being perceived as substandard to what they are looking for, in cases where the names of these entities differ from those of the drugs they are familiar with, to being, individually and as a particular object, a more affordable way of improving their health. This shaping will depend on a patient's position in the market and

---

4 See also Ecks and Basu (2009).

their own income, in a country where income differences are significant. In addition, it is important to remember that the perception of generics as being 'similar to' or 'different from' innovator brands is itself dependent on levels of awareness of the mechanisms of production, patenting and branding that for many patients are relatively low. As a result, some patients will choose certain medicines over others, sometimes based upon misconceptions about their actual comparativity as chemical entities, while others will simply go with the option that they can afford:

> Certain products are afforded by the poor people and the more affluent, who go for the other most imported products. They can afford these ones...Some pharmacists concentrate on imported products for a certain category of people. Some want to concentrate on the cheaper products. (private pharmacist)

Progressively, a double market in generics has emerged, with a lower-end category of products offered to poorer patients, but also an increasing demand for upper-end products, branded generics and innovator brands from more wealthy patients:

> As more people move into the middle-income brackets and as awareness and availability of the drugs came and was all over the place. You still have a lot of the market depending on the Indian market. They are very cheap. Obviously, those who cannot afford will go for the Indian one. But some, the elite, look for the branded. The thing is that, because of...the rate of illiteracy in Ghana and...ignorance as well. You might have the same product that they've seen, but you give them a generic, they don't want it. Some of them go with the empty box to the pharmacy and [say] 'I want this one.' If the pharmacist says, 'No. It's the same thing as this is, it's just the same brand,' They say, 'No...I want this one. If you don't have it I can go somewhere else.' (medical doctor)

The significant differences in income, as well as the wariness of generics that I expand on below, have resulted in those drugs being fundamentally different objects for different groups of patients and, as a result, different pharmacies/pharmacists. Importantly as well, their meaning for health professionals in Ghana is unclear, and within the practice of health professionals the labels and significance attributed to generics shift constantly, making them as terms, as well as materials, largely indeterminate. Previous research has shown that, although doctors are familiar with the definition of generic medicines – but retaining an ambivalence towards it that I return to below – other prescribers, nurses in particular, are often unable to define what a generic might be (Ghana Ministry of Health, 2008). This uncertainty is, again, central to the fragility of generics as medicinal tools. This overall fluidity, however, can only be genuinely seized if bringing back questions about generics into the broader context of the Ghanaian market for drugs and the generalized concerns for low-quality medicines.

Generics and their other: how counterfeit medicines impact the role of generic drugs in the health system

> Generics, I think it started in 97 and then it gained ground in 2000...I think it was there that counterfeit started coming up more. People felt the counterfeits more with [the] generics. (private pharmacist)

In the politics of generic medicines in Ghana, in the way in which resistance to generics is taking place and in the various shifts that animate discourses on generics, the presence of counterfeit medicine as a problematic actor is crucial. Here, I turn to counterfeit medicines to provide a clearer understanding of the way in which generics are constructed in Ghana and argue that the meanings attached to generics are fundamentally dependent on the market for counterfeits. Here, I certainly do not wish to argue that generic drugs are of lesser quality than branded medication; instead, I unpack the local understandings of generics and counterfeits and show that the associations and shifts between both categories are a significant aspect of the challenges met when trying to enrol generics in the local pharmaceutical system. The global politics of counterfeit medicines and the definition of what is contained under this label are key to understanding the difficulties met by generics in the market of Ghana.

Counterfeit medicines provide an unusual site of entanglement of shifting legal-labelling and socio-technical practices. The term counterfeit medicine is loosely applied to a set of very different actors and highly contrasting legal situations, each entangled in a very specific set of production networks (Outterson and Smith, 2006). This is both problematic to the practice of medicine and public health and conceptually challenging. The deployment of different types of counterfeit drugs in health networks also has a differentiated impact on life and health, producing different realities of the material product. The collusion of these different realities under the same term, however, has significant impact on practices and the management of (il)legality, and of risks. This assimilation of contrasting realities results in processes of exclusion that are not necessarily warranted by the particular risk that is being targeted. Returning to the legal analysis of the loosely used term 'counterfeit drug', and unpacking the 'counterfeit blackbox', allows a questioning of the performed relationships of power that are at play in the global pharmaceutical market.

Counterfeit medicines are revealing entities, both for what they show of public health practices and of the relative position of different brands in the public health priorities of Africa, but also because they illustrate further some of the difficulties in drawing boundaries around the legal space. Therefore, they demonstrate how the notions of fluidity and heterogeneity that are central to actor-network theory (ANT) become relevant to unpacking very practical actors of day-to-day healthcare. I use this example to demonstrate the importance of careful attention to processes of legal-labelling and creating (il)legalities and argue that this is a significant part of any ANT analysis of a socio-techno-legal network. Nonetheless, the setting of boundaries around a strictly defined legal domain is empirically and conceptually challenged by the ideas of entanglement and shifting realities that are at the core of ANT.

Defining counterfeit drugs

The value and nature of a drug is derived partly from its chemical make-up – which may or may not differ between the 'real' and the 'fake' – and partly from the legal and economic networks in which it is inscribed. Questioning the very nature of what constitutes a drug, one of my Ghanaian informants explained that: 'The problem with drugs is quality. If you lower quality, they are not drugs.' (public health policy-maker) Issues of material and socio-cultural identity are at play here, and the very identity of the chemical entity is at stake when defining counterfeit drugs. This identity is contingent both on the type of situations covered by the term 'counterfeit', and on definitions of what makes a drug real, valid, or legitimate. The different legal situations covered by the term means that some counterfeit drugs may be identical to the legitimate/real drug in its material composition and in its physical effects on the patient's body. It is therefore common to label as counterfeit some medicines that are effective but breaching a law, as well as chemical entities that are not what they claim to be (Outterson and Smith, 2006). The concept of counterfeit drugs hides situations that differ more vastly from each other than is the case in other areas of counterfeiting. There is an assumption that for a medicine to be 'just a medicine' as opposed to a counterfeit one, it needs to belong to certain legal but also (consequently) socio-economic networks, predominantly neoliberal and responding to set regulatory frameworks. These networks are formed around patterns of power and shaped to perform and reinforce the rights of some over others. At the same time, the collusion of different legal situations under the same label complicates the position of legitimate generic medicines in public health networks.

To explain this conundrum more clearly, I start by detailing the categories of drugs that are covered by the label 'counterfeits'. By unpacking this term, at least three broad categories can be identified that vary significantly in terms of public health impact, potential solutions and legal issues. The first category of drugs labelled as counterfeit, and those that are most problematic from a health point of view, are the ones that are of substandard quality. Those can be chemical entities that contain no active product, or low levels of active product only. They can also be drugs that contain actively harmful substances. These two situations can be distinguished to some extent, but also overlap in the concern they create for the management of public health, and their existence justifies the many global actions currently taken to tackle the counterfeit market.[5] Whilst the latter drugs present an immediate danger to patients' health, leading in some cases to serious consequences, including death, the former are dangerous because patients will be lacking the medicinal treatment that they believe to have been given. In turn, the consequences of this will vary depending on how closely patients are being followed: follow-up medical appointments may be able to identify this, but in contexts where access to health professionals is often difficult, this can have dramatic consequences. The exact share that these medicines occupy on the global market is contested and research shows that the profusion of figures that are put forward by the World Health Organization (WHO) and other organizations are conflicting and uncertain (Obi-Eyisi and Wertheimer, 2012). Their widespread presence across Africa is well-established and their role both in Ghana and Djibouti (more recently) has been demonstrated during this research, but the very nature of the system makes it very difficult to evaluate the specific share they occupy – as will become clear when looking at how they are used and distributed in Ghana, for example. In any case, the fake drugs are the ones that, from a chemical point of view, and as put in the words of the informant quoted earlier 'not real drugs', tend to be the ones that capture most generally public imaginaries and global discourses on counterfeits and the risk they represent for health.

The second category of drugs that are labelled as fake or counterfeit are those that are in breach of a number of regulations. They may in fact be chemically similar to the real drug, but in breach, for example, of IP rights. In this category, ARVs produced without a licence having been granted to the producer can and have been labelled as counterfeits even when the chemical composition and effects on patients' bodies were identical. More generally, any generic version of a patented entity that has not been authorized by a licence is commonly labelled as counterfeit. So, whilst the generic versions of drugs that are out of patent are 'generics' as long as their chemical features are similar to those of the original, generic versions of drugs that are still under patents can be generics when they have been produced under licence, and counterfeit when they have not – bringing potentially the same drug,

---

[5] See, for example, the International Medical Products Anti-Counterfeiting Taskforce (IMPACT) and the Council of Europe Convention (ElBishlawi, 2012; Liberman, 2012).

produced by the same producer and under similar manufacturing conditions to be labelled very differently and with very different connotations and implications.[6] As well as IP rules, the breach of other regulations can make drugs tip into the category of counterfeit; for example, prescription drugs bought abroad and their import within a territory where they cannot be legally used or procured. Interestingly, in purely medical or medicinal terms, the material sold and used in this context is entirely similar or comparable to the original or real drug, and assimilating this and the first category of counterfeit is problematic as usable and dangerous medicines are merged under the same label.

Finally, a more blurry category of drugs that are chemically equivalent to the original medicine, but different in the route that they take to meeting patients, can be identified. These drugs may be sold in outlets where they should not legally be sold,[7] they may be labelled in ways that are incomplete, in a language other than the official languages of the country, packaged poorly, potentially stored in inadequate conditions. These may cause public health concerns, not necessarily due to the chemical constituents of the drug but to the networks that surround them – be those material (storage) or expertise-related (advice to patient). This is particularly the case for drugs that breach laws on points of sale. A significant part of the illegal market is therefore constituted by drugs that reach the patient by illegal means. Again, there is a differential set of impacts here depending on the networks we are referring to.

What is at stake under all these different labels is the very nature of what we consider as being a real drug or not. The boundary may be easy to draw at one level, when distinguishing the chemical components of a drug – although contestations surrounding the effects of specific drugs are common, and emerges from some of the quotes I refer to later in this chapter. When looking at two entities with the same components, we may attach different levels of importance to the networks immediately surrounding the drug when the patient encounters it – is a drug still a drug if the patient is not offered enough information on how to take it or use it? If it is bought for the wrong condition or in the wrong dosage, or given with inadequate advice in relation to its posology? As phrased by an informant from the Pharmacy Council:

> I would not look at access as having the medicine in hand. I would look at access as having the medicine in hand and having the appropriate information…if you have access to medicines which you use wrongly, in the end it will kill you. I have had dealings with people who don't know how to use them. Will you

---

6 For a problematization of 'generics', 'copies' and the licit/illicit divide in a different context, see Hayden (2011).
7 Or on the 'grey market' for pharmaceuticals (Ghosh, 2002).

call this access? They have the medicines [sic] and it is prescribed they have it. They can't use it properly.

The extension of the term counterfeit to drugs that are not complying with IP regulations is also very controversial (Attaran et al., 2011). Whether these drugs are 'problematic' from a legal and economic perspective or not could be debated, but is not the key issue here – the core of the problem here is one of labelling and of the impact of using, for breach of IP and licensing conditions, a term that is also used to refer to medicines that can endanger the health of patients, through containing harmful substances or by being ineffective in fighting disease. The difficulty with this and the role of discourses, including from the pharmaceutical industry, in using a legal label to blur socio-technical boundaries has started to be brought to public attention recently (Anderson, 2009; Oxfam, 2011). Similarly, current initiatives, such as the controversial Anti-Counterfeiting Trade Agreement (ACTA), often maintain some of this blurriness, prioritizing IP reinforcement while using a term commonly associated elsewhere with harmful products (McManis and Pelletier, 2011; Rens, 2011; Liberman, 2012).

Overall, at the moment, under the same label of counterfeit, these very different socio-techno-legal tools co-exist. The difficulty in any such collusion in labelling is to see a degree of confusion and assimilation in the identification of specific objects.[8] Although the healthcare concerns of each differ, a certain movement or shift away from counterfeit as a whole can result in a drift away from legitimate, or healthy, medicines. In the rest of this chapter, I relocate the role and impact of counterfeit medicines in Ghana, before exploring the porous boundaries between branded/generic/counterfeit systems of drug distribution and some of the issues raised by this collusion of terms. In particular, the drive against the 'risky' counterfeits results in a more general drive towards a limited number of (principally Western) producers.

Counterfeit drugs in Ghana

The widespread use and distribution of counterfeit medicines is a significant concern in Ghana. An analysis of the discourses of health professionals and policy-makers on the issue illustrates how this is articulated and how the networks of counterfeit medicines are shaped. It also opens up questions about the impact of the fluidity of the term counterfeit, and demonstrates some of the practical effects that the fluid labelling of products that are different in their nature and their relation to the patient can have. The interchangeable use of the term counterfeit, to refer to products that may or may not have a certain level of toxicity, may or may not carry active

---

8 For an example of how IP issues and threats to life are mixed in legal discourses, see Bunker (2007) and Yar (2008).

substances, and may or may not be entangled in criminal networks, leads to an extension of the label to drugs that are, in fact, outside of any of the three definitions that are given above. In particular, the assimilation of the inactive/toxic counterfeit, with the illegally produced counterfeit and with the unlicensed generic, under the same label, also results in an assimilation of the 'illegitimate generic' with generics in general. In the discourse of health professionals and policy-makers, the broad use of the term counterfeit that can be noted in international discourses is echoed, and there is no systematic effort to differentiate between different 'types' of counterfeits, with different degrees of risks for the patient. Interestingly, the amalgam that is produced under the term counterfeit also results in an assimilation of fakes and generics that is not specific to Ghana – generics have commonly been received with significant distrust by patients – but is interesting to retrace and deconstruct here. In particular, the concerns over counterfeits appear to also result in a backlash against all generic medicines and a return to branded medicines in many cases. Counterfeits therefore appear to have a significant impact on the market for generics in the country and, potentially, extend the scope of the influence of patents.

When discussing access to healthcare and the issues that contemporary Ghana is facing, all informants spontaneously brought up the topic of counterfeit drugs. They were presented as a risk for practitioners to be aware of and a danger to patients, as well as being one of the most significant healthcare issues the government is facing. The perspective of each participant and their description of what was 'the problem' of counterfeits varied depending on their own positionality within health networks, but, for all, they represented a certain *risk* that had to be acknowledged and avoided. The key concern for all, however, was that of drug quality, and the core of the risk to be avoided was that of health risks to the patients – in other words the only actual risk of concern to practitioners and policy-makers was that of the supply and distribution of medicines that were not of the right quality or not administered in the right way. This was expressed in slightly different ways in different interviews:

> We have an issue of quality control, so a lot of these cheap medicines have no active ingredients...Oh yes, counterfeits are in Ghana. They are here. Ghana is a loose country...In terms of medicines, some don't have any active ingredients. But also some have lower levels of active ingredients. (public health policy-maker)
>
> The problem we found was with some imported drugs. They come in, and they are cheap, but with no active ingredient. (public health policy-maker)
>
> Not harmful, but some basically there is nothing [in] it. Others, probably half strength. Not something harmful. We don't have that detail yet. It leads to resistance, especially antibiotics and

stuff like that. Even malaria. That's where we have a problem. Malaria almost 50 per cent of our health budget. It means the potential to make money there is quite huge. That is where we see a lot of counterfeits... (private pharmacist)

Doctors translated these concerns in relation to their own practice:

> It's a huge, massive problem. Firstly, your reputation is on the line. Whenever you write, giving a patient any treatment that doesn't respond, obviously you are asking yourself questions like 'Was my diagnosis correct?' Also, 'The drug I gave, was that any good to the patient?' And also, forget about your reputation, the most important person is the patient. They have got to get better. Sometimes they are really really sick and you are giving them a drug that may be really half strength of what it's supposed to be. Basically, you are under-dosing them. They aren't getting enough of the drug. They aren't getting enough of the treatment and also you are building up resistance to these sicknesses. It's a massive problem. I would wish that every time I write a particular drug, I get a really really good drug, a really good – if it's an antibiotic, it's a real antibiotic of the right concentration of the right dosage that the patient will get. I would wish that. It doesn't always happen. (medical doctor)

The underlying causes of the thriving market for substandard medicines are numerous, and their production is a global phenomenon that happens in many places and at many times (Obi-Eyisi and Wertheimer, 2012). Here, I try to capture some of the specific factors that arose in this research and represent, unsurprisingly, a mixture of poverty, lack of education, access and difficulties in pre- and post-market control – each reminding us of the tight inscription of health practices within the broader socio-cultural and economic context of any locality. Poverty is clearly one of the key elements that creates a demand for counterfeit medicines and, in fact, makes them a significant actor within the public health networks of Ghana – some of them replacing legitimate drugs, some taking up a space that would not have been occupied by legitimate drugs anyway because potential patients would have been priced out:

> Some people only look at the bottom line. They go for the cheapest and if you are not lucky you have some of these fake one[s]. (medical doctor)

For the poorest people, counterfeit medicines (in most of their meaning defined above) occupy a space that is left empty by the formal networks of healthcare, partly because some people are priced out, but also partly for issues of physical access to the formal system of care. Interestingly as well, the difficulties in tackling counterfeits comes from issues of identification – of the counterfeit drug itself, as opposed to the quality drug, but also of the networks that are legitimate for the sale of a particular type of medicine. The bulk of counterfeit medicines are thought to be found in the hands of the chemical sellers that I introduced briefly earlier. Little control is operated in those premises in terms of quality and the market for these counterfeit medicines is constituted essentially of patients with limited resources. Chemical sellers are often found in places where hospitals are difficult to access and pharmacies absent, including rural areas, and their very role is to respond to the lack of pharmacies in particular localities. Their enrolment of and with counterfeit becomes symbolic of some of the difficulties of spatial access for patients. As a result, the rural market is particularly heavily saturated with poorly controlled drugs. The system of chemical sellers was developed to try to extend access to some basic medicines in the most remote areas to those who could not access pharmacies, and to respond to the concentration of pharmacies around the larger urban areas – in particular, a significant proportion of the pharmacies in Ghana are located in Accra, leaving inhabitants in the rural areas of the country sometimes very far from a pharmacy. Although the chemical sellers have participated in increasing access to some modern medicines in the countryside, they have also created many difficulties:

> They came about as a result of the fact that we don't have enough pharmacies as well as pharmacists. Every pharmacy is supposed to have a pharmacist. The number of pharmacists in Ghana is very small. Most of the pharmacists from my class are no longer in the country. They are in the US, UK practising. So, we decided, let's get some people trained and let them have access to some group of medications that people need and allow them to sell those drugs. That is how the chemicals came in. Also, all the pharmacists even as of now, close to 60 per cent of pharmacies in Ghana are located in Accra. Very few are in the rural areas. Because it's liberalized and it's market-driven. Every pharmacy wants to go to where the money is. Your chemicals sellers are, sort of, we give them training and they are supposed to, you know, fill the gap. They are not properly monitored. There are also a lot of things there that are not supposed to be there. And there are so many. Every town, city, hamlet, some small towns you see over there. They are all over. They are all over. They play a very important role in our health system, but because they are not properly regulated... they tend to create problems for our health. (private pharmacist)

Interestingly, the difference between pharmacies and chemical sellers, though clearly emphasized by all interviewees, seemed much more blurry from a patient's perspective – and myself and my co-researcher spent a significant amount of time trying to clarify the status of individual outlets. Labelling was uncertain, chemical sellers do in practice sell more than they are allowed to, and although the difference between a top-end pharmacy and a small chemical seller is obvious, the spectrum and range of shops that we encountered made the boundary seem slightly ill-defined, and we suspected that patients could easily be mistaken or not clearly aware of the difference between a real chemist and the owner of a small shop selling medicines displaying a board saying 'chemist'. Understanding the difference between different outlets and the relative expertise or right to sell particular products of different individual providers requires a degree of understanding of a system of qualification, authorization and licensing that many patients, not familiar with the intricacies of public health systems, will not have. This excerpt from an interview with a wholesaler is illustrative of some of the difficulties in drawing the visible and practical boundary between those different outlets and representative of several other conversations we had with participants:

Res: A chemical shop is not registered to sell, a chemical shop, first of all doesn't need a pharmacist.
Int: But how do you know the difference?
Res: When you walk in you know the chemical shops are, like, the deprived ones. They don't have prescription drugs.... they might sell anti-malaria, paracetamol, over-the-counter products. Some of them sell Amoxicillin. They don't sell, like, the hard core prescription drugs... First of all it's [a] chemist shop. Ok, some pharmacies are chemist shops as well... [pause] Ok, you can see the set up. You see a pharmacy shop and you know it's a pharmacy shop, because it's well decorated and everything looks quite... chemist shops don't make that much money to be able to afford to make the place look good... They usually don't sell, like, the UK products. They usually sell the local products and the Indian products, they are cheaper products. If I have, like, a headache and I need a painkiller, I can go there and buy it. Ok, when you go into a pharmacy there is a separate box where they keep the prescription drugs. That is where they keep the prescription drugs and the rest are OTCs [over-the-counters]... They have different compartment[s] there. In the mall they have, like, a different compartment. Behind the counter, that's where they keep all the prescription drugs. You see them exhibited there. Observe next time. Over the counter... Usually air-conditioned. They are, like, open. Chemical sellers... They are not big. Usually, the operator is not that well educated. All he knows is what he's selling. He will tell me what he's selling or Lemsip, you know, over the counter products. OTCs.

The ability to judge the legality of selling a particular product, or the ability to provide expert advice on its use, is therefore essentially dependent on patients being able to judge the nature of a shop and its owner by looking at its size and setting. This is not always easy, and the difference between a small pharmacy and an upper-end chemical seller is not necessarily obvious, and, as a result, it can be difficult to judge the limitations that exist both to the entitlement of the owner to sell particular products and to the extent of their expertise.[9]

In the background of this problem is also the recurrent issue of expertise, at its most basic level – and also of the distribution of expertise, not only amongst health professionals, but also amongst patients. And if identifying outlets and understanding what they can legitimately be expected to sell, plus checking and evaluating are all difficult, identifying a fake from a genuine drug is even more difficult, even for the trained eye – which of course is part of what makes their proliferation so difficult to slow down:

> Some of them look so genuine... Recently, we saw same packaging from somewhere that have [sic] come onto the market. They look so close to the original... (private pharmacist)

But some of the difficulties that Ghana and other African states face – in terms of illiteracy and the lack of patients' familiarity with the healthcare system, or at least with this very specific part of the healthcare system (made up of competing pharmaceutical producers, labels in a language that may not be familiar and in letters than may not be readable, distinctions between the qualifications of those advising on the tablets that may not be obvious without familiarity with a certain form of educational system etc.) – have made the problems particularly acute. Again, the 'two-speed' nature of the healthcare system and the obvious links this has with the gaps between rich and poor, educated and uneducated, right across the country are visible in this dilemma:

> So it is a big problem, not only in Ghana but all over Africa. I was reading a research [report] by someone in Kenya, and a lot of the malaria tablets, they are fake... so it is a problem... but the root of it is poverty and illiteracy. Because if you work at the pharmacy you realize that those who are educated, they ask a lot of questions, they want to know where the medication came from, before they buy it... at least from my experience... but people who aren't educated, they can't even read, even if it is written on it they can't even read... (private pharmacist)

---

9 A photo gallery of a chemical seller provided by Pfizer (interestingly, and as part of the advertising of its assistance programmes) gives a sense of these difficulties: www.pfizer.com/responsibility/global_health/mam_photo_gallery.jsp.

Avoiding substandard medicines

The diffuse nature of the networks through which counterfeit drugs are produced – be they low-quality or simply in infringement of licensing rules – makes the problem of control particularly difficult to solve. Many of them come by road, often from neighbouring Nigeria. The porous borders being Nigeria and Ghana, but also across the region, and the difficulties in controlling what is imported by sea are all facilitating factors. The government in Ghana has taken various steps in order to try to slow down the counterfeit market, but the level of resources that would need to be involved is significant and in excess of what is currently available. In practice, much of the surveillance system is delegated to practitioners rather than being systematic. The task is made particularly difficult by the widespread nature of the phenomenon. The number of potential outlets, informal as well as formal, the form of the selling points, the entry of drugs through ports as well as by road, packaging that is constantly transformed and made to resemble that of legitimate drugs, all contribute to make the problem a very difficult one to solve. The government has tried to put a system into place:

> We have a consumer complaint desk for people, the public, to inform us of anything – if they come by some medicines for which they have a reason to suspect anything then they will have to call in and we will have market surveillance…go and investigate. And then later, we get to the lab to do the verifications and whatnot. And…there are various sanctions. We work with the police and then hand it to the police. Sometimes they will do raids and some investigative activities with the police. Especially with the Criminal Investigation Department and sometimes with Interpol. They will do the prosecution if that is a preference. And then the other things they also do is revoke the licence if we had already given it…(member of the Pharmacy Council)

In practice, the system encounters, once again, the limitations that I highlighted with respect to other areas of governmental control:

> They are working hard to cut it out. As I told you, the training, the manpower, equipment. We don't have a lot of things. We've come a long way, but we still have a long way, very long way to go. (private pharmacist)

> The government still don't have a grasp of the situation. It's also another problem. Most of those guys who are in occupations packaging them and selling them have contacts at the highest level of the political structure. Sometimes, when we come to take

> them on, they are not being kicked out. Very powerful, yes. It's a big problem. It's a very big problem. (private pharmacist)

In this difficult context, checks and controls become dependent on individual practitioners taking their own steps to try to avoid counterfeits interacting with their practice. Some have specific expertise that enables them to distinguish carefully the different categories of drugs that they are dealing with:

> Because of that I do all purchasing myself. I also have some training in detection of contact with drugs. I worked with Food and Drugs and I was trained in the UK for some time. By virtue of the fact that I used to work at the main regulator of medications in Ghana, I know who are the accredited agents for every product. If I'm looking for a particular product, I just go to that or I call them and they supply. (private pharmacist)

Patients also adapt their practices – but only those patients that have sufficient education to be aware of the problem of counterfeits:

> Fake medications is [sic] a problem all over the world. Especially in Africa, because our controls are very very poor. Borders are very poor. Regulations not up to scratch. We still have a long way to go. Fake medications is [sic] a problem. People have that at the back of their minds. It serves as a guide where to go to for your medication. (member of the Pharmacy Council)

Often, however, individual efforts to avoid substandard medicines result in a return to branded medication, or to using supplies from Europe or multinational companies as a guarantee of safety and quality. In the absence of specific expertise or faith in the checks and controls provided by the government, patients and practitioners commonly turn to an avoidance strategy of the drugs that they do not have full trust in, or of providers and producers that they are not familiar with. This is where the issue of counterfeit and the intertwining of different types of drugs under the same label becomes most interesting. The global issues of counterfeit medicines and of access to drugs can be brought together in a number of ways, but one of the ways to look at them is to question the back-and-forth movement between branded and generics, and how this is affected by counterfeit medicines. In the next section, I look at some of these movements.

'Fake' drugs, avoidance strategies and the impact on legitimate cheap medicines

Analysing in more detail attitudes towards generic medicines demonstrates the close interdependency between generics and counterfeits – of all kinds. In particular, strategies to avoid substandard medicines often result in a return to branded drugs and a pulling away from official efforts to increase reliance on generic medicines. This is linked to frequent assimilations in discourses between generics and counterfeit and a wariness that has been associated with generics in other contexts. Nonetheless, in the context of Ghana and of the efforts made to decrease the cost of medicines, this is a useful issue to look at in detail – in particular because the high price of medicines is itself one of the causes of the proliferation of counterfeits, maintaining a vicious cycle.

The concern of health professionals, and of patients, is not for patents or licensing issues but primarily based on fears of low-quality drugs that are not part of a well-established system of distribution – here being essentially that of large pharmaceutical groups. The assimilation and confusion over what is meant by counterfeits and how the different networks of brands, generics and counterfeits work is problematic, and also leads to policy decisions that are ill adapted to some of the difficulties faced in Africa. If wanting to address simultaneously the problems of the high cost of quality drugs and of the low quality of some of the cheapest drugs that are sold, a careful look at definitions, networks and strategies is essential – but not necessarily implemented in practice:

> The WHO is trying to harmonize the rules for pharmaceuticals and counterfeiting. But I tell them, it is not all about counterfeits. And some people also refer to generics as counterfeits, and this is wrong. I tell them that it is about definition. (IP policy-maker)

The difficulty of dealing with counterfeits without compromising the global campaign for access to cheap medicines was pointed out by non-governmental organizations in slightly different terms. In a recent report, for example, Oxfam claimed that the proactive role of the global pharmaceutical industry in targeting counterfeit medicines was an indirect way of reinforcing IP and took advantage of the ambivalence of the notion of counterfeits (Oxfam, 2011). Controversies about legal efforts to tackle counterfeits, without clearly focusing on health rather than IP issues, have similarly emerged, both in relation to global measures (ACTA being the clearest example) and national legislation (such as the Kenyan Anti-Counterfeiting Bill 2008 or the Ugandan Counterfeit Goods Bill 2009) (Liberman, 2012). The direct influence of the pharmaceutical industry on this general and often uncertain and ill-defined mobilization is not always clear. The global campaigns on counterfeit medicines are certainly effectively supported by a range of actors whose first focus will not be those of Ghanaian health professionals; but the difficulties of solving the issues at stake here also run deeper than simply a manipulation of campaigns by multinational companies – although their role in maintaining and performing ambivalence in the term is certainly part of the confusion that surrounds it. In practice, this ambivalence has already become embedded in the day-to-day practices of the key actors of public health, performing ambiguous realities of what are 'real' and 'fake', 'good' and 'bad' medicines. When discussing with doctors their approach to prescription and selection of particular brands over others, some of the inherent ambivalence of those discourses appeared. For example, in the following conversation I tried to find out how doctors identified, in their practice, low-quality medicines; soon the discussion became one in which the notion of 'low quality' was assimilated with that of generics:

Res: Sometimes you get a fairly straightforward case. You've picked up maybe a urinary tract infection and you expect a response to a particular drug. As far as you know there isn't a resistance to it. But the patient keeps on coming back to you and saying it's not working. Sometimes when you change the medication there is an immediate response. So then you know that, okay, fine, this drug didn't work. Sometimes you get very good results with a particular antibiotic, brand of antibiotics, in a way that you don't get normally if you just ask them to get a generic.
Int: That's interesting. They are supposed to be the same...if they are good quality generics, they are supposed to be the same, aren't they?
Res: They are supposed to be the same, but sometimes you don't [know]. Maybe also it's...maybe it's out of habit. Maybe it makes doctors feel comfortable with a particular drug...maybe there is a bias in that...But it's not only about having a bias. I think some of these biases are based on real experience that happen on the ground...It's the same base drug but just by a different company, different brand and you get good results. Anti-malarials typically as well. The patient has malaria and you start treatment with a certain brand, just write a generic, okay, cool. A patient comes back and is still unwell and still sick and if you check through the lab: still there. You alter the drug and go with the brand name and you get really good results. It can be really frustrating, because the patient keeps on going back and forth and then obviously if they have to pay they have to pay double, and the inconvenience as well to the patient, and [they] are sicker for longer.

This wariness towards generics is not unique to Ghana and, indeed, the controversies around bioequivalence have a long history in which the brand-name manufacturers played a proactive role for many years (Carpenter and Tobbell, 2011). It does not necessarily mean either that generics are not prescribed at all, or that doctors will avoid them, but certainly slows down the use of generics in some particular situations and limits the enrolment of generics within the mainstream hospital networks – and as a result within public health networks, as the drugs prescribed will tend to be the ones patients seek. In cases where treatment needs to act fast, the 'safest' option will be that of using a known and tried medicine:

> In some cases, you just don't want to take any chances with anything generic, especially in the very young kids. I don't want to take any chances with something I'm not familiar with...One was made by this five-star company...I have seen it work...I have seen the research and it's been proven. I want to use something good, proven to be good. No offence to those who haven't proven their products. I just don't want to take any chances. With the more expensive popular brand names, you know that there has been some research done. They are more convincing. The generic things kind of come out of nowhere, no offence. I don't really know too much about them. Probably haven't seen a presentation or read a paper about some research that was done on them. They have put out this legal document that says 'My drug contains this and this and this'. If it's made in some village in Kumasi it is still the drug. If that's what the patient go[es] for then, cool. You pray that it's not chocolate inside the medication...You see if the person gets better. Sometimes it's a learning process for you, an indirect way of actually studying the effectiveness of that drug. (medical doctor)

In establishing the definition of what are trusted medicines, a number of factors then come in, which participate in establishing the influence of large multinational companies into the local public health networks, in spite of any policy efforts to encourage a broader range of suppliers onto the market. Some of this transpires from the previous quote. The origins of the drug, and the settings in which it is produced and advertised, are all significant in positioning its importance. Again, the advantages that innovator brands have in that respect are crucial. Similarly, research active companies are in a very different position from companies seeking to emerge and establish their products onto new markets, and the pharmaceutical industry also supplies expertise: 'companies are producers not only of pills but also knowledge about their safety and efficacy, and their gifts to doctors of travel to conferences and workshops provide access to the latest expertise' (Lakoff, 2005, p. 140).

The phenomenon at play here is not simply one of direct and aggressive advertising, but a more subtle and maybe even more problematic process in which the enrolment of cheaper generic medicines is threatened by the joint works of innovator brands on the one hand, and low-quality counterfeits on the other. Advertising by large companies will be one of the elements that influences and shapes these relationships, as explained below by a young hospital doctor, but are only part of a very complex story:

> Most of my seniors have more experience with the drugs than we do. Most of them are familiar with them in the pharmaceutical reps and have even been on some seminars and stuff, organized by these pharmaceutical companies. Even if I don't have first-hand experience with that drug I can always ask them, 'What do you recommend?'

The phenomenon itself is also embedded into broader patterns of trust that link into places of origin as much as they link to manufacturers themselves; for example, even when generics are imported, a clear distinction appeared in discourses between the 'cheaper' Indian products and 'UK generics', that I have already referred to. This is not necessarily something unique to the pharmaceutical field, and it forms part of the landscape in which the respective enrolment of products occurs, in a context where trust is difficult to achieve but essential to the practices of doctors and the choices of many patients:

> People tend to have the insurance that if it's coming from the UK that is good quality. That is something that works here in Ghana.
> I guess anything made in the UK comes with some standard.
> (private pharmacist)

Overall, the significant problems that are caused by counterfeit medicines and the overlap in discourses and perceptions of what makes a legitimate and/ or effective medicine render the links between patents and access to health even more difficult to define. In markets where medicines remain too expensive for many, the proliferation of cheaper products, some of poor quality, is almost inevitable and very difficult to manage for a government with limited resources and a limited ability to reach remote places. At the same time, the blurriness of the boundaries between different types of drugs and an amalgam of concepts under same or similar labels in public discourses result in a turn to more expensive branded products that only aggravates the problem. Any solution to this conundrum can only be found in a deeper engagement with the complex weaknesses of the import and distribution system and with a closer engagement with the strategies deployed by practitioners of medicine to select trustworthy sources.

Conclusion

A close look at the pharmaceutical market and public health system of Ghana raises many questions in relation to the actual and potential role of patents with regard to access to medicines. In particular, the role of these socio-techno-legal tools is inherently entangled with processes of construction of different types of medicines, and different types of patients. In these processes, the role of patents and their influence is linked to their official term and official purpose in very loose terms. As well as ensuring exclusivity for a period of time, patents result in building a particular version of a drug as 'unique' in the perception of its practitioners. Reciprocally, drugs that are attached to patents almost exclusively emerge from an industry that has a positional advantage as compared to others in establishing its products, acting at a distance, and generating its relative power. The perpetuation of these patterns through practices, and in a context that facilitates reliance on the most established networks and the most established products, is illustrated here. In this context, governmental regulatory actions that aim to encourage the enrolment of a broader range of affordable medicines are reshaped and limited by the personal connections and habits of doctors, and the generics are repeatedly faced with resistance in which their enrolment in health networks is constantly challenged by established brands. The role of counterfeit medicines and the fluid and at times highly political use of this label are also determinant of the possibilities offered to generics. As a result, the influence of patents cannot be thought of in a purely binary way in which they would either 'exist' or 'not exist', be 'respected' or 'breached', but is codependent on much broader patterns of practical and discursive inclusion and othering. In all these processes, the proactive role of the innovator pharmaceutical industry, in marketing its products, plays a historical role in positioning some products over others. Nonetheless, these activities alone do not fully explain the complex set of relationships that inscribes some drugs over others in the daily routines of practitioners of health (Healy, 2006; Ecks and Basu, 2009).

In Chapter 6, I turn to the task of unpacking a final aspect of the relationship between IP and access to medicines and question how the processes of mobilization, resistance and responses that have been opposed to the Trade Related Aspects of Intellectual Property Rights agreement have resulted in global movements that inherently transform the landscape of healthcare in Djibouti and Ghana. I argue that a deep understanding of IP is dependent on acknowledging that those movements are also an inherent part of the ontological links between IP and health.

6
Global Movements, Changing Markets and the Reshaping of Health and Disease

The role of the Trade Related Aspects of Intellectual Property Rights (TRIPS) agreement, within the public health landscape of African states cannot be understood as a static image. Rather, TRIPS is about transformations. In the previous chapters, I have introduced some of these transformations as enacted through the movements generated by the implementation of TRIPS – or at times, their unexpected lack of movement. I have then questioned how the influence of pharmaceutical patents can be explored aside from their role as legal regulation, through their action within markets, and in particular in markets that are still heavily influenced by past and current forms of imperialism. Here, I reflect on the changes, innovations and transformations that have occurred within the public health context of Djibouti and Ghana in recent years, and in particular those that can be viewed as a reflection of the broader movements generated by TRIPS at the global level. My starting point here is that TRIPS can only be explored fully if we also engage with the various global movements that is has produced or been entangled with. The analysis provided in Chapter 2 is built upon in this chapter, and I start from the understanding of TRIPS as a complex assemblage that has come to produce and become entangled into the access to medicines campaign and its different effects. I explore two main issues here: first, I look at some of ways in which medicines and diseases have become reshaped in Ghana and Djibouti following the new global emphasis on access to affordable medicines. I then turn specifically to AIDS, as a site in which the complexity of the coproductive processes linking TRIPS and disease can be explored in more specific depth. I argue throughout that these movements and transformations need to be considered carefully if we wish to understand the full extent of the relationship between public health and intellectual property (IP). This approach is both informed by my theoretical conceptualization of TRIPS and by the entanglement of TRIPS, IP and recent global programmes in the discourses of participants to this research. In their views, discussions of IP were inherently linked to a broader questioning of the movements that animate the landscape of disease and treatment that they engaged with on a day-to-day basis. TRIPS is an event that happens in many places, that generates changes in many networks, that is embedded in multiple actions and practices, and, in order to understand what it 'does' in Djibouti or in Ghana, it is essential to have a clearer idea of the effects it has in these many other places, and the indirect repercussions this has on these localized contexts.

Dislocated effects of TRIPS and the reordering of health networks

TRIPS is a complex assemblage that manifests itself through a constant process of entanglement and disentanglement, and through the production of new effects, each of which is inherently linked to a wider networked space.[1] In Susan Sell's words 'without TRIPS, there would be no access to medicines campaign' (Sell, 2002a, p. 481), or, at least, not in the form that it has been adopted over the past 15 years. In this section, I follow the theoretical and empirical conceptualization of TRIPS as a multidimensional assemblage that cogenerates discourses and actions relative to affordable medicines. This is exemplified by some of the movements that animate public health in Djibouti and Ghana. I focus on two specific sets of movements: a renewed emphasis on making modern drugs available for particular diseases; and a more general emphasis on access to affordable drugs. I describe some of the implications of these programmes and their relationship to TRIPS before questioning their limitations and where the various issues of power and exclusion that have permeated debates on IP are left in the localized contexts of these sub-Saharan African states.

As introduced in Chapter 1, the history of TRIPS is a complex story of making and remaking, in which the role of global IP needs to be conceptualized in terms of performance and coproduction. Amongst the many things it did, TRIPS generated a new form of resistance and opposition; new actors in the public health field joined around TRIPS and connected in new ways. The mobilization of those opposed to TRIPS resulted in turn in emphasis being put on new problems, including that of access to medicines. By triggering a new set of critics, TRIPS has also generated a new set of pressures on governments and international organizations to deal with the issues raised in poor countries, and to deal more specifically with the issue of access to medication.

---

1 This relates to actor-network theory approaches to 'globality', as being the manifestation of the expansion of networked connections and the creation of links across localities (Law, 1999a; 2002).

The large networks of opposition that TRIPS generated (and that I described in Chapter 1) have resulted in redirecting public attention towards the daily difficulties in accessing affordable medicines that many poor people face across the world, and in particular in sub-Saharan Africa. Their intense lobbying efforts transformed the possibilities for access for many people and also reshaped significantly the networks of distribution of medicines in many locales (Klug, 2010). I do not wish by this to claim that TRIPS is in any way a positive development, in its politics, for the poor in their general struggle to access healthcare. Many of the new programmes are still riddled with the limitations that are symbolic of the patterns of dependency and exclusion that created TRIPS in the first place, as I will develop below. In addition, the access to medicines campaign was produced as a response to TRIPS, but also because of the relentless efforts by individuals and organizations to resist what remained a new set of burdens on struggling localities (Sell, 2002a). Conceptually, however, a full analysis of where TRIPS has left the poor can only be achieved with careful attention to the localized manifestations of the access campaigns. In Djibouti and in Ghana, the shifts produced by the new global attention to IP and access to medicines have adopted two main forms: a new system of financing for the treatment of particular diseases; and a more general new focus on affordability and generic medicines. Here, I introduce briefly some of these programmes, before questioning their inherent limitations and the persistent difficulties for the poor.

Global movements and the making of affordable medicines

A first effect of the access to medicines campaign has been to shift attention to generic and affordable medicines in general. Global programmes aiming to encourage governments to rethink practices that impacted on prices were proposed, more or less successfully, both in Ghana and Djibouti. This was apparent in both case studies, although the effects of the different programmes varied greatly, and were much clearer in Djibouti. I have already mentioned, in Chapter 4, the changes to the market for generic medicines that were sought by a World Bank project in 2002. The project is a useful illustration of some of the complex movements that occurred in response to the new public attention to affordable medicines that the access campaign triggered. The project was resolutely external to Djibouti in its shaping, and came as part of movements in global policies:

> The way it works here is generally that the World Bank whispers an idea and asks us to officially apply for this particular fund. That's what basically happened in this case. (member of the Ministry of Health)

Interestingly, this project is illustrative of the processes of production and transformation that have animated the links between IP and health in recent years. While TRIPS is progressively making pharmaceutical patents part of the official landscape of Djibouti, the new system of import and distribution has been creating a new concurrent network from which they are newly excluded. Here, I suggest that the Centre d'Achat des Medicaments et Matériel Essentiels (CAMME) should be viewed as part of a broader international emphasis on access to affordable medication for the poor, which has become inherently entangled with TRIPS. It is an essential part of these networks, and this role is itself an integral aspect of TRIPS, a dimension that cannot be put aside. Again, the broadening of the market to new entities and new types of medicines is also itself entangled within other movements that animate the market. As generics became normalized in this alternative network of affordable medication, they progressively made their way into the public and private systems of distribution more broadly – albeit within strict limitations. These transformations also opened a new space in which counterfeit medicines progressively started entering the market.

In Ghana, efforts from the government to integrate generics have emerged at the national level. Nonetheless, outside funding to encourage further rationalization of expenses and the promotion of affordable and quality medicines to the population were also introduced. As a significant example, one of the pilot programmes for the Medicines Transparency Alliance (MeTA) was implemented in Ghana. The initiative is jointly funded by the UK Department for International Development, the World Health Organization (WHO), Health Action International Africa, Transparency International, the World Bank and the International Federation of Pharmaceutical Manufacturers and Associations. The programme is illustrative of how new, smaller programmes are constantly emerging in this field, and how a broader awareness of the high cost of medicines in various parts of Africa triggers responses emerging from various sources, and with slightly different emphasis. The programme set by MeTA presents its ultimate goal as being 'to improve access to medicines for poor people'.[2] It is highly visible on the internet and presents a carefully drawn workplan of how its multi-stakeholder approach will result in more transparency and a better control of prices of quality drugs than is currently the case. Full details of the workplan are available on the internet and do not need to be presented again here. Perhaps more interesting was the fact that all the Ghanaian participants to MeTA that we interviewed emphasized its lack of practical impact, and how the project seemed to have quickly evaporated – criticisms

---

2 www.medicinestransparency.org/about-meta/.

I return to below. The following quote provides a general sense of how the project was described:

> MeTA came about because of the high cost of medication for people. It was originally Tony Blair, following from the efforts to give aid in the 90s...this was one of the ideas to make medicines more affordable. We realized the issue was not only one of production, but also one of distribution. So MeTA then came about because the Ministry of Health applied to the global programme. It started in 2008 and ran for two years. It is being revised now, but many of us have opted out...(public health policy-maker)

I return to the issue of stability and longevity below. The new emphasis on affordability is interesting at several levels. Fundamentally, it poses a conceptual dilemma in delimiting the boundaries of TRIPS, and in that respect demonstrate the blurry boundaries of such a controversial transnational legal agreement. In spaces, counter-intuitively, patents and their influence through established brands may in fact have become more proactively challenged. This does not make TRIPS any less problematic, and the problem of access perseveres within the many new restrictions put on future possibilities by the new layer of global regulations. The movements generated by TRIPS, and by the access to medicines campaign, are also more complex than simply being one of access or restriction to access in general. In fact, the access to medicines campaign also participated in transforming the ways in which access to particular treatment, for particular diseases, is shaped.

Aside from a renewed attention to generic and affordable medicines, access to medicines has also translated in practice into a subsidized form of access to specific medicines, for particular diseases. Specifically, the provision of affordable medicines for tuberculosis (TB), malaria and AIDS has been very closely supported, as well as monitored, in the past decade. These diseases need treatment that, for reasons specific to each condition, is generally expensive, needs frequent revisiting and, in the cases of TB and AIDS, close monitoring. Because of the nature and the cost of the treatment, these have become important focal points of the access to medicines campaign and of global funding programmes. The creation of the Global Fund in 2002 has been particularly determinant in stabilizing the position of these diseases as the key burdens that poor people were facing in various parts of the world, including sub-Saharan Africa. The Global Fund has been closely associated with other global initiatives that manage and distribute resources to partners and in localities and determine the general lines of global policies in the management of disease. The Roll Back Malaria initiative and the Global Drug Facility for TB have, for example, been determinant in providing what appears as an agreed and unified approach to disease and treatment management. The complexity of these global programmes is beyond the scope of this project, and here I wish to focus essentially – and succinctly – on some of the effects that global responses to disease, and in particular to malaria and TB (I return to AIDS below), have on the landscape of access to affordable medicines.[3]

Those were most visible, and for the moment most successful, in Ghana, where tablets for malaria and TB treatment have become free, or very affordable, for patients. Malaria treatment has been heavily subsidized in the past few years in Ghana. As a result, the price of artemisinin-based combination therapies (ACTs) has been reduced very significantly, making them available to patients for a nominal price. The price of anti-malarials has dropped significantly as a result of the programme, increasing affordability and, as result, limiting the opportunities for the counterfeit market in these products to grow. Similarly, the treatment of TB has become largely subsidized, although funding is also directed there at ensuring an early detection of the disease. The approach to distribution of the relevant medicines differs in each case, with the availability of anti-malarials being progressively facilitated by increasing their points of distribution (and making them available, for example, from some chemical sellers), while the treatment of TB has remained centralized and closely monitored, to limit the risks of resistance. In both cases, the significant amount of funding directed to the diseases is the result both of their significance as public health concerns, but also of the growing concern for the cost of modern medicines, symbolizing the entanglement of patents, access and particular conditions.

Contesting global projects

The movements generated by TRIPS and the access to medicines campaign have therefore become inherently linked to the reshaping of health systems and of the diffusions of medicines, or discourses surrounding medicines, in Djibouti and Ghana. The fragility of the new networks that have emerged remains salient, however, and the questions and critiques made of the particular programmes referred to here are linked to broader questions about the meaning of these transformations. The core of these criticisms relates to issues of stability and the longevity of programmes that are dependent on external resources. The fluidity of boundaries between diseases, conditions and treatments raises a second set of issues that I explore briefly here and return to when looking at AIDS in the next section.

---

3 For an insightful analysis of the entanglement of modern and traditional, local and global in the treatment of malaria, see Langwick (2007).

Stability

The first criticism of the global programmes that were deployed in order to facilitate access to medicines was their lack of stability. In particular, the processes of displacements that they are dependent on means that most decisions, the availability of funds and the prioritizing of areas are often settled by actors that have little direct experience of the localities in which treatments will be distributed. As a result, projects remain fragile assemblages that can at any point crumble or lose effects and significance. The detachment of the decision-makers from the interests at stake was commonly seen as being centrally interlocked with this dislocated process of decision-making:

> They come and they do what they like. Sometimes they walk away. They don't solve any problems. Of course we have systems running. You can ride on the back of the systems. But first and foremost you must understand the people. So they say, okay, we will give you affordable medicines. We pay at the factory gates, so the medicines come to you at its [sic] cost. Now you go round and see if you see the medicines. They are not there. So, the question is, it's not coming, and throwing things in for a few minutes [doesn't help] ... [when] you walk away. You don't solve anybody's problem. (member of the Pharmacy Council)

> Malaria for instance. There was this global support and now we are going back. The funding is no longer coming in. There are problems all over the world. When that programme was on it was really good, you know. If there is a way we can make them [anti-malarials] cheaper that will also help. Then there would be no incentive for people to counterfeit. I would wish that it was coming from our government. I would have wished. Something coming from our side you don't have to approve. Now we are no longer getting it. (private pharmacist)

The case of MeTA was presented as particularly illustrative of this, and the progressive disinteressement of its Ghanaian members is illustrative of how nodes of a network gradually separate until it has virtually crumbled. Those who had been part of MeTA and were interviewed in this research all emphasized that it, and other programmes of this type, only had a limited meaning within the broader picture of the challenges and practice of healthcare in Ghana:

> The issue about META is that META is hanging in because it's foreign funded, again. It is not built into the systems. It was built outside the systems. No money no META. The pilot phase is over now, so we don't know what will happen. But I don't have much to say about META. (member of the Pharmacy Council)

Again, the dislocation of decision-making is at the core of the critique provided here and crucial to many development programmes, beyond the example of healthcare and access to medicines.

The repetitive processes of dependency that critiques of TRIPS have emphasized remain inherently built into the very answers that are currently given to the problem. In spite of the achievements of the access to medicines campaign, the difficulties faced by the poor reappear and are often displaced rather than solved. Each of the programmes, and each of the promises therefore made by the international community, is also in itself transformative of the complex chain of events that surround each individual disease, and each particular patient. When a programme crumbles, the knowledge that treatment could be available makes the experience of each patient a different one from what it would otherwise have been. The process of entanglement of these different effects therefore has repercussions within each node of the network that becomes redefined as possibilities are reshaped:

> Some new drugs they have introduced are not available anymore in the teaching hospitals. You reverse [sic] back to the ones that are no good. There was a reason for the change. You educated people, told them this drug had problems. You had to convince them that drug A has these problems. So don't use Drug A again. Drug B doesn't have all those problems... But now Drug B is not available. They'll say: 'You've told me Drug A was no good, so why go back to Drug A?' (member of the Pharmacy Council)

> So the combination medicines were inaccessible and unaffordable. Now you have made it [sic] accessible and affordable. Now it is not accessible or the people cannot afford [it]... You don't cure the issue. You create more complicated issues and you confuse the people. (member of the Pharmacy Council)

Significant diagnoses

The uncertainty surrounding diseases and treatment runs further than the continuity of funding and is closely linked to the difficulty of diagnosis in both Ghana and Djibouti. The approach to funding has resulted in different conditions bringing patients into very distinct networks, in which diagnosis will condition the affordability of treatment. For example, in Ghana, while treatment for TB is financed under the Stop TB partnership, pneumonia or other serious chest infections are dependent on the payment possibilities under the National Health Insurance Scheme and may or may not be fully financed:

> They go to the hospital... they test you and if you are not positive they refer you to a different clinic... Once it is TB, treatment

is free. That is paid by the Global Fund. Everything about TB is free...If it's not TB, they refer you and you pay for treatment! (member of Stop TB)

Here, a particular diagnosis may or may not enable free treatment for patients, and the limitations of the compartmentalized nature of disease management comes to life in the day-to-day experiences of patients. In a context where diagnosis itself is difficult, with very limited facilities and problems with accessing medical professionals (highlighted in Chapters 4 and 5), this important diagnosis is often difficult to make. In the case of malaria, conditions that look like malaria will be treated as such and treatment provided free of charge. The management of TB is overseen more closely to avoid risks of resistance. At each level of this process, the difficulties that cripple the health system as a whole participate in limiting the effectiveness of programmes that remain inherently fragile.

Overall, the movements that animate access to medicines in both Djibouti and Ghana have become so inherently linked to discourses on and resistance to TRIPS and IP that it becomes methodologically problematic to evaluate the impact of TRIPS without observing some of these more general movements. In both contexts, the movements that animate the pharmaceutical field are multidirectional, and not simply an issue of increased or decreased access. It is also one in which patterns of interlocking and dependency – of patients on particular diagnoses, but also of the affordability of medicines when decision-makers are in far-away locations – are all very visible. The political critique of TRIPS here links back to its underlying process of making and unmaking: TRIPS is a complex assemblage that was made possible by the relative influence of some actors over others, the material enablement of some actors over others; although its ultimate effects have been more complex than simply one of immediate reinforcement of patents in all their dimensions, the underlying problematique of persistent patterns of ordering and loss of control remains visible in each of the nodes of these new networks. I return to some of these issues in conclusion, but, first, I turn to one of the key sites of entanglement between IP and health by looking at the making and remaking of AIDS and its treatment in Djibouti and Ghana.

Stories of AIDS

Nowhere is the complexity of the IP/health and global/local nexuses clearer than in the example of AIDS. The complexity of AIDS is a well-explored topic, and a rich literature has engaged with different aspects of this multifaceted disease. A section in a book can in no way claim to reflect exhaustively the nature of these different layers, different aspects of complexity. Yet, writing about patents in Africa and interrogating the interface of global/local movements and reshapings that occur in this area cannot be complete without engaging with AIDS. At the same time, AIDS is, in many ways, a particular case rather than illustrative of the general issues raised by patents and access to health. Too often, the case of AIDS has been chosen to symbolize more broadly a debate which is very different when other diseases or conditions are looked at. Here, I want to explore critically some of the connections at play when AIDS and patents are brought under the same research umbrella, but it is important to understand that this is a specific case rather than an example of the overall situation.

Here, I focus specifically on stories of AIDS in Djibouti and in Ghana, from the perspective of access to treatment, and I want to convey some of the core aspects of the politics of treatment in these two localities. I also want to use this example to reflect on how global policies affect the local, and how in fact global and local phenomena become entangled to the point of being indistinguishable. In particular, I question how debates on access to medicines and IP have produced yet another new version of AIDS and affected its positioning in global policies and local strategies, and in fact how a process of disempowerment of local actors to the benefit of external networks has operated, enabling action at a distance in responding to this particular concern in a way that is partly problematic (Biehl, 2007; Epstein, 2007).

In the first part of this section, I return to some of the elements of the complexity of AIDS highlighted by others, and briefly explore what these demonstrate about the multiple nature of AIDS and the specific constitution of AIDS in sub-Saharan Africa. The politics of AIDS in particular settings is best understood with some exploration of the inherent multiplicity of disease that is seldom engaged with in literature on TRIPS. AIDS and its complex history – its entanglement in networks of poverty and deprivation, postcolonial patterns of power and relationships, global/local political conflicts and discourses, the stigmatization of sexuality, racial and social stereotypes – is a unique illustration of the constant fluidity and complexity that compose a 'single-ized' disease. This section starts by trying to define this object of study and seize some snapshots of this travelling actor.

The making of AIDS

In *Impure Science*, Stephen Epstein (1996) provides what remains one of the most detailed histories of the making of AIDS. In particular, he rewrites the history of the disease as one of controversies and settlements, and of the successive closing and reopening of debates and uncertainties. The book is a fascinating story in many respects, but most unusually in its parallel questioning of the making of AIDS as a medical, identified and broadly agreed upon disease and of a particular approach to treatment and the politics of participation in the development of an answer to AIDS. The history of the definition of AIDS that he provides illustrates how the disease emerged from being a set of isolated symptoms in small groups of patients to an agreed and labelled condition. In this process, contestations across medical researchers, politicians and publics were constant and often positioned against backgrounds of cultural and social contestations about personal practices. The thick description he provides is telling in reminding us of the fragility of diseases and of the 'impurity' of their nature and definition – constantly challenged and transformed by the networks in which they are enrolled and by which they are created in a particular form and under a particular label. In the 30 years since the first cases of AIDS were identified, the disease has known many more socio-political controversies and become transformed in yet new, possibly endless ways. Contestations as to its very existence and nature have travelled across the world, generating new political debates and a sense of outrage from parts of the global public. And the politics of its treatment have become problematized and controversial beyond the original US sites where they were first opened. New forms of citizens' engagement with the production and distribution of treatment for AIDS became visible in many new locales, as Biehl (2007) illustrates in the case of Brazil. AIDS has become one of the themes on which global citizenship is both visible, through the engagement of extensive networks of actors across the world, and questionable, as the positionality of individuals is so disparate in the face of this disease (Bastos, 1999).

Africa became a focal point of discourses and debates around AIDS, due partly to the high rates of the disease and its fast progression across the continent and partly because of the concerns that were soon raised in socio-economic terms, but also due to the controversial positions taken by some African political leaders. Many of those debates are not directly relevant here, but form an important background to the question of AIDS anywhere in Africa today, and to the difficulties of approaching and deconstructing this area in ways that encompass both the suffering of people, the intensity of the political controversies and the practical difficulties of responding to a major health crisis – both global and very localized. Didier Fassin (2006) follows some of the controversies that have animated AIDS in the South-African context and provides a fascinating ethnography of how AIDS is permanently transformed in the different discursive and material networks through which it travels. The entanglement of the political and cultural tensions within South-African society during the controversies surrounding AIDS triggered by President Thabo Mbeki provide us with some insight into the complexity of this disease in another very specific national context. More generally, the politics of AIDS and its treatment have given rise to new forms of cultural and social networks, and new forms of citizenships, that are illustrative of the responsive and contingent nature of the links between disease, healthcare and societies (Nguyen, 2005).

AIDS as a postcolonial object

Over the years since its appearance and discovery, AIDS has become strongly entangled in the postcolonial and racialized networks that cut across Africa and most of the world. The emergence of AIDS and the controversies that first animated debates on its origins were tainted with heavy preconceptions about racialized practices and the cultural origins of AIDS as a disease. The identification of the virus and a clearer understanding of the disease enabled the debates to move away from some of the underlying misconceptions, but discourses on AIDS have remained heavily tainted by racialized stereotypes. Those pertaining to the sexualization of particular populations, especially in Africa, are the clearest example of the stereotypes that have been perpetuated by the AIDS epidemics, and in turn by some of the campaigning around AIDS. Carol Heimer (2007) points out, furthermore, how the production of family relations and sexuality within Africa have themselves been transformed by the policies of the colonial era.

In addition, the epidemic came to inscribe itself in the new politics of Africa, played out both on the continent itself and within other globalized sites, where a significant part of the decision-making is being made. In South Africa, the contestation of the global scientific consensus on AIDS became entangled within post-apartheid politics, creating some of the most salient examples of the clashes between Western forms of scientific knowledge, localized contestation and the links between specific knowledge and the broader conflicts between knowledge systems (Fassin, 2006). In those debates, as retraced by Didier Fassin and others, the nature of science itself is at stake, and the illustration of the enrolment of scientific controversies within political projects is clearest. The challenges sought by the anti-scientific and 'anti-AIDS' statements are also meaningful for what they show of the contestation of Western knowledge systems in general, and some of the challenges that are faced by 'global science' today – of achieving a consensus that is truly global and allows space for local happenings and histories.

Over the years, controversies surrounding the origins of AIDS, on the causes and transmissions of the disease, and of some of the strategies to avoid contamination and facilitate treatments have become settled globally, including in Africa. Dissident individual voices persist, awareness is still limited amongst some populations, discrepancies still persist between theory and practice, but a set of controversies have now been settled, in which the 'science' of AIDS has become predominantly agreed upon. Disagreements and controversies, however, have become displaced on the politics of AIDS, and new debates have been opened in terms of how the epidemic should be approached and how it links to other crises that Africa is facing. The controversies relative to the treatment of AIDS are to be understood within the tensions of colonial policies that turned the treatment of venereal diseases into specific sites of violence and stigma and, therefore, caused it to remain entangled in complex social histories (Heimer, 2007). Current wariness and the difficulty in enlisting patients within the official networks of AIDS needs to be traced back to a long history of constituting sexually transmitted diseases in this particular way.

AIDS and global IP

Amongst the many persistent controversies surrounding AIDS and its treatment are the debates on patents and access to anitretrovirals (ARVS), and I want to briefly unpack some of the relationships between AIDS and TRIPS. My position here is that TRIPS has played a significant part in reshaping AIDS as a disease and creating new controversies on the global scene in terms of the very nature of AIDS. TRIPS has in this way played a part in creating AIDS as we know it. As much as TRIPS has also become a part of the AIDS assemblage, AIDS has participated in building the TRIPS assemblage as we experience it today.

Since TRIPS was adopted, AIDS and IP have become entangled in very complex ways. Part of it is linked to the effects – actual or potential – of IP on access to ARVs. ARVs are patented, and therefore the cost of ARVs is significantly affected by IP, and consequently by the extension of IP that TRIPS has generated (e.g. Joni, 2002; Matthews 2004a). Consequently, the second level of entanglement of TRIPS and AIDS appeared as the campaign against TRIPS by access to medicines activists became significantly focused on access to ARVs. As explained in Chapter 2, a few key moments participated in the transformation of AIDS and of its various actors. The emergence of the '$1 a day treatment' participated in transforming AIDS significantly: from an inevitable death sentence to one contingent on regulation and corporate strategies. The pharmaceutical industry itself experienced significant transformations, following on from this, but also from the actions of a group of pharmaceutical companies against the South-African government in the 'Pretoria trial' that progressively problematized it in relation to AIDS, to Africa and ultimately to the poorest AIDS sufferers (Barnard, 2002; Klug, 2010). Notions of fairness and inequalities also became linked to IP in a way that was new for a significant part of the general public. These different events and the inherent links between the novelty of ARVs, and therefore the patenting of many of these medicines, has meant that a significant part of the access to medicines campaign and of the commentaries on this campaign have become focused on the question of AIDS. In other words, the debate on patents and access to medication has often been dominated by the more specific debate on access to anti-HIV/AIDS drugs (Sell, 2002a). The movements linking TRIPS and AIDS then became processes of transformation as well as entanglement, in which TRIPS and the controversies surrounding TRIPS were being progressively rewritten by the emergence of new pressures linked to access to ARVs and where the politics of AIDS was being rewritten by the new opportunities that had in fact been opened by TRIPS in fostering global support and resistance to the practices of 'Big Pharma'. In turn, these transformations had some very practical impacts in reshaping policy programmes and the global response to the AIDS crisis, and in turn created a renewed interest in the academic literature both for TRIPS and for the politics of access to ARVs (Fleet, 2003; McGoey et al., 2011). As the campaign on access to medicines started growing, one of its main impacts was in redefining how we respond to AIDS and, in the process, what AIDS means and in fact is for patients, health professionals and policy-makers, drawing out conflicting interests in the shaping of political opportunities (Biehl, 2004; 2007; Shadlen, 2007).

Local challenges and global programmes – AIDS in Djibouti

If exploring the ways in which IP, disease and access to health have become entangled in global scenarios, the specific attention to AIDS in these debates is a key feature. At the same time, the relative 'importance' of AIDS, as opposed to other conditions, and of ARVs as opposed to other, often basic, medication, has started to be questioned in public health circles. These are types of challenges to AIDS policies that are very different from the South-African resistance explored above and that originate from a variety of sources. They do not tend to deny the gravity of AIDS, or the need to tackle its transmission and alleviate the suffering of AIDS patients. Instead, they question the balance that is being struck between investments in AIDS and investment in other areas of suffering. In this section, I use the example of Djibouti to explore some of those resistances and debates and question another dimension of the interaction between global and local sites in the constitution of AIDS and the entanglement of discourses on IP from the local distribution of medicines. Here, challenges are brought mainly to the distribution of funds and critiques question how global discourses on access and IP have shifted attention to modern as opposed to basic medication.[4] The growing attention of the international community to AIDS is by no means exclusively the result of the issue of cost and IP and stems both from the severity of the epidemics and the growing awareness of the challenges that Africa has faced in tackling the disease (Halbert, 2002; Mercurio, 2004). However, the links

---

4 Including an early focus of academic writings on HIV/AIDS medicines (Schoell, 2002; Matthews, 2004a).

between TRIPS and AIDS remain important. In Djibouti, actors challenged the impact that global discourses had on specific localities, such as Djibouti's, whose health concerns and possibilities may be radically different from those of more explored spaces may be. The questions I am interested in here are both practical and methodological – what can we learn from AIDS and resistance to AIDS in Djibouti, and how can these stories enable us to reconceptualize an approach to the effects of global IP law? Underlying this question is the fact that the issues raised by access to HIV have come to symbolize, for many, the problems raised by IP. Instead, I argue that they are a unique site in which these issues are made visible, but that they are also unique in their acute dimension. The performance of AIDS as somehow representative of the difficulties created by IP in relation to access to medicines has also resulted in overshadowing the many complex challenges to access that sub-Saharan Africa faces. According to Duncan Matthews:

> In many respects, the debate about how best to ensure access to essential medicines to combat the HIV/AIDS virus has come to typify anxieties about the World Trade Organization (WTO) Agreement on Trade-Related Aspects of Intellectual Property (the TRIPS agreement) and its potential to have adverse socio-economic impacts on developing countries. (2004a, p. 2)

Here, I argue that the discourses surrounding TRIPS have stabilized a focus and an assimilation that is not reflective of the complex nexuses in which IP, disease and health are entangled more generally.

Since 2003, Djibouti has become a key recipient of global attention and global funding in relation to AIDS. Here, I question the progressive reshaping of AIDS as a health priority in Djibouti and the resistance opposed to this framing by some key local actors. I argue that an analysis of IP needs to account for the dislocated effects of TRIPS and question what the campaigns TRIPS has generated have changed in relation to the experience and existence of particular diseases. In those terms, the networked nature of TRIPS means that understanding the links between IP and access to health is best done by allowing space to question the repercussions that resistance to those instruments has had on health systems. TRIPS is therefore a central actor in reshaping understandings of AIDS as central to public health priorities and understandings of ARVs as essential elements in access to health.

The global response to AIDS in Djibouti has been the result of investments by the World Bank and the Global Fund, which are managed overall under the Cadre National Stratégique Intersectoriel de Lutte contre le Sida. The programme as a whole has seen investments of over $25 million between 2003 and 2008, making Djibouti an important recipient of international money for AIDS. Most significant was the implementation in 2004 of a World Bank project, directed at financing treatment for AIDS, malaria and TB (essentially tackled as 'risk co-factors') (World Bank, 2003), AIDS being its most central and innovative aspect – the project is referred to in Djibouti as 'the AIDS project'.

The narratives of the project provided by official documents and by actors in Djibouti involved in the project are in significant contrast. Whilst the official documents list the range of aspects of the multisectoral approach to AIDS embedded in the project, those in charge locally described it in much more patient-focused terms, as being essentially designed in practice to offer 'free HIV treatment to 250 patients in Djibouti' (medical doctor involved in the AIDS project) – eight years after its implementation, the Global Fund estimates that 1100 patients are on antiretroviral therapy. The funds officially, however, also aim to develop the infrastructure necessary to deal with the disease – although:

> many questions remain unanswered – and in particular that of social structures. It is crucial that patients get the appropriate social support that is needed, and for the moment we don't have the means to give them that. (member of the Ministry of Health)[5]

The impact of the project on restructuring the local management of and response to AIDS has been considered in post-implementation studies by the World Bank, but is not in fact the main concern of this chapter. More interesting here are the apparent resistance and opposition of many health professionals in Djibouti to the implementation of this project and their overall scepticism as to the appropriateness of the project to the needs of patients in Djibouti – adding up to a general scepticism within the population over the project and the adequate use of the resources. The focus of this resistance was not about the necessity, globally or in Djibouti, to address the AIDS epidemics, but one of relative urgency and of health priorities in a context where resources are limited. In particular, the high priorities of AIDS as a public health concern and of ARV drugs as a public health solution in Djibouti, as compared to other diseases and other treatments, were questioned. None of these reservations questioned the suffering of AIDS patients, or the ultimate desirability of relieving them from some of this pain and enabling them to work and live in the way that treatment makes possible. However, in the current medical and socio-economic context of Djibouti, for professionals who dealt with the daily sufferings of the local population as a whole, the difficulties in treating other conditions appeared as being just as urgent as

---

5 The links between an increased availability of drugs and state investment in infrastructures have been explored previously (e.g. Nattrass and Geffen, 2005). For a critique of the global strategies surrounding AIDS treatment more generally, see Epstein (2007).

a large-scale project to treat AIDS. A number of reasons were put forward to explain this position, and these chime with some of the criticisms of global AIDS politics.

A first ground for this scepticism was based on cost and the allocation of resources and, of course, the cost of treatment. If working in a context where resources are limited, funding is often insufficient to treat all patients and choices have to be made. The cost of treating particular diseases will be one of the elements that health professionals think of when seeing money being distributed towards one particular disease. Some of the resistance towards the high levels of funding directed at AIDS, in particular, stemmed from the fact that this money could have saved 'more lives' if allocated to other conditions or health emergencies. As stated by one of the medical doctors involved in the deployment of the World Bank project:

> From a public health point of view, it is complete nonsense. With all that money, we are going to treat 250 people, while it could have been used to solve all the problems of maternal death, which is a key problem here. It could also have been directed at basic treatment for childhood diseases that we cannot cure at the moment. But at the moment, internationally, AIDS is the question...so we have to 'do' AIDS – it looks good. (member of the Ministry of Health)

However, other factors also came into explaining why there were strong reservations about the project and opposition to the significant investment, making the cost of medication only one of the elements cited. Some aspects of the controversies surrounded the statistics provided in relation to AIDS, where these located the prevalence of AIDS as opposed to other diseases, and on what informants from the public health field stated 'seeing' in Djibouti (namely that other diseases are currently causing more damage to the population in Djibouti). The statistical evidence provided to determine AIDS rates, in a place where patients may not be coming forward with symptoms of AIDS, or may not be able to access medical care and diagnosis, has been contested (Dray et al., 2005). This is not unique to AIDS, or to Djibouti, and interviews with the Stop TB partnership in Ghana have, for example, similarly raised the difficulties of establishing statistical certainty and the discrepancy between official statements by global organizations and what seemed to be a more realistic estimate based on their own experiences. AIDS also still carries a cultural taboo, and many health actors interviewed emphasized that many patients would refuse to come forward and face the fact that they had AIDS, because of the social stigma still attached to the disease:

> There is a bit of AIDS, but we are mainly concerned with TB. And to be fair, we have very few patients coming forward and willing

to talk about AIDS, it is still a real taboo. (medical doctor involved with the AIDS project)[6]

Finally, some of the concerns expressed were more deeply linked to the underlying difficulties faced by the public health networks of Djibouti, and whether a stabilized network for the treatment of AIDS could realistically emerge in the current political and socio-economic context. The global projects are certainly ambitious in their purpose of developing a cross-sectorial answer to AIDS, and in aiming to develop a network of support, treatment and prevention that cuts across governmental disconnections and instability. Many had reservations, however, as to the feasibility and sustainability of such an ambitious project. When the global community started investing in AIDS in Djibouti, the range of social support and infrastructures that needed to be developed to offer treatment to patients with AIDS, and ensure that they would follow a long-term treatment programme, were not available in any form. In fact, a significant part of the financial investment was aimed at fostering and creating this new network. But, as we have seen in the context of IP, the creation of cross-sectorial answers in a context where connections are weak, and any project's longevity is difficult to guarantee, can be a real problem, and these issues played a significant part in actors' scepticism over 'Projet Sida'.

Overall, the difficulties that could be foreseen in implementing this ambitious project, the prevalence of AIDS as compared to other diseases present in Djibouti, the ease with which some of these diseases could be cured in contrast with the challenges of treating AIDS were all part of what made several of the health professionals most directly involved with the project highly sceptical. While none of them questioned the need to deal with AIDS, their main concern was that the attention devoted to AIDS did not seem replicated when dealing with other diseases. The question here is really one of *priority*, and the scepticism expressed in Djibouti has been echoed in other commentaries about the global politics of AIDS (Shiffman, 2008). Interestingly, the redirection of global funds towards this particular disease in Djibouti has both produced it as a public health concern (in the sense of a concern that could and would be addressed) and as a contested actor in its relative positionality in the network. In a sense, contestation flows from conflicting shapings of AIDS in absolute terms on the one hand, and of AIDS in relative terms on the other. While the position of Djiboutian actors does not deny the importance of engaging with it medically as such, their perception of health concerns as a more general and entangled problematique brings them to question the distribution of funds and attention.

---

6 Biehl (2009) explores in depth the difficulties that social stigma create in large-scale programmes for the treatment of AIDS, in the case of Brazil.

Methodologically, the effects of TRIPS as an assemblage also participate in creating competing versions of diseases. AIDS may not be quite the same problem, relative to other diseases, in Djibouti as it is in other spaces where AIDS is more predominant, where other issues may not be as pressing, or where health facilities offer different prospects. The dislocated effects of TRIPS and of the access to medicines campaign not only enable more medicines to be delivered, or the pharmaceuticalization of global markets, but create a multidimensional system in which some diseases and some treatments become relocalized and understood differently in global imaginaries. The effects of TRIPS in terms of access to health are not simply about enabling research or increasing costs, they have become more blurry and complex as an increasing number of actors have come to perform contrasting stories of TRIPS and of its immediate impact. Indeed, for the purpose of this research, what is most interesting is to question, once again, whether TRIPS itself might be embedded in this particular project and to what extent its role in generating new resources for AIDS, and a large international focus on the treatment of AIDS, might need to be read when questioning what it *does* in a specific developing country, or in a particular localized context. Any such analyses also need to account for AIDS as a complex network and transformative actor, understood and lived differently by all those that it affects. As is the case for any disease, and as has been demonstrated in other examples, there is not one story or one reality about AIDS, but multiple and co-existing stories that all merge together (Law and Singleton, 2000a; Mol, 2003). The relationship between AIDS and TRIPS, or pharmaceutical patents in any of their forms, is played out at several levels and is the result of multiple performances rather than unidirectional 'impacts'.

The making of affordable drugs – global opportunities and local productions in Ghana

In Ghana, the transformations experienced by AIDS, and their surrounding controversies, following from global investment in AIDS, were of a different nature. Although challenges to the discrepancies between globally produced expectations and local entanglements arose, they did not question as such the validity of the investments made towards AIDS. Instead, in a context where local strategies pre-existed global projects, and where local production has materialized, the focus turned more specifically to the regulatory constraints placed on the making of ARVs. I start by introducing briefly the background of access to ARVs in Ghana before focusing on this issue.

The distribution of ARVs in Ghana is organized separately from the main pharmaceutical market – again, shaping the disease as not being 'typical' of the links between IP and access to health, but having an unusual system of procurement and distribution. Drugs are centrally obtained through the global programmes and only drugs approved by the WHO can be provided. Quality ARVs are therefore selected, and the carefully controlled distribution system ensures that resistance is not unnecessarily built:

> For ARVs for instance, they are centrally procured. So that we can take advantage of all the quality things that needed to be done and yet achieving value for money. So we go through approval processes; we go through evaluation processes before the products come in. (representative of the National Drugs Programme)

> When I was in the district, my facility had a clinic, an HIV/AIDS clinic that we ran. Whenever we had patients who were seen in a private facility they would be referred to this clinic. The patients would come in and they would have the initial work-up done, the baseline labs and all that, before they started treatment. As soon as they started treatment the response is [sic] also monitored. If there is any indication there is resistance, the drugs are changed. (medical doctor)

Before the implementation of this programme, the issue of cost-control for the government was very different in nature, and the links between patents and the cost of medicines was much more acute. The government had tackled these very directly by using compulsory licences to enable the local production of ARVs:

> Remember that patents are private rights...and the fact that they are private rights does not mean that we cannot take advantage of what has been provided internationally for countries, and that is exactly what we have done in the past. So, we try to work together with the other ministries, departments and agencies that have something to do with TRIPS so that they can help us. By that agreement, we issued a compulsory licence in 2005 for four antiretroviral drugs. (representative of the National Drugs Programme)

Patents, cost and balancing needs and possibilities

As was the case in Djibouti, AIDS in Ghana is built largely in relation to the other health concerns faced by the country, in an environment where resources are limited. The control of resources for AIDS is essential in the overall organization of the health system, and the relationship between the price of these medications and the treatment of other diseases is very tight:

> You know that HIV is a developmental disease and the mere fact [is] that we need the numbers and if we have to buy ARVs for people living with HIV, the cost alone would drain all the

> budgetary allocations for other diseases. And so how do we balance that with the fact that we need other medicines for other diseases apart from the ones for ARVs? So, we have to find a way for getting value for money; and that way of getting value for money caused us to search and find out which medicines can we buy, which ones are on the market in which the generic versions are available that we can buy without infringing on the patent rights of the owners? (representative of the National Drugs Programme)

AIDS is therefore tightly linked to other diseases, and the processes of diagnosis and shifting positionality of patients that I evoked in relation to TB are similarly visible in relation to AIDS. For example, when discussing the cost of medicines for conditions such as diarrheic or respiratory infections, a doctor explained:

> If there is some underlying HIV or some other immunal suppression or TB... then they get back into those programmes. Then it is free... (medical doctor)

The diagnosis of AIDS, which, because of limited facilities, is not systematically carried out for patients who are on the margins of the health system, will significantly affect the possibility of access for the poor. Ultimately, access, when provided, will radically change the health and life of patients, and it is useful to remind ourselves here that at the centre of this system is also the alleviation of the suffering of many patients, an aspect of the story that is always worth remembering when discussing other aspects of the conceptual politics of AIDS:

> Because we have the drugs coming in, the antivirals coming in, it's really really helped with the management. It reduces not only infectivity, because if a patient is on treatment the chances of them spreading the illness is reduced. Not only that then, also the quality of life is affected. You have people who just come in and they are really sick, very sick, can't do anything. Probably they have had their condition complicated by diarrhoea and vomiting and come in really weak and unwell. As soon as you are able to start them on the antiviral drug, it's such a dramatic improvement in your life. It's a big problem. It's a massive problem. But the anti-HIV virals coming in right now are really helpful. Just improving people's quality of life, and then obviously a reduction in infectivity as well. (medical doctor)

Headlines on AIDS are a regular mix of positive statements, regarding the growing number of patients who are successfully enrolled in networks of care and medicines that transform the experience of AIDS (a great achievement of the access to medicines campaign) and of sceptical views about the possibility of genuinely addressing the epidemic. The day-to-day reality of the deployment of ARVs is similarly ambivalent and often reminds us of the limits that persist in shaping what can be achieved in contexts where resources remain limited. The psychological and social structures that enable the longevity of these treatments and the stabilization of the slow process of treatment that will shape a patient's life from the moment it is initiated are still not present in Ghana any more than they are in Djibouti:[7]

> It's not just about giving them the meds. The psychological and psychiatric angle to the management is not something that has also caught on here... and it's for the rest of their lives, it's a lifetime commitment. It's like marriage counselling, you are going to commit to the medication, the treatment, the follow-up and all that. (medical doctor)

In another example, a participant recalled the transformations that technologies of treatment and prevention undergo when they are released into new networks, expressing a broader scepticism about the conflicts between global programmes and practical encounterings that echoes questions raised earlier in this chapter:

> I can give you one good example of these female condoms. People buy it and, where you sit at the back, you will think maybe, 'Oh, female condoms are being used and unwanted pregnancies are being cut. They use the bangle.' But for me even I don't know how, because you [could actually *not*] use it [a female condom] and then [still] wear the bangle. Are you getting me? If that bangle could serve... showing how many female condoms are used, then that would be fine. If I [saw] them wearing them I [would] know they are being very protective. [But in reality] If I see [you wearing the bangle then I know] you've wasted 10 of those condoms. That is what it means. So the acceptability and everything need to be worked out properly. (member of the Pharmacy Council)

Overall, the programmes deployed at the global level to address AIDS in Ghana make it both unique medically, in terms of potential resistance and of the specificities of its management, and socially, in terms of how it is addressed and of the specific networks of treatment that surround it. At the same time, AIDS remains in the day-to-day experience of doctors and patients as a disease

---

7 For an analysis of the system of ARV distribution in Uganda, by comparison, see Reynolds Whyte et al. (2006).

that is only part of a broader network of suffering in which choices need to be repeatedly made, and where full workable solutions are still not available. As was the case in Djibouti, any financial commitment to ARVs, by the global community or by the Ghanaian government, is done at the expense of not investing in another of the many diseases that still need further funding. The dependency on global funding is also problematic in the many ways that I highlighted earlier in this chapter – be they practical or political.

However, the Ghanaian example is also enlightening for what it demonstrates about a further aspect of the tight entanglement of global policies and local opportunities, and about the relationship between patents and health. Here, I turn to the issue of enrolment of locally produced ARVs into the networks of treatment and question the role of the WHO pre-qualification system in shaping relationships of power around pharmaceutical capacity for production.

Growing local capacity

Since the distribution of ARVs is organized through the Global Fund, any medicines that will be enlisted in the system need to have been processed through the WHO pre-qualification process. This mechanism has been put in place in order to offer some guaranteed standards of the quality of medicines, which are crucial in relation to ARVs where the concern for resistance is always present. However, the pre-qualification system has also created a new layer of socio-technical and regulatory pressures and expectations for medicines, that de facto excludes some producers in parts of the world – in particular sub-Saharan Africa. The process is a difficult one, not only in relation to the quality of the drugs that are scrutinized, but also in relation to the broader network within which each drug is enrolled. Any company wanting to apply for pre-qualification therefore needs to have a basis of expertise that also enables it to be enrolled in the difficult networks of standardization and administrative regulation that have been set up at the global level. The result is that, in Ghana, at the moment, although a compulsory licence was issued in 2006, and although one of the local manufacturers is therefore allowed to produce ARVs, those drugs cannot reach Ghanaian patients, as they are prevented from entering the distribution networks set up by the Global Fund. When discussing issues of IP and the weight of patents in relation to access to medicines, the question of pre-qualification was therefore brought up several times:

> Most pharmaceutical patent applications that we get, about 95 per cent, are foreign. Damanan took over a patent but luckily they were the agent for the company. But sometimes I feel sad [that] the Ghanaian government doesn't have fund[s] to buy it. The Global Fund was very strict in its rules. We would need to have a new lab, pass the WHO pre-qualification system...we don't have WHO

> recognition, so we can't sell to our own government! So Danaman is selling to Congo and Ivory Coast, but not here because we use the Global Fund, and for this you need WHO pre-qualification! So how do we compete?... We have very good laws but if the government can't use its own companies because of the pre-qualification agreement, we have an issue. (IP policy-maker)

The issue here is one of industrial development as well as one of public health, and the two dimensions of debates on pharmaceutical patents meet most explicitly here. Although access to ARVs is facilitated by the Global Fund, the possibilities for them to become disentangled from broader issues of dependency are limited. Whilst the approach to HIV/AIDS treatment provided in Ghana addresses one of the issues raised by IP in relation to access to health – namely the immediate provision of affordable medicines to patients – it perpetuates the difficulties of the local industry to grow and emerge as a potential long-term supplier of medicines for the local market:

> They keep saying... I have forgotten this word. Improve the quality through qualification. There should be a balancing act. How do you strengthen the... systems here to get a good quality medicine. Rather than to tell me that you can get me good quality medicine from India, or from China, or from the US, and when you can't afford or when everything goes wrong, the medicines don't come. But then you have crippled the systems within. Of course, if I set up [a] factory and I'm producing some drug and the price with the overheads is just about two dollars. Do you come from our side with the same company and you say 'Well, this is from a pre-qualified factory and it has the best of qualities and it is one price asked, two pounds or two dollars.' Against that, I would have to fold up. (member of the Pharmacy Council)

This is particularly problematic in a context where the stability, longevity and adequacy of international programmes for the treatment of AIDS are subject to significant critiques (Biehl, 2007). While Ghana has successfully and without much political pressure, used compulsory licences and the flexibility thereby offered by TRIPS, the more general unfolding of the AIDS networks has made this effort redundant. The exclusionary nature of the pre-qualification programme is not exclusive to Ghana and, indeed, a review of the ARVs that have received pre-qualification from the WHO shows that only three African manufacturers (in Zimbabwe, Kenya and South Africa) have received pre-qualification.[8] No pre-qualified drug for the treatment of malaria or TB is produced in Africa. Whilst those new regulatory measures

---

8 Lists of pre-qualified medicines are available at http://apps.who.int/prequal/.

are important to guarantee quality, they also raise a new set of issues for capacity-building and for an industry that now needs to be able not only to produce medicines in cases of emergency and health crises, but also to respond to complex regulatory guidelines and requirements. Again, some of the issues that animate the debates surrounding TRIPS become displaced into a new locus.

Conclusion

Over the past 15 years, the landscape for the global governance of healthcare has been significantly modified. In particular, the access to medicines campaign has radically reshaped responses from global institutions to health crises in Africa, and the positioning of the Big Pharma has shifted to become increasingly complex (Pollock, 2011). In these movements, the role of TRIPS has been a determinant, as has the shape of these programmes and the access to medicines campaign as a whole. Consequently, the impact of TRIPS on access to medicines in Africa cannot be fully conceptualized without some engagement with the broader movements that have animated healthcare. In both Djibouti and Ghana, these movements have brought some significant improvements, but remain entangled in recurrent limitations. The main transformations generated by responses to the inequalities embedded in TRIPS have played at two levels: first, in a renewed emphasis on the importance of affordable drugs; and, second, in a shift of attention to particular diseases. Amongst these, AIDS has been most radically transformed in its deployment and management since the emergence of TRIPS. In the various movements and transformations that have occurred over the past 15 years, however, certain patterns of inequality and exclusion seem to persist. Those were at the core of TRIPS, and TRIPS, by inscribing them into law, has stabilized some of the patterns of dominance that allowed it to emerge. At the same time, the material ability of some to act at a distance and over others, which enabled the making of TRIPS, is also visible in each of the complex networks that TRIPS has come to transform. Methodologically, the questioning of TRIPS is complicated by its entanglement within both broader, apparently globalized movements, that are in fact constituted of a mixture of ambivalent local effects. I now turn to bringing together the various insights of this research to explore further the conceptual issues that it has raised.

Conclusion: Pharmaceuticals and Socio-Legal Ambivalence

In conclusion, I return to the various processes that this study has highlighted of the relationship between socio-legal tools and health for the poor. Throughout this study, I have sought to demonstrate the complex ways in which intellectual property (IP) links to access to medicines in Djibouti and Ghana. This complexity can broadly be identified in three sets of directions, each providing a particular form of empirical critique of more linear narratives commonly attached to IP and health, and that others have at times provided in different contexts. At the same time, this study has raised questions about the process of studying law in its social deployment and the very nature of legal tools.

From texts to social orderings

At a first level, the case studies of Djibouti and Ghana demonstrated that the complex links between IP and access to health are shaped by potential discrepancies between law in the books and law in its daily practices and deployment. The many steps needed to transform law as text into social ordering are contingent on the pre-existence of materials, expertise and other objects that condition the ability of the law to act at a distance on new actors. In contexts where resources are limited, and where the immediate relevance of IP may be contested, this can radically impact on the ability of IP rules to have any effect on social ordering and, in fact, transform radically what IP may look like, and its very nature, in these new contexts. The transformation of IP took on a different shape in Djibouti and Ghana, but the various challenges that the deployment of law into social ordering may meet were salient in both contexts. In Djibouti, the difficult and contested translation of transnational rules into local regulation has been the most central event in this domain in the past ten years. In Ghana, where patent laws have existed for many years, these challenges appeared both at the level of the translation of new transnational obligations into existing laws and in the deployment of patents as working tools in daily practices.

The vantage points offered by Djibouti and Ghana provide new opportunities to carefully reassess the meaning of the Trade Related Aspects of Intellectual Property Rights (TRIPS) agreement and of IP in less explored examples of developing countries. Although studies of TRIPS have often focused on states that have hosted the most substantial generic industries, it would be simplistic to assume that the impact of IP on other localities can be deduced from looking at those who have traditionally provided them with medicines. In fact, the examples provided here not only participate in producing a more complete picture of the sites of entanglement between IP and health, but also of the practical workings of a highly technical legal field in environments in which these legal tools fail to mobilize actors. The discrepancy between the letter of the law and its practice, suggests, at one level, that TRIPS may simply not have the significance that has been lent to it in other commentaries regarding the impact it would have on 'developing countries' and, indeed, on the radical changes that it may have triggered in other contexts. Nonetheless, the political cynicism that many commentators have shared remains justified in contexts like Djibouti and Ghana, where TRIPS may not have had the dramatic effects anticipated, but where it remains an unnecessary drain on already limited resources, in contexts where it is unlikely to bring any benefits to those whose lives need improving.

Law, regulations and the day-to-day

The importance of providing a more careful reassessment of the relationship between TRIPS and IP is reinforced by observing closely the links between regulation and routines that affect the pharmaceutical market. The complexity of the links between regulations and pharmaceutical markets has been increasingly highlighted in recent scholarship, but, interestingly, primarily outside the literature that paid close and specific attention to the debates surrounding TRIPS and access to medicines (Hayden, 2007; Pollock, 2008; Greene, 2011a). The markets of Djibouti and Ghana illustrate the subtle and unexpected ways in which socio-legal events complicate the movements that animate pharmaceutical markets and processes of (de)pharmaceuticalization (Cloatre and Pickersgill, forthcoming). In both case studies, the ability of patents to generate effects aside from and beyond their legal term was visible. The market of Djibouti is a particularly clear illustration of the interesting ways in which tools that are officially absent from a particular jurisdiction manage to generate effects, nonetheless. Medicines that had been patented at any point in their lifespan therefore maintained a privileged position in a market where their existence was not officially recognised. This privileged position of innovator brands was also visible in Ghana, in spite of proactive policies by the government to turn 'bioequivalence' into social equivalence of branded and generic products. The role of patents in both cases is subtle, and tightly entangled with the power of brands. Those cannot in fact be fully dissociated and, although brand fidelity is a well-recognised phenomenon, it is also shaped very substantially by the ability of particular brands to have a monopoly for many years. Brands and patents themselves are tightly entangled with a particular industry, located within very few countries, and whose practices have been criticized for many years.

The blurring of legal and non-legal, official and non-official, is particularly acute in this context. The movements of patents, brands and particular drugs within local markets are not necessarily linked in expected or predictable ways with the legislation of given jurisdictions. Similarly, the position and influence of the pharmaceutical industry is dependent on relationships that are not necessarily direct and proactive, but have become over the years entangled in very subtle, repetitive patterns of control. Although some of these are proactively targeted at exercising this control at a distance, the ways in which branded medicines come to be dominant in particular markets or maintain their strength even when challenged by governmental programmes seeking to integrate generics more substantially cannot be fully explained through the deliberate actions of the global industry (Ecks and Basu, 2009). In practice, an array of routines, habits, preferences and wariness – some of which is not merely directly grounded in the direct actions of the industry – shapes the ways in which selected versions of drugs are being chosen. Politically, challenging the influence of innovator brands in these localized contexts can only be done by engaging with the specific instances in which ambivalence towards competitors is experienced. The handling of the crisis generated by counterfeit medicines in much of Africa is an example of such an instance, where the tackling of low-quality counterfeits should be associated with a careful engagement with the current relationship between counterfeits and quality generics. In both Djibouti and Ghana, the influence of the pharmaceutical industry was not only the result of proactive actions, but was also expressed in ways that were perhaps more determinant of the successful and historical enrolment of their products, brands and relationships in sets of daily routines.

TRIPS and the transformations of global/local health governance

The effects of TRIPS on particular localities are also rendered complex by the indirect, unexpected and ambivalent links between TRIPS, access to medicines campaigns and the 'global' governance of health – I return below to the problems raised by the term 'global' here. The mobilization and campaigning that TRIPS has generated has transformed health governance in international politics and local practices, but not only by a linear process of restriction of the number of medicines which poor people are able to access – or processes of depharmaceuticalization. In fact, concerns about lessened access have reinforced discourses on the necessity of medicines for the health of the poor. In turn, this has generated new programmes for access and mobilized communities and practitioners of medicine and health to offer some cheaper medicines to some poor people. However, these processes themselves displaced contestations onto new issues, which are not always taken up or confronted in international discourses that are quick to emphasise the 'success' or 'failure' of particular policies.

Again, these took different shapes in Djibouti and Ghana, but common to the different critiques made by informants to these health programmes was a contestation of the dependency still experienced by local health systems, and therefore by the poor, towards decentred decisions, often taken outside of the Djiboutian or Ghanaian context. In these new programmes, once again, the positionality of different types of producers and different medicines is codependent on sets of regulatory demands that aim to guarantee safety but do little to ensure an equal distribution of how and where 'safe' medicines are produced and 'constructed'. Similarly, the positionality of particular diseases and the specific needs of local health crises are influenced by dominant understandings of the risks that IP poses and the particular medicines for which access needs to be facilitated. The politics of AIDS have therefore become inherently shaped and transformed by their positioning at the very centre of the IP debates, generating contestation of their management in localities, like Djibouti, that are less traditionally influential in shaping these discourses. Again, in this context, the links between the pharmaceutical industry and the poor are ambivalent. At one level, the significant controversies that have surrounded the industry in the light of TRIPS have required it to try to transform its image, and the industry has increasingly engaged with programmes in which the prices of its medicines were lowered and negotiated. However, the subtle ways in which the influence of the innovator industry remains expressed in places such as Djibouti or Ghana are still exercised through the day-to-day experiences of its health actors, but also through the new forms of regulatory entanglement, or disentanglement, of specific drugs and providers with particular programmes.

In this complex set of patterns within which patents and TRIPS are inscribed, and which they participate in producing, the very idea of globality becomes ontologically questionable and empirically unhelpful. Many of the movements described here are the result of effects and happenings that travel in directions that are always very clearly grounded and embedded into localised events. TRIPS, no more than patents, remains global in its deployment, and the image of global IP does little to convey its inscribing within the daily experiences of the poor. Global health programmes, though distributing their effects broadly across the globe, are still largely and commonly experienced in both Djibouti and Ghana as being constructed 'elsewhere', being dislocated rather than truly global for those who receive them. Once practices are taken into account, the global becomes little less than an aggregate of local effects (Law, 2003b).

Legal movements and boundaries

These different movements, as well as being illustrative of some of the challenges of making medicines affordable to all and of the complexity of the movements that influence this access, exemplify the fluid boundaries of legal tools and their effects. Throughout these case studies, the movements of TRIPS and of patents are illustrative of much of the processes and effects that actor-network theory (ANT) has traditionally emphasized as constitutive of social relationships. Legal tools in this context, be they TRIPS or patents, are not fundamentally different in their nature from other types of actors and constitute only a part of a general process of ordering. In both contexts, the action of patents was made more effective through their entanglement in daily routines than through the official channels that are meant to create and maintain them. Legal analysis may indicate that efforts to implement or enforce patents are failing, but this would be missing their extensive entanglement within other processes of ordering. In these, the role of patents becomes co-constitutive of habits that they are not unique in shaping, but that would not have adopted this form had this temporary monopoly not been granted, or had particular inventors not been repeatedly rewarded through patents.

Like other actors, legal tools are also highly contestable and contingent on the deployment of a particular set of heterogeneous connections to be able to bear effects. Their contingency is particularly salient in contexts and situations where they have been imported rather than needed, and where their immediate relevance to those whom they are expected to engage is weak. In environments where material resources are limited, the contingency of the legal – though not a new finding – is illustrated in particularly visible ways. Transnational tools, such as TRIPS, are subjected to a vast set of transformations that make them unpredictable and potentially more 'fragile' than anticipated, as they are revisited with each of the new spaces and movements in which they are enrolled. At the same time, the scripts that legal tools carry, including their political history, may re-emerge, as those legal tools are deployed, and remain part of the stories that unfold and become displaced. The inherent set of influences that are entangled within TRIPS, whilst they are not directly effective in either Djibouti or Ghana, are visible in new controversies that result from the unfolding of IPs in different sites that come back to affect localized contexts differently. The attention to the local, to particular moments and controversies, to a specific set of heterogeneous connections that ANT suggests, provides a useful way of returning to issues that disappear from view when generalizations are drawn, or when repeated patterns become taken for granted, or reduced under the label of a general phenomenon.

The case studies provided here only offer a snapshot of the many ways in which IP links to and affects access to healthcare for the poor. The processes exposed in Djibouti and Ghana are specific to these localities and, although they share similarities, and certainly also share similarities with other contexts, they are only illustrative of a much more varied set of practices and effects. TRIPS is a multiple tool that affects agents in ways that are contingent on previous and parallel events, and patents adopt a radically different meaning in each context where they are questioned. The global pharmaceutical industry and its grasp on local markets throughout the world are established and perpetuated through mechanisms that are not always direct and visible. The improvement of the health of the poorest, in Africa and elsewhere, is a slow process, and the constant erection of new hurdles, the disappearance of opportunities and the recurring set-backs are disheartening for the observer, and even more so for those who experience them on a day-to-day basis. Although the immediate impact of TRIPS in Djibouti and Ghana is more subtle than only restricting the availability of drugs, the story of IP in each country is also one where the burden of disease is aggravated by a political and regulatory context in which private interests often remain strongly embedded in the materiality of treatment.

Bibliography

Abbott, F M (1998) 'First Report to the Committee on International Trade Law of the International Law Association on the Subject of Parallel Importation' (1) *Journal of International Economic Law* 607–36

Abbott, F M (2002) 'The Doha Declaration on the TRIPS Agreement and Public Health: Lighting a Dark Corner at the WTO' 5(2) *Journal of International Economic Law* 469–505

Abbott, F M (2005) 'Managing the Hydra: The Herculean Task of Ensuring Access to Essential Medicines' in K E Maskus and J H Reichman (eds), *International Public Goods and Transfer of Technology under a Globalized Intellectual Property System* (Cambridge: Cambridge University Press), pp. 393–425

Abraham, J (1995) *Science, Politics and the Pharmaceutical Industry: Controversy and Bias in Drug Regulation* (London: UCL Press)

Abraham, J (2010) 'Pharmaceuticalization of Society in Context: Theoretical, Empirical and Health Dimensions' 44(4) *Sociology* 603–22

Adewopo, A (2002) 'Global Intellectual Property System and Sub-Saharan Africa: A Prognostic Reflection' 33 *Toledo Law Review* 749–71

Akrich, M and B Latour (1992) 'A Convenient Vocabulary for the Semiotics of Human and Non-human Actors' in W Bijker and J Law (eds), *Shaping Technology, Building Society: Studies in Sociotechnological Change* (Cambridge MA: MIT Press), pp. 205–24

Amsterdamska, O (1990) 'Surely, You Must be Joking, Monsieur Latour!' 15 *Science, Technology and Human Values* 495–504

Anderson, T (2009) 'Confusion over Counterfeit Drugs in Uganda' 373 (9681) *The Lancet* 2097–8

Anderson, W (2002) 'Introduction: Postcolonial Technoscience' 32(5/6) *Social Studies of Science* 643–58

Anderson, W and V Adams (2008) 'Pramoedya's Chickens: Postcolonial Studies of Technoscience' in E J Hackett, O Amsterdamska, M Lynch and J Wajcman (eds), *The Handbook of Science and Technology Studies* (Cambridge MA: MIT Press) (3rd edn), pp. 181–204

Association of the British Pharmaceutical Industry, *Code of Practice for the Pharmaceutical Industry* (2012 edn) www.abpi.org.uk/our-work/library/guidelines/Pages/code-2012.aspx

Attaran, A (2004) 'How do Patents and Economic Policies Affect Access to Essential Medicines in Developing Countries?' 23(3) *Health Affairs* 155–66

Attaran A, R Bate and M Kendall (2011) 9(2) 'Why and How to Make an International Crime of Medicines Counterfeiting' *Journal of International Criminal Justice* 325–54

Attaran A and L Gillepsie-White (2001) 'Do Patents for Antiretroviral Drugs Constrain Access to AIDS Treatment in Africa?' 286 *JAMA* 1888–91

Bala, K, O Lanza and S R Kaur (1998) 'Retail Drug Prices: The Law of the Jungle' (April) *HAI News* 1–16

Bala, K and K Sagoo (2000) 'Patents and Prices' (April/May) *HAI News* 1–9

Balasubramaniam, K (2002) 'Patents, Prices and Public Policy' in P Drahos and R Mayne (eds), *Global Intellectual Property Rights: Knowledge, Access and Development* (London: Palgrave MacMillan), pp. 90–107

Bale, H E (1997) 'Patent Protection and Pharmaceutical Innovation' 29(1/2) *New York University Journal of International Law and Politics* 95–107

Bale, H E (1998) 'The Conflicts between Parallel Trade and Product Access and Innovation: The Case of Pharmaceuticals' 4(1) *Journal of International Economic Law* 637–53

Barad, K (2007) *Meeting the Universe Halfway: Quantum Physics and the Entanglement of Matter and Meaning* (Durham NC: Duke University Press)

Barnard, D (2002) 'In the High Court of South Africa, Case No 4138/98: The Global Politics of Access to Low-Cost AIDS Drugs in Poor Countries' 12(2) *Kennedy Institute of Ethics Journal* 159–74

Barrett, S (2004) 'Implementation Studies: Time for a Revival? Personal Reflections on 20 Years of Implementation Studies' 82(2) *Public Administration* 249–62

Barry, A (2001) *Political Machines: Governing a Technological Society* (London and New York: Athlone Press)

Barry, A (2002) 'In the Middle of the Network' in J Law and A Mol (eds), *Complexities: Social Studies of Knowledge and Practice* (Durham NC: Duke University Press), pp. 142–65

Barry, A (2005) 'Pharmaceutical Matters: The Invention of Informed Materials' 22(1) *Theory, Culture and Society* 51–69

Barry, A and D Slater (2002) 'Technology, Politics and the Market: An Interview with Michel Callon' 31(2) *Economy and Society* 285–306

Barton, J (2004) 'TRIPS and the Global Pharmaceutical Market' *Health Affairs* 146–54

Bass, N (2002) 'Implications of the TRIPS Agreement for Developing Countries: Pharmaceutical Patent Laws in Brazil and South Africa in the 21st Century' 34 *George Washington University International Law Review* 191–222

Bastos, C (1999) *Global Responses to AIDS: Science in Emergency* (Bloomington IN: Indiana University Press)

Berkman, A, J Garcia, M Muñoz-Laboy, V Paiva and R Parker (2005) 'A Critical Analysis of the Brazilian Response to HIV/AIDS: Lessons Learned for Controlling and Mitigating the Epidemic in Developing Countries' 95(7) *American Journal of Public Health* 1162–72

Biehl, J (2004) 'The Activist State: Global Pharmaceuticals, AIDS, and Citizenship in Brazil' 22(3) *Social Text* 105–32

Biehl, J (2007) 'Pharmaceuticalization: AIDS Treatment and Global Health Politics' 80(4) *Anthropological Quarterly* 1083–26

Biehl, J (2009) *Will to Live: AIDS Therapies and the Politics of Survival* (Princeton NJ: Princeton University Press)

Bierlich, B (2007) *The Problem of Money: African Agency and Western Medicine in Northern Ghana* (New York: Berghahn Books)

Black, J (2001) 'Decentring Regulation: Understanding the Role of Regulation and Self Regulation in a "Post-Regulatory" World' 54(1) *Current Legal Problems* 103–46

Black, J (2002) 'Critical Reflections on Regulation' 27(1) *Australian Journal of Legal Philosophy* 1–35

Bond, P (1999) 'Globalization, Pharmaceutical Pricing and South African Health Policy: Managing Confrontation with US Firms and Politicians' 29(4) *International Journal of Health Services* 765–92

Boyle, J (1996) *Shamans, Software and Spleen: Law and the Construction of the Information Society* (Cambridge MA: Harvard University Press)

Bowker, G (1994) 'What's in a Patent?' in W Bijker and J Law (eds), *Shaping Technology/ Building Society: Studies in Sociotechnical Change* (Cambridge MA: MIT Press)

Braithwaite, J and P Drahos (2002) *Information Feudalism: Who Owns Knowledge Economy* (London: Earthscan)

Bunker, A (2007) 'Counterfeit Pharmaceuticals, Intellectual Property and Human Health' 89 *Journal of the Patent and Trademark Office* 493

Callon, M (1986a) 'Some Elements of a Sociology of Translation: Domestication of the Scallops and the Fishermen of Saint Brieuc Bay' in J Law (ed.), *Power, Action and Belief: A New Sociology of Knowledge?*, Sociological Review Monograph (32) (London: Routledge & Kegan Paul), pp. 196–233

Callon, M (1986b) 'The Sociology of an Actor-Network: The Case of the Electric Vehicle' in M Callon (ed.), *Mapping the Dynamics of Science and Technology* (London: Macmillan), pp. 19–34

Callon, M (1991) 'Techno-economic Networks and Irreversibility' in J Law (eds), *A Sociology of Monsters, Essays on Power, Technology and Domination* (London: Routledge), pp. 132–61

Callon, M (1998) 'An Essay on Framing and Overflowing: Economic Externalities Revisited by Sociology' in M Callon (ed.), *The Laws of the Markets* (Oxford and Keele: Blackwell)

Callon, M (1999) 'Actor-Network Theory: the Market Test' in J Law and J Hassard (eds), *Actor Network and After* (Oxford and Keele: Blackwell and *Sociological Review*), pp. 181–95

Callon, M (2007) 'What Does It Mean to Say that Economics is Performative?' in D MacKenzie, F Muniesa and L Siu (eds), *Do Economists Make Markets? On the Performativity of Economics* (Princeton NJ: Princeton University Press), pp. 311–57

Callon, M and B Latour (1981) 'Unscrewing the Big Leviathan: How Actors Macrostructure Reality and How Sociologists Help Them to Do So' in K D Knorr-Cetina and A V Cicourel (eds), *Advances in Social Theory and Methodology: Toward an Integration of Micro- and Macro-Sociologies* (Boston MA: Routledge), pp. 277–303

Callon M and B Latour (1992) 'Don't Throw the Baby Out with the Bath School! A Reply to Collins and Yearley' in A Pickering (ed.), *Science as Practice and Culture* (Chicago IL: Chicago University Press), pp. 343–68

Callon, M and J Law (1995) 'Agency and the Hybrid Collectif' 94 *South Atlantic Quarterly* 481–507

Callon, M, P Lescoumes and Y Barthe (2009) *Acting in an Uncertain World: An Essay on Technical Democracy* (Cambridge MA: MIT Press)

Campbell, C (2003) *'Letting Them Die': Why HIV/AIDS Prevention Programmes Fail* (Bloomington IN: Indiana University Press)

Carpenter, D and D A Tobbell (2011) 'Bioequivalence: The Regulatory Career of a Pharmaceutical Concept' 85(1) *Bulletin of the History of Medicine* 93–131

Castells, M (1996) *The Rise of the Network Society: The Information Age* (Cambridge MA: Blackwells Publishers)

Castells, M (2000) 'Materials for an Explanatory Theory of the Network Society' 51(1) *British Journal of Sociology* 5–25

Chakrabharty, D (2000) *Provincializing Europe: Postcolonial Thought and Historical Difference* (Princeton NJ: Princeton University Press)

Challu, P M (1995) 'Effects of the Monopolistic Patenting of Medicine in Italy since 1978' 10(2/3) *International Journal of Technology Management* 237–51

Chaudhuri, S (2005) *The WTO and India's Pharmaceuticals Industry* (New Delhi: Oxford University Press)

Cloatre, E (2008) 'TRIPS and Pharmaceutical Patents in Djibouti: An ANT Analysis of Socio-legal Objects' 17(2) *Social and Legal Studies* 263–87

Cloatre, E and R Dingwall (forthcoming) '"Embedded Regulation": The Migration of Objects, Scripts and Governance' *Regulation and Governance*, published in 2012 as Early View (online version of record before inclusion in an issue) http://onlinelibrary.wiley.com/doi/10.1111/j.1748–5991.2012.01152.x/abstract

Cloatre, E and M Pickersgill (forthcoming) 'International Law, Public Health and the Meanings of Pharmaceuticalisation'

Cohen, J C, M Gyansa-Lutterodt, K Torpey, L C Esmail and G Kurokawa (2005) 'TRIPS, the Doha Declaration and Increasing Access to Medicines: Policy Options for Ghana' 1 *Globalization and Health* 17

Collins, H M and S Yearley (1992) 'Epistemological Chicken' in A Pickering (ed.), *Science as Practice and Culture* (Chicago IL: Chicago University Press), pp. 301–26

Comaroff, J and J Comaroff (eds) (1999) *Civil Society and the Political Imagination in Africa* (Chicago IL: University of Chicago Press)

Correa, C M (1998) 'Implementing the TRIPS Agreement in the Patent Field: Options for Developing Countries' 1(1) *Journal of World Intellectual Property* 75–100

Correa, C M (2000) *Intellectual Property Rights, the WTO and Developing countries: The TRIPS agreement and policy options* (London: Zed Books)

Correa, C (2001) 'Public Health and Patent Legislation in Developing Countries' (3) *Tulane Journal of Technology and Intellectual Property* 1–53

Correa, C (2003) 'TRIPS and Access to Drugs: Towards a Solution for Countries without Manufacturing Capacity' 17 *Emory International Law Review* 389–406

Cowan, D and H Carr (2008) 'Actor-Network Theory, Implementation and the Private Landlord' 35(1) *Journal of Law and Society* 149–66

Crampes, C (2000) 'La recherche et la protection des innovations dans le secteur pharmaceutique' (1) *Revue Internationale de Droit Economique,* Numero Special: Brevets pharmaceutiques, Innovation et Sante Publique 125–45

Cunningham, A and B Andrews (eds) (1997) *Western Medicine as Contested Knowledge* (Manchester: Manchester University Press)

Das, A and R Jeffery (2009) 'Pharmaceuticals, Physicians and Public Policy: Unravelling the Relationships' 2(1/2/3) *Journal of Health Studies* 6–12

Davies, K and M Trebilcock (2008) 'The Relationship Between Law and Development: Optimists vs Sceptics' 56(4) *American Journal of Comparative Law* 895–946

de Laet, M (2000) 'Patents, Travel, Space: Ethnographic Encounters with Objects in Transit' 18(2) *Environment and Planning D: Society and Space* 149–68

de Laet, M and A Mol (2000) 'The Zimbabwe Bush Pump: Mechanics of a Fluid Technology' 30 *Social Studies of Science* 225–63

Deere, C (2010) *The Implementation Game: The TRIPS Agreement and the Global Politics of Intellectual Property Reform in Developing Countries* (Oxford: Oxford University Press)

Dimasi, J A, R Hansen and H Grabowski (2003) 'The Price of Innovation: New Estimates of Drug Development Cost' 22 *Journal of Health Economics* 151–85

Dinwoodie, G and R Dreyfuss (2009) 'Designing a Global Intellectual Property System Responsive to Change: The WTO, WIPO and Beyond' 26 *Houston Law Review* 1187

Direction de la Pharmacie et des Laboratoires du Tchad, Ministere de la Sante Publique, Republique du Tchad (2004) 'Enquete sur le Prix des Medicaments au Tchad' (May) www.haiweb.org/medicineprices/surveys/200405TD/survey_report.pdf#search='enquete%20sur%20le%20prix%20des%20medicaments%20au%20tchad

Dolmo, B C (2001) 'Examining Global Access to Essential Pharmaceuticals in the Face of Patent Protection Rights: The South African Example' (7) *Buffalo Human Rights Law Review* 137–60

Drahos, P (2002) 'Negotiating Intellectual Property Rights: Between Coercion and Dialogue' in P Drahos and R Mayne (eds), *Global Intellectual Property Rights: Knowledge, Access and Development* (London: Palgrave), pp. 161–82

Drahos, P and J Braithwaite (2002) *Information Feudalism: Who Owns the Knowledge Economy* (London: Earthscan)

Dray, X, R Dray-Spira, J A Bronstein and D Mattera (2005) 'Séroprévalence des virus de l'immunodéficience humaine et des hépatites B et C parmi les donneurs de sang en République de Djibouti' 65 *Médecine Tropicale* 39–42

Dutfield, G and D Posay (1996) *Beyond Intellectual Property: Towards Traditional Resources Rights for Indigenous People and Local Communities* (Ottawa: International Development Research Centre)
Ecks, S and S Basu (2009) 'The Unlicensed Lives of Antidepressants in India: Generic Drugs, Unqualified Practitioners, and Floating Prescriptions' 56(1) *Transcultural Psychiatry* 86–106
Elam, M (1999) 'Living Dangerously with Bruno Latour in a Hybrid World' 16(4) *Theory, Culture and Society* 1–24
ElBishlawi, K (2012) 'International Politics Become Involved in the Fight Against Counterfeit Medicines' in A Werteimer and P Vang (eds), *Counterfeit Medicines: Policy, Economics and Countermeasures* (London: ILM Publications)
Engelberg, A B (2002) 'Implementing the Doha Declaration: A Potential Strategy for Dealing with Legal and Economic Barriers to Affordable Medicines' www.cptech.org/ip/health/pc/engelberg.html
Epstein, H (2007) *The Invisible Cure: Africa, the West, and the Fight Against AIDS* (New York: Farrar, Strauss, & Giroux)
Epstein, S (1996) *Impure Science: AIDS, Activism and the Politics of Knowledge* (Berkeley CA: University of California Press)
Escobar, A (1994) *Encountering Development: The Making and Unmaking of the Third World* (Princeton NJ: Princeton University Press)
Farmer, P (1992) *AIDS and Accusation: Haiti and the Geography of Blame* (Berkeley CA: University of California Press)
Farmer, P (2003) *Pathologies of Power: Health, Human Rights, and the New War on the Poor* (Berkeley CA: University of California Press)
Fassin, D (1992) *Pouvoir et Maladie en Afrique* (Paris: Presses Universitaires de France)
Fassin, D (2006) *Quand les Corps se Souviennent: Experiences et Politiques du Sida en Afrique du Sud* (Paris: La Decouverte)
Faure, J (1999) 'Le Service de Sante des Armees: les defis de la professionalisation', *Rapport d'Information au Senat fait au nom de la commission des Affaires étrangères, de la défense et des forces armées* www.senat.fr/rap/r98-458/r98-458.html
Fleet, J (2003) 'UN Approach to Access to Essential AIDS Medications, Intellectual Property Law and the WTO TRIPS Agreement' 17 (summer) *Emory International Law Review* 451–66
Ford, N (2003) 'Patents, Access to Medicines and the Role of Non-governmental Organisations' 1(2) *Journal of Generic Medicines* 137–45
Fox, R C and E Goemaere (2006) 'They Call it "Patient Selection" in Khayelitsha: The Experience of Médecins sans Frontières-South Africa in Enrolling Patients to Receive Antiretroviral Treatment for HIV/AIDS' 15 *Cambridge Quarterly of Healthcare Ethics* 302–12
Gervais, D (ed.) (2007) *Intellectual Property, Trade and Development: Strategies to Optimize Economic Development in a TRIPS-Plus Era* (Oxford: Oxford University Press)
Ghana Ministry of Health (2008) 'A Knowledge, Attitude, Beliefs and Practices Study on Low Generic Medicines Prescribing in Ghana' http://apps.who.int/medicinedocs/en/m/abstract/Js16498e/
Ghosh, S (2002) 'Pills, Patents, and Power: State Creation of Grey Markets as a Limit on Patent Rights' 14(2) *Florida Journal of International Law* 217–60
Grabowski, H (2002) 'Patents, Innovation and Access to New Pharmaceuticals' 5(4) *Journal of International Economic Law* 849–60
Grabowski, H G and J M Vernon (1992) 'Brand Loyalty, Entry, and Price Competition after the 1984 Drug Act' 35 *Journal of Law and Economics* 331–50
Greene, J A (2011a) 'Making Medicines Essential: The Emergent Centrality of Pharmaceuticals in Global Health' 6(1) *BioSocieties* 10–33

Greene, J A (2011b) 'What's in a Name? Generics and the Persistence of the Pharmaceutical Brand in American Medicine' 66(4) *Journal of the History of Medicine and Allied Sciences* 468–506

Grubb, P (1999) *Patents for Chemicals, Pharmaceuticals and Biotechnology* (Oxford: Oxford University Press)

Halbert, D J (2002) 'Moralized Discourses: South Africa's Intellectual Property Fight for Access to AIDS Drugs' 1(fall/winter) *Seattle Journal for Social Justice* 257–88

Halbert, D J (2005) *Resisting Intellectual Property* (Abingdon: Routledge)

Hammer, P J (2002) 'Differential Pricing of Essential AIDS Drugs: Markets, Politics and Public Health' 5(4) *Journal of International Economic Law* 883–912

Hammersley, M and P Atkinson (1995) *Ethnography: Principles and Practice* (London: Routledge)

Harding, S (1998) *Is Science Multicultural? Postcolonialisms, Feminisms, and Epistemologies* (Bloomington IN: Indiana University Press)

Harding, S (2008) *Sciences from Below: Feminisms, Postcolonialisms, and Modernities* (Durham NC: Duke University Press)

Harman, G (2009) *Prince of Networks: Bruno Latour and Metaphysics* (Melbourne: Re-press)

Hayden, C (2003) 'From Market to Market: Bioprospecting's Idioms of Inclusion' 30(3) *American Ethnomethodologist* 359–71

Hayden, C (2007) 'A Generic Solution? Pharmaceuticals and the Politics of the Similar in Mexico' 48(4) *Current Anthropology* 475–95

Hayden, C (2011) 'No Patent, No Generic: Pharmaceutical Access and the Politics of the Copy' in M Biagioli, J P Aszi and M Woodmansee (eds), *Making and Unmaking Intellectual Property: Creative Production in Legal and Cultural Perspective* (Chicago IL: University of Chicago Press), pp. 285–304

Heath, C (1997) 'Parallel Imports and International Trade' 28(5) *International Review of Industrial Property and Copyright Law* 623–32

Heimer, C (2007) 'Old Inequalities, New Disease: HIV/AIDS in Sub-Saharan Africa' 33 *Annual Review of Sociology* 551–77

Henderson, E (1997) 'TRIPS and the Third World: The Example of Pharmaceutical Patents in India' 19(11) *European Intellectual Property Review* 651–63

Hermer, J and A Hunt (1996) 'Official Graffiti of the Everyday' 30(3) *Law and Society Review* 455–80

Heywood, M (2002) 'Drug Access, Patents and Global Health: Chaffed and Waxed Sufficient' 23(2) *Third World Quarterly* 217–31

Heywood, M (2009) 'South Africa's Treatment Action Campaign: Combining Law and Social Mobilization to Realize the Right to Health' 1(1) *Journal of Human Rights Practice* 14–36

Hiltgartner, S (2009) 'Intellectual Property and the Politics of Emerging Technologies' 84(1) *Chicago-Kent Law Review* 197–224

Hunt, A (1996) *Governance of the Consuming Passions: A History of Sumptuary Law* (New York: St Martin's Press)

Jeffery, R, S Ecks and P Brhlikova (2007) 'Global Assemblages of Pharmaceuticals: Rethinking TRIPS and GMP' 30(3) *Biblio* 45–52

Johnson, J (2005) 'Stopping Africa's Medical Brain Drain' 331 *BMJ* 2–3

Joni, J (2002) 'Access to Treatment for HIV/AIDS: A Human Right Issue in the Developing World' 17 *Connecticut Journal of International Law* 273–80

Kapczynski, A (2008) 'The Access to Knowledge Mobilization and the New Politics of Intellectual Property' 117 *Yale Law Journal* 804–85

Kapferer, J N (1997) 'Marque et médicaments: le poids de la marque dans la prescription médicale' 165 *Revue Francaise du Marketing* 43–51

Keyala, B K (1999) *Pharmaceutical Industry and Patent System in India: A Case Study, in TRIPS Agreement on Patent Law: Impact on Pharmaceuticals and Health for All* (New Delhi: Centre for the Study of Global Trade Systems and Development)

Kirim, A S (1985) 'Reconsidering Patents and Economic Development: A Case Study of the Turkish Pharmaceutical Industry' 13 *World Development* 219–36

Klug, H (2010) 'Law, Politics and Access to Essential Medicines in Developing Countries' 36(2) *Politics and Society* 207–46

Koshy, S (1995) 'The Effect of TRIPS on Indian Patent Law: A Pharmaceutical Industry Perspective' 4 *Boston University Journal of Science and Technology Law* 1–56

LaCroix, S J and A Kawaura (1996) 'Product Patent Reform and its Impact on Korea's Pharmaceutical Industry' 10(1) (spring) *International Economic Journal* 109–24

Laing, R, B Waning, A Gray, N Ford and E Hoen (2003) '25 Years of the WHO Essential Medicines Lists: Progress and Challenges' 361 *The Lancet* 1723–29

Lakoff, A (2005) *Pharmaceutical Reason: Knowledge and Value in Global Psychiatry* (Cambridge: Cambridge University Press)

Lamptey, P (2003) 'Future Challenges in the Global Fight against HIV/AIDS in Developing Countries' 17 *Emory International Law Review* 645–50

Langwick, S A (2007) 'Devils, Parasites, and Fierce Needles: Healing and the Politics of Translation in Southern Tanzania' 32(1) *Science, Technology, and Human Values* 88–117

Larrieu, J and G Houin (2001) 'Medicament generique et propriete intellectuelle' (1) *Revue Internationale de Droit Economique* Numero Special: Brevets pharmaceutiques, Innovation et Sante Publique 173–85

Latour, B (1987) *Science in Action: How to Follow Scientists and Engineers Through Society* (Milton Keynes: Open University Press)

Latour, B (1988a) *The Pasteurization of France* (Cambridge MA: Harvard University Press)

Latour, B (1988b) *Irréductions*, Pasteurisation of France (Cambridge MA: Harvard University Press)

Latour, B (1993) *We Have Never Been Modern* (Brighton: Harvester Wheatsheaf)

Latour, B (1999a) 'On recalling ANT' in L Law and J Hassard (eds), *Actor-Network Theory and After* (Oxford: Blackwells), pp. 15–25 (republished in 2004 as B Latour (2004) 'On Recalling ANT' (Lancaster: Department of Sociology, Lancaster University) www.lancs.ac.uk/fss/sociology/papers/latour-recalling-ant.pdf

Latour, B (1999b) 'For David Bloor…and Beyond: A Reply to David Bloor's "Anti-Latour"' 30(1) *Studies in the History and Philosophy of Science* 113–29

Latour, B (2002) *La Fabrique du Droit* (Paris: La Decouverte)

Latour, B (2004) *Politics of Nature: How to Bring the Sciences into Democracy* (Cambridge MA: Harvard University Press)

Latour, B (2005) *Reassembling the Social: An Introduction to Actor-network Theory* (Oxford: Oxford University Press)

Latour, B (2009a) 'Will Non-humans Be Saved? An Argument in Ecotheology' 15(3) *Journal of the Royal Anthropological Institute* 459–75

Latour, B (2009b) *On the Modern Cult of Factish Gods* (Durham NC: Duke University Press)

Latour, B (2010) 'Networks, Societies, Spheres: Reflections of an Actor-Network Theorist' 5 *International Journal of Communication* 796–810

Latour, B, J Jensen, T Venturini, S Grauwin and D Boullier (2012) 'The Whole is Always Smaller than its Parts: A Digital Test of Gabriel Tarde's Monads' *British Journal of Sociology*

Latour, B and S Woolgar (1979) *Laboratory Life: The Social Construction of Scientific Facts* (Los Angeles CA: Sage)

Law, J (1986) 'On the Methods of Long Distance Control: Vessels, Navigation and the Portuguese Route to India' in J Law (ed.), *Power, Action and Belief: A New Sociology of Knowledge? Sociological Review Monograph* (London: Routledge), pp. 234–63

Law, J (ed.) (1991) *A Sociology of Monsters? Essays on Power, Technology and Domination*, Sociological Review Monograph (London: Routledge)

Law, J (1992) 'Notes on the Theory of the Actor-Network: Ordering, Strategy and Heterogeneity' (Lancaster: Centre for Science Studies, Lancaster University) www.lancs.ac.uk/fss/sociology/papers/law-notes-on-ant.pdf, also published in (5) *Systems Practice* 379–93

Law, J (1994) *Organizing Modernity* (Oxford: Blackwells)

Law, J (1997a) 'Topology and the Naming of Complexity' (Lancaster: Centre for Science Studies, Lancaster University) www.comp.lancs.ac.uk/sociology/papers/law-topology-and-complexity-pdf

Law, J (1997b) 'Traduction/Trahison: Notes on ANT' (Lancaster: Centre for Science Studies, Lancaster University) www.comp.lancs.ac.uk/sociology/stslaw2.html

Law, J (1999a) 'Materialities, Spatialities, Globalities' (Lancaster: Centre for Science Studies, Lancaster University) www.comp.lancs.ac.uk/sociology/soc029jl.html

Law, J (1999b) 'Objects, Spaces and Others' (Lancaster: Centre for Science Studies, Lancaster University) www.comp.lancs.ac.uk/sociology/papers/law-objects-spaces-others.pdf

Law, J (2000) 'Ladbroke Grove, or How to Think about Failing Systems' (Lancaster: Centre for Science Studies, Lancaster University) www.comp.lancs.ac.uk/sociology/papers/law-ladbroke-grove-failing-systems.pdf

Law, J (2003a) 'Making a Mess with Methods' (Lancaster: Centre for Science Studies, Lancaster University) www.comp.lancs.ac.uk/sociology/papers/law-making-a-mess-with-method.pdf

Law, J (2003b) 'And if the Global were Small and Non-Coherent? Method, Complexity and the Baroque' (Lancaster: Centre for Science Studies, Lancaster University) www.comp.lancs.ac.uk/sociology/papers/law-and-if-the-global-were-small.pdf

Law, J (2004) *After Methods: Mess in Social Science Research* (London: Routledge)

Law, J (2008) 'Actor-Network Theory and Material Semiotics' in B S Turner (ed.), *The New Blackwell Companion to Social Theory* (Oxford: Blackwell) (3rd edn), pp. 141–58

Law, J and J Hassard (1999) *Actor-Network Theory and After* (Oxford: Blackwell)

Law, J and A Mol (1995) 'Notes on Materiality and Sociality' 43(2) *Sociological Review* 274–94

Law, J and A Mol (eds) (2002) *Complexities: Social Studies of Knowledge Practices* (Durham NC: Duke University Press)

Law, J and V Singleton (2000a) 'This is not an Object' (Lancaster: Centre for Science Studies, Lancaster University) www.lancs.ac.uk/fss/sociology/papers/law-singleton-this-is-not-an-object.pdf

Law, J and V Singleton (2000b) 'Performing Technology's Stories' (Lancaster: Centre for Science Studies, Lancaster University) www.comp.lancs.ac.uk/sociology/soc036jl.html

Law, J and J Urry (2002) 'Enacting the Social' (Lancaster: Centre for Science Studies, Lancaster University) www.lancs.ac.uk/fss/sociology/papers/law-urry-enacting-the-social.pdf

Lazzarini, Z (2003) 'Making Access to Pharmaceuticals a Reality: Legal Options under TRIPS and the Case of Brazil' 6 *Yale Human Rights and Development Law Journal* 103–38

Lessig, L (1999) 'The Limits in Open Code: Regulatory Standards and the Future of the Net' 14 *Berkeley Technology Law Journal* 759–69

Levi, R and M Valverde (2008) 'Studying Law by Association: Bruno Latour Goes to the Conseil d'Etat' 33(3) *Law and Social Inquiry* 805–25

Liberman, J (2012) 'Combating Counterfeit Medicines and Illicit Trade in Tobacco Products: Minefields in Global Health Governance' 40(2) *Journal of Law and Medical Ethics* 326–47

Light, D W and R Warburton (2011) 'Demythologizing the High Costs of Pharmaceutical Research' 6(1) *BioSocieties* 34–50

Lippert, R (2009) 'Signs of the Surveillant Assemblage: Privacy Regulation, Urban CCTV, and Governmentality' 18(4) *Social and Legal Studies* 507–22

Lury, C (2004) *Brands: The Logos of the Global Economy* (London and New York: Routledge)

Mallavarapu, S and A Prasad (2006) 'Facts, Fetishes, and the Parliament of Things: Is There any Space for Critique?' 20(2) *Social Epistemology* 185–99

Marsland, R (2007) 'The Modern Traditional Healer: Locating "Hybridity" in Modern Traditional Medicine, Southern Tanzania' 33(4) *Journal of Southern African Studies* 751–65

Maskus, K E (2000) *Intellectual Property Rights in the Global Economy* (Washington DC: Institute for International Economics)

Maskus, K E and J H Reichman (eds) (2005) *International Public Goods and Transfer of Technology* (Cambdrige: Cambridge University Press)

Matip, N (2008) 'La mise en conformité du droit des brevets de l'Organisation africaine de la propriété intellectuelle (OAPI) avec les prescriptions de l'accord ADPIC' 13(1) *Lex Electronica*

Matthews, D (2004a) 'Is History Repeating Itself? The Outcome of Negotiations on Access to Medicines, the HIV/AIDS Pandemic and Intellectual Property Rights in the World Trade Organisation' 1 *Law, Social Justice and Global Development Journal* www2.warwick.ac.uk/fac/soc/law/elj/lgd/2004_1/matthews/

Matthews, D (2004b) 'The WTO Decision on Implementation of Paragraph 6 of the Doha Declaration on the TRIPs Agreement and Public Health: a Solution to the Access to Essential Medicines Problem?' 7(1) *Journal of International Economic Law* 73–107

May, C (2004) 'Capacity-Building and the (Re)production of Intellectual Property Rights' 25(5) *Third World Quarterly* 821–37

May, C (2007) *World Intellectual Property Organization (WIPO): Resurgence and the Development Agenda* (Oxford: Routledge)

McGoey, L, J Reiss and A Wahlberg (2011) 'The Global Health Complex' 6(1) *BioSocieties* 1–9

McManis, C and J Pelletier (2012) 'Two Tales of a Treaty Revisited: the Proposed Anti-Counterfeiting Trade Agreement (ACTA)', Legal Studies Research Paper Series (St Louis LA: Washington University in St Louis, School of Law)

Mercurio, B C (2004) 'TRIPS, Patents and Access to Life-saving drugs in the developing world' 8(2) *Marquette Intellectual Property Law Review* Summer 211–50

Mol, A-M. (2003) *The Body Multiple: Ontology in Medical Practice* (Durham NC: Duke University Press)

Mol, A-M and M de Laet (2000) 'The Zimbabwe Bush-pump: Mechanics of a Fluid Technology' 30(2) *Social Studies of Science* 225–63

Moser, I (2008) 'Making Alzheimer's Disease Matter: Enacting, Interfering and Doing Politics of Nature' 39(1) *Geoforum* 98–110

Médecins sans Frontières (MSF) (2003a) 'Doha Derailed: A Progress Report on TRIPS and Access to Medicines', 27 August 2003 www.accessmed-msf.org/prod/publications.asp?scntid=27820031110385&contenttype=PARA&

Médecins sans Frontières (MSF) (2003b) 'TRIPS, Pharmaceutical Patents and Access to Medicines: Seattle, Doha and Beyond', 24 July 2003 www.accessmed-msf.org/prod/publications.asp?scntid=24720031521553&contenttype=PARA&

Médecins sans Frontières (MSF) (2003c) 'Chairman's Text Brings New Difficulties to WTO Paragraph 6', 27 August 2003 www.msf.org/msfinternational/invoke.cfm?component=article&objectid=77830ACA-8EC5-419A-82AB7D7ED6A2E1ED&method=full_html

Muennich F E (2000) 'Les Brevets Pharmaceutiques et l'Acces aux Medicaments' (1) *Revue Internationale de Droit Economique* Numero Special: Brevets Pharmaceutiques, Innovation et Sante Publique 71–81

Mullin, T (2002) 'AIDS, Anthrax and Compulsory Licences: Has the United States Learnt Anything? A Comment on Recent Decisions on the Intellectual Property Rights of Pharmaceutical Patents' 9 *ILSA Journal of International and Comparative Law* 185

Murdoch, J (1997) 'Inhuman/nonhuman/human: Actor Network Theory and the Prospects for a Non-Dualistic and Symmetrical Perspective on Nature and Society' 15 *Environmental Planning D: Society and Space* 731–56

Murdoch, J (1997) 'Towards a New Geography of Heterogeneous Associations' 21(3) *Progress in Human Geography* 321–37

Murdoch, J (1998) 'The Spaces of Actor-Network Theories' 29(4) *Geoforum* 357–74

Muriu, D (2009) 'Third World Resistance to International Economic and Structural Constraints: Assessing the Utility of the Right to Health in the Context of the TRIPS Agreement' 11 *International Community Law Review* 409–29

Nattrass, N and N Geffen (2005) 'The Impact of Reduced Drug Prices on the Cost-Effectiveness of HAART in South Africa' 4(1) *African Journal of AIDS Research* 65–7

Nelken, D (1981) 'The Gap Problem in the Sociology of Law: A Theoretical Review' 1 *Windsor Yearbook of Access to Justice* 35

Nelken, D (1987) 'Law in Action or Living Law? Back to the Beginning in Sociology of Law' 4 *Legal Studies* 157–74

Nerozzi, M (2002) 'The Battle over Life-Saving Drugs: Are Developing Countries being TRIPed by Developed Countries?' 47 *Villanova Law Review* 605–41

Nguyen, V-K (2005) 'Antiretroviral Globalism, Biopolitics, and Therapeutic Citizenship' in A Ong and S J Collier (eds), *Global Assemblages: Technology, Politics, and Ethics as Anthropological Problems* (Malden MA: Blackwell), p. 126

Noehrenberg, E (2006) 'The Realities of TRIPS, Patents and Access to Medicines in Developing Countries' in M Perez Pugatch (ed.), *The Intellectual Property Debate: Perspectives for Law, Economics and Political Economy* (Cheltenham: Edward Elgar)

Nogueira, J (2002) 'Intellectual Property Rights, the World Trade Organisation and Public Health: The Brazilian perspective' 17 *Connecticut Journal of International Law* 311–18

Nogues, J (1990) 'Patents and Pharmaceutical Drugs: Understanding the Pressures on Developing Countries' 31 *Developing Economies* 24–53

Nogues, J (1993) 'Social Costs and Benefits of Introducing Patent Protection for Pharmaceutical Drugs in Developing Countries' 31(1) *Developing Economies* 24–53

Obi-Eyisi, O and A Wertheimer (2012) 'The Background and History of Counterfeit Medicines' in A Werteimer and P Vang (eds), *Counterfeit Medicines: Policy, Economics and Countermeasure* (London: ILM Publications)

Ong, A and S Collier (eds) (2004) *Global Assemblages: Technology, Politics, and Ethics as Anthropological Problems* (London: Blackwell)

Otten, A (2000) 'Les Brevets Couvrant les Produits pharmaceutiques et l'Accord sur les ADPIC' (1) *Revue Internationale de Droit Economique* Numero Special: Brevets Pharmaceutiques, Innovation et Sante Publique 161–6

Outterson, K and R Smith (2006) 'The Good, the Bad and the Ugly' 16 *Albany Law Journal of Science and Technology* 525

Oxfam International (2001) 'Priced out of Reach: How WTO Patent Policies Will Reduce Access to Medicines in the Developing World' www.oxfam.org.uk/what_we_do/issues/health/downloads/priced.rtf

Oxfam (2011) 'Crisis of Poor Quality Medicines Being Used as an Excuse to Push up Prices for Poor' www.oxfam.org/en/pressroom/pressrelease/2011-02-02/crisis-poor-quality-medicines-being-used-excuse-push-prices-poor

Park, J S (1993) 'Pharmaceutical Patents in the Global Arena: Thailand's Struggle between Progress and Protectionism' 13(1) *Boston College Third World Law Journal* 121–54

Petryna, A, A Lakoff and A Kleinma (eds) (2006) *Global Pharmaceuticals: Ethics, Markets, Practices* (Durham NC and London: Duke University Press)

Pires de Carvalho, N (2002) *The TRIPS Regime of Patents Rights* (London: Kluwer Law International)

Pires de Carvalho, N (2010) *The TRIPS Regime of Patents Rights* (The Hague: Kluwer) (3rd edn)

Pogge, T (2008) 'Access to Medicines' 1(2) *Public Health Ethics* 73–82

Pollock, A (2008) 'Pharmaceutical Meaning-Making Beyond Marketing: Racialized Subjects of Generic Thiazide' 36(3) *Journal of Law, Medicine and Ethics* 530–6

Pollock, A (2011) 'Transforming the Critique of Big Pharma' 6(1) *BioSocieties* 106–18

Pottage, A (2012) 'The Materiality of What?' 39(1) *Journal of Law and Society* 167–83

Pottage, A and B Sherman (2010), *Figures of Invention: A History of Modern Patent Law* (Oxford: Oxford University Press)

Pound, R (1910) 'Law in Books and Law in Action' 44 *American Law Review* 12–18

Press, I (1969), 'Urban Illness: Physicians, Curers and Dual Use in Bogota' 10(3) *Journal of Health and Social Behavior* 209–18

Pretorius, W (2002) 'TRIPS and Developing Countries: How Level is the Playing Field?' in P Drahos and R Mayne (eds), *Global Intellectual Property Rights: Knowledge, Access and Development* (London: Palgrave)

Ray, A and E Selinger (2008) 'Jagannath's Saligram: On Bruno Latour and Literary Critique After Postcoloniality' 18(2) *Postmodern Culture*

Redwood, H (1994) *New Horizons in India: The Consequences of Pharmaceutical Patent Protection* (Felixstowe: Oldwicks Press)

Rens, A (2011) 'Collateral Damage: The Impact of ACTA and the Enforcement Agenda on the World's Poorest People' 26(3) *American University International Law Review* 783–809

Reynolds Whyte, A, M A Whyte, L Meinert and B Kyaddondo (2006) 'Treating AIDS: Dilemmas of Unequal Access in Uganda' in A Petryna, A Lakoff and A Kleinman (eds), *Global Pharmaceuticals: Ethics, Markets, Practices* (Durham NC: Duke University Press), pp. 240–62

Riles, A (2000) *The Network Inside Out* (Ann Arbor MI: University of Michigan Press)

Riles, A (2010) 'Collateral Expertise: Legal Knowledge in the Global Financial Markets' 51(6) *Current Anthropology* 795–818

Riles, A (2011) *Collateral Knowledge: Legal Reasoning in the Global Financial Markets* (Chicago IL: University of Chicago Press,)

Rogers, E (1995) *The Diffusion of Innovations* (New York: Free Press)

Romanucci Schwarts, L (1969) 'The Hierarchy of Resort in Curative Practices: The Admiralty Islands, Melanesia' 10(3) *Journal of Health and Social Behavior* 201–9

Rozek, R and R Berkowitz (1998) 'The Effects of Patent Protection on the Prices of Pharmaceutical Products: Is Intellectual Property Raising the Drug Bill in Developing Countries' 1 *Journal of World Intellectual Property* 179–244

Schegloff, E A (1997) 'Whose Text? Whose Context?' 8(2) *Discourse and Society* 165–88

Scherer, F M (2000) 'Le Systeme des Brevets et l'Innovation dans le Domaine Pharmaceutique' (1) *Revue Internationale de Droit Economique* Numero Special: Brevets Pharmaceutiques, Innovation et Sante Publique 109–24

Scherer, F M and J Watal (2002) 'Post-TRIPS Options for Access to Patented Medicines in Developing Nations' 5(4) *Journal of International Economic Law* 313–19

Scherer, F M and S Weisburst (1995) 'Economic Effects of Strengthening Pharmaceutical Patent Protection in Italy' 26 *International Review of Industrial Property and Copyright Law* 1009–24

Scott, C (2004) 'Regulation in the Age of Governance: The Rise of the Post Regulatory State' in J Jordana and D Levi-Faur (eds), *The Politics of Regulation: Institutions and Regulatory Reforms for the Age of Governance* CRC series on Competition, Regulation and Development (Cheltenham: Edward Elgar), pp. 145–74

Seeratan, N N (2001) 'The Negative Impact of Intellectual Patent Rights on Developing Countries: An Examination of the Indian Pharmaceutical Industry' 3 (spring) *St Mary's Law Review on Minority Issues* 339–412

Sell, S (2002a) 'TRIPS and the Access to Medicines Campaign' 20(2 Summer) *Wisconsin International Law Journal* 481–522

Sell, S (2002b) 'Industry Strategies for Intellectual Property and Trade: The Quest for TRIPS and Post-TRIPS Strategies' 10(1) *Cardozo Journal of International and Comparative Law* 79–108

Sell, S (2003) *Private Power, Public Law* (Cambridge: Cambridge University Press)

Sell, S (2004) 'The Quest for Global Governance in Intellectual Property and Public Health: Structural, Discursive and Institutional Dimensions' 77 (summer) *Temple Law Review* 363–99

Sell, S (2007) 'TRIPS-Plus Free Trade Agreements and Access to Medicines' 28 *Liverpool Law Review* 41–75

Shadlen, K (2007) 'The Political Economy of AIDS Treatment: Intellectual Property and the Transformation of Generic Supply' 51 *International Studies Quarterly* 559–81

Shadlen, K, S Guennif, G Guzman and N Lalitha (eds) (2011) *Intellectual Property, Pharmaceuticals and Public Health: Access to Drugs in Developing Countries* (Cheltenham: Edward Elgar)

Sheperd, C and M Gibbs (2006) '"Stretching the Friendship": On the Politics of Replicating a Dairy on East Timor' 36(3) *Science, Technology, and Human Values* 668–701

Sherman, P B and E F Oakley (2004) 'Pandemics and Panacea: The World Trade Organization's efforts to Balance Pharmaceutical Patents and Access to Drugs' 41(2/3) *American Business Law Journal* 353–411

Shiffman, J (2008) 'Has Donor Prioritization of HIV/AIDS Displaced Aid for Other Health Issues?' 23(2) *Health Policy and Planning* 95–100

Shoell, S (2002) 'Why Can't the Poor Access Lifesaving Medicines? An Exploration of Solving the Patent Issue' 4 *Minnesota Intellectual Property Review* 151–82

Silbey, S and P Ewick (2003) 'The Architecture of Authority: The Place of Law in the Space of Science' in A Sarat, L Douglas and M Umphrey (eds), *The Place of Law* (Ann Arbor MI: University of Michigan Press)

Star, S L (1991) 'Power, Technologies and the Phenomenology of Conventions: On Being Allergic to Onions' in J Law (ed.), *A Sociology of Monsters* (London: Routledge), pp. 26–56

Strathern, M (1996) 'Cutting the Network' 2(3) *Journal of the Royal Anthropological Institute* 517–35

Strathern, M (1999) 'What is Intellectual Property After?' in J Law and J Hassard (eds), *Actor Network Theory and After* (Oxford: Blackwells), pp. 156–80

Sun, H (2004) 'The Road to Doha and Beyond: Some Reflections on the TRIPS Agreement and Public Health' 15(1) *European Journal of International Law* 123–50 't Hoen, E (2010) 'The Revised Drug Strategy: Access to Essential Medicines, Intellectual Property and the World Health Organisation' in G Krikorian and A Kapczynski (eds), *Access to Knowledge in the Age of Intellectual Property* (New York: Zone Books)

Third World Network, *Tackling AIDS with Cheap Generic Drugs* (2004) 6 December www.twnside.org.sg/title2/gtrends35.htm

Vaistos, C (1971) 'Patents Revisited: Their Function in Developing Countries' *Science, Technology and Development* 71–97

Vaughan, M (1991) *Curing their Ills: Power and African Illness* (Palo Alto CA: Stanford University Press)

Velasquez, G (2000) 'Medicaments Essentiels et Mondialisation' (1) *Revue Internationale de Droit Economique* Numero Special: Brevets Pharmaceutiques, Innovation et Sante Publique 38–44

Verran, H (2002) 'A Postcolonial Moment in Science Studies: Alternative Firing Regimes of Environmental Scientists and Aboriginal Landowners' 32(5/6) *Social Studies of Science* 729–62

Waberi, A (2002) *Balbala* (Paris: Gallimard)

Waberi, A (2003) *Transit* (Paris: Gallimard)

Watal, J (1999) 'Introducing Product Patents in the Indian Pharmaceutical Sector: Implications for Prices and Welfare' 20 *World Competition* 5–21

Watal, J (2000) *Access to Essential Medicines in Developing Countries: Does the WTO TRIPS Agreement Hinder It?* Science, Technology and Innovation Discussion Paper No 8 (Cambridge MA: Center for International Development, Harvard University)

Watson, M (2011) 'Cosmopolitics of the Subaltern: Problematizing Latour's Ideas of the Commons' 28 *Theory, Culture and Society* 55–79

World Bank (2002) *Djibouti: Health Sector Development* Report No PID10697 (Washington DC: World Bank)

World Bank (2003) *Updated Project Information Document (PID), Djibouti – HIV/AIDS, Malaria and Tuberculosis Control Project* Report No AB7 (Washington DC: World Bank)

World Health Organization (WHO) (2001) 'Globalization, TRIPS and Access to Pharmaceuticals' www.who.int/3by5/amds/en/regulations1.pdf

World Health Organization (WHO)/World Trade Organization (WTO) (2002a) 'Implications of the TRIPS Agreement and the Doha Declaration and Public Health' www.who.int/medicines/areas/policy/WHO_EDM_PAR_2002.3.pdf

World Health Organization (WHO)/World Trade Organization (WTO) (2002b) 'WTO Agreements and Public Health' (Geneva) www.wto.org/english/res_e/booksp_e/who_wto_e.pdf#search='WTO%20agreements%20and%20public%20health

Yar, M (2008) 'The Other Global Drugs Crisis: Assessing the Scope, Impacts and Drivers of the Trade in Dangerous Counterfeit Pharmaceuticals' 1(1) *International Journal of Social Inquiry* 151–66

Zainol, Z A, L Amin, K Jusoff, A Zahid and F Akpoviri (2011) 'Pharmaceutical Patents and Access to Essential Medicines in Sub-Saharan Africa' 10(X) *African Journal of Biotechnology* 12376–88

Index

access to medicines campaign
  AIDS/ARVs 39, 156, 164, 165
  counterfeit medicines 147
  diagnosis of 168, 172
  effects of 10, 154, 156, 157, 166, 170, 172–3, 176
  history of 36–40, 154
  malaria 156
  TRIPS 9, 10, 31, 36, 43, 152, 153, 179, 180
  tuberculosis 156
  see also disease
acting at a distance
  AIDS 161
  in Djibouti 103–5, 112–14
  in Ghana 84, 87, 130, 151
  law 177
  pharmaceutical industry 105, 112–14, 151, 179
  TRIPS 30, 31, 43, 46, 176
actor-network theory (ANT)
  actor-network (concept of) 14, 17
  introduction to 11–17
  capitalism 15, 16, 26
  disease 18–20
  embeddedness (concept of) 17–18
  enlisting (process of) 14, 108, 174
  ethnography 8, 16–17, 21, 27
  globality (concept of) 9, 153, 180–1
  heterogeneity (concept of) 12, 24, 26, 136
  intellectual property 29
  interessement (process of) 14, 22, 59
  irreduction (principle of) 15–16, 20–1, 26, 28
  law 20–2, 43, 67–8, 136, 181
  materiality (concept of) 8, 12–14, 21, 40
    counterfeit medicines 135–6, 138
    generic medicines 134
    patents 95–100
    TRIPS 30
  postcolonial context 22–9
  technologies 26–7, 45
  translations of 17–18
  see also assemblage; Callon, Michel; disease; entanglement; Harding, Sandra; Latour, Bruno; Law, John; Mol, Anne-Marie; Pottage, Alain; Riles, Annelise
advertising 103–7, 123, 144, 149, 150
affordable medicines
  AIDS 156
  generics 108, 110–13, 132–5
  global programmes 154–9
  IDA 108
  in Djibouti
    access to 108, 110–13
    CAMME 110–11, 154, 155
  in Ghana 155, 157, 175
    access to 124–7, 133–135, 151, 175
    Medicines Transparency Alliance (MeTA) 155–6
  Malaria 156
  pharmaceutical patents 2
  tuberculosis 156
  TRIPS 153, 154, 176
  see related access to medicines campaign; compulsory licences; generic medicines
AIDS 1, 152, 157
  complexity of 19, 160–2, 170
  crisis 37
  diagnosis of 172
  history of 161–3
  impact on TRIPS 43
  in Djibouti 92, 94, 165–70
    Cadre National StratégiqueIntersectoriel de Lutte 166
    World Bank ('the AIDS project') 166–9
  in Ghana 117, 170–4
  intellectual property 70, 164–5
  knowledge system 163
  politics of 161–9, 172, 180
  postcolonial object 163–4
  public health priority 166–9
  South Africa 162–3
  taboo 168–9
  technologies of treatment 173
  see also access to medicines campaign; affordable medicines; assemblage; disease; entanglement

Anderson, Warwick 23, 27–9, 139
antiretrovirals (ARVs)
    access to 164–5
    generic medicines 98, 109–10
    in Djibouti 98, 109–10, 166–7
    in Ghana
        access to 116, 171–3
        allocation of resources 171–4
        global fund 53, 167, 174, 175
        local capacity 174–6
        pre-qualification 174–5
        see also compulsory licences
    price of 39, 164
    TRIPS 164–5
    see also AIDS; access to medicines campaign; counterfeit medicines
assemblage
    ANT as 17
    drugs as 32
    legal texts as 21–2
    TRIPS as 10, 29–44, 152, 153, 160, 170
    TRIPS and AIDS 164

Barry, Andrew 15, 72
Big Pharma
    advertising 104, 107
    generic medicines 103, 107
    hegemony of 40
    influence in Djibouti 103, 107
    positioning of 176
    resistance to 165
bioequivalence 148, 179
blackboxing
    concept of 14
    counterfeit medicines 135
    disease 19
    intellectual property
        networks 72
        rules 29
    legal texts 21–2
    TRIPS 31–40, 42–4
Bolar exemption 41, 51
    in Djibouti 51
    in Ghana 54
boundaries
    legal/law 4, 8, 21, 99, 136, 139, 181
    pharmaceutical patents 91, 99, 100
    traditional medicines 123–4
    TRIPS 30, 156
brand fidelity 106, 179

brands
    influence of in Djibouti 9–10, 91, 97, 99–101, 103–4, 106–7, 111, 113, 125, 178–80
    influence of in Ghana 116, 130–1, 133, 149, 178–80
    pharmaceutical patents 43–4

Callon, Michel
    ANT (general) 12, 17
    actor-networks 14
    capitalism 15
    expertise 55
    interessement 22, 84
    law 22
    materiality 13
    obligatory passage points 86, 114
    performativity 42
capacity-building
    in Djibouti 70
    generic medicines 33
    in Ghana 174–6
    WHO 70
    WIPO 58–9, 70
    WTO 70
capitalism *see* actor-network theory
Centre d'Achat des Medicaments et Matériel Essentials (CAMME) 110–11, 154, 155
Chakrabharty, Dipesh 24–5
compulsory licences
    anthrax scare 39
    Doha Declaration 41, 51
    in Djibouti 51, 106
    in Ghana 53–4, 57
        ARVs 53, 171, 174, 175
    least developed countries 106
    TRIPS 36, 42, 43
Consumer Project on Technology (US) 38
counterfeit medicines
    Anti-Counterfeiting Bill 2008 (Kenya) 147
    Anti-Counterfeiting Trade Agreement 139, 147
    ARVs 137
    Counterfeit Goods Bill 2009 (Uganda) 147
    in Djibouti 95, 112, 155
    fluid nature of 131–5, 140, 151
    in Ghana 81, 84, 139–51, 157
        access to 142
        expertise 144, 146

government control 145–6
  malaria 141, 144, 158
  risk 140
impact on generic medicines 10, 179
  in Ghana 139–51
legal-labelling 131, 135–6
multiple meanings 135–9
politics of 135
site of entanglement 135
WHO 137, 147
see also access to medicines campaign; ANT; ARVs; blackboxing; entanglement; expertise

De Laet, Marianne 14, 26–7, 29, 31, 42
Deleuze, Gilles 17, 23
dengue fever 109
(de)pharmaceuticalization 170, 178, 180
developing countries
  AIDS crisis in 37
  pharmaceutical patents and access to health 37, 98
  travel of drugs in 20
  TRIPS
    generalizations 5
    impact in 29, 49, 53, 61, 71, 166, 170, 178
    meaning for 46, 178
    negotiations on 35
  see also Doha Declaration; pharmaceutical patents, flexibilities; TRIPS-plus
developed states 42
diagnosis
  AIDS 168, 172
  significance of 159–60
disease
  access to medicines campaign 38–9
  in ANT 12, 18–20, 44
  framing of 43
  management of 156, 160
  prioritization of 108–9, 157, 169, 174
  reshaping of 154–60, 180
    AIDS 164–76
  social significance of 40
  see also blackboxing
dislocation, of legal effects 153–60, 166, 170, 181
Djibouti
  Chambre du Commerce 73–4, 101
  CAMME 110–11, 154, 155
  Hôpital Bouffard 93–4, 100–2
  Hôpital Peltier 93

international donations 100–3
Ministry of Health 7, 70, 73–8, 130
Ministry of Trade and Industry 7, 50, 73–5, 77
Organisme de Protection Sociale
  free health services 94
  import and distribution 100, 101, 109
  independence 101
  patents 114–15
  preferred by patients 93
  use of generic medicines 97–8, 101, 108
Pharmacies communautaires 110, 112
Pharmappro 100–3
public health in 92–5
Securité Sociale 107
see also imports
Doha Declaration 40, 41, 51 *see related* Bolar exemption; compulsory licences; parallel imports; pharmaceutical patents, extended deadlines
drugs
  in ANT studies 20
  as assemblage 32
  enabling power of 39
  inventing 33
  'modern' 2, 70, 95, 123, 153
  non-patented 108
  as objects of protection 32
  see also affordable medicines, brands, counterfeit medicines, generic medicines, imports, pharmaceutical patents, registration

Economic Community of West African States 59
embeddedness
  of pharmaceutical patents 95, 96, 98, 99, 100, 108, 130, 131
  of political and cultural value in Western medicine 124
  principle of 17–18
  of private interests and the materiality of treatment 182
  of TRIPS 45, 46, 153, 170, 176
enlisting
  of drugs within essential medicines list 108
  of patients (AIDS) 164
  process of 14

Index 199

entanglement
 of AIDS 160–5
 in ANT 21, 25, 136
 counterfeit medicines as site of 135
 essential medicines list (EML), as site of 108
 of intellectual property 3, 35, 165, 178
 of patients, disease and patented drugs 106–8, 109
 of pharmaceutical patents 37–40, 80, 111–12, 157, 179, 181
 process of 17–18, 123, 159
 regulatory 8, 180
 of TRIPS 36, 153, 159, 176
Epstein, Steven 19, 55, 161–2
ethnography
 AIDS 162
 methodology 7–8, 72
 see also actor-network theory
expertise
 in ANT 12, 19, 55, 56
 in Djibouti
  CAMME 111
  intellectual property 48, 50, 57, 59, 60, 64, 68
  patents 49, 51, 52, 62, 74, 96
  TRIPS 68
 fluidity of 55
 in Ghana
  counterfeit medicines 143, 144, 146
  intellectual property 54, 57, 59, 60, 63, 64, 69, 80, 88
  patents 53, 58, 62
  pre-qualification 174
  testing 126
 and intellectual property 36
 local 9, 41, 45, 46
 nature of 56
 TRIPS 30, 42, 65
externalization, process of 24

Fassin, Didier 162–3
fieldwork 7, 72–5
Foucault, Michel 17, 23

generic medicines
 attention to 154, 156
 availability of 9, 111–12, 155
 branded 97, 106, 125, 134
 capacity-building 33
 in Djibouti
  central procurement of 110–13
  exclusion of 92, 97–9, 103–10
  normalization of 155
 in Ghana
  central procurement 125–7, 155
  enrolment of 116, 117, 124–35, 149
  impact of counterfeit medicines 139–51
  use of non-proprietary names 130–1
  see also health insurance
 meaning of 97–8
 parallel imports 95
 and patent systems pre-TRIPS 33–4
 see also actor-network theory; affordable medicines; antiretrovirals; Big Pharma; World Bank
Ghana
 Attorney General's Chambers 7, 53, 57
 chemical sellers 118–19, 142–3, 157
 Food and Drugs Board 7, 12, 67, 79–88, 124
 National Drugs Programme 7, 125–7
 Pharmacy Council, market surveillance 82–3, 86–7
 public health 117–24, 142–4
Global Fund 156
 in Djibouti 166–7
 in Ghana 53, 160, 174–5
global/local
 AIDS 160, 161, 165–70
 networks 99
 and TRIPS 179–80
global pharmaceutical industry 23, 30, 33, 39, 114, 130, 147, 182
global programmes
 dependency on external resources 157–9
 longevity of 157
 stability of 157, 158–9

Harding, Sandra 23, 24, 26
Harman, Graham 12–14
Haraway, Donna 24
Health Action International 38, 155
health insurance, in Ghana 125, 127–30, 159
heterogeneity, concept of 12, 26, 136
hospitals
 access to
  in Djibouti 93
  in Ghana 119, 120, 124
 and medicines
  in Djibouti 100, 102
  in Ghana 125–8

quality
    in Djibouti 93, 94, 110
    in Ghana 119
use of generics in
    in Djibouti 97
    in Ghana 131, 132, 159

IDA Foundation 101, 102, 108, 109
imports
    Djibouti 100–10, 114, 155
        lack of government control 103
        reliability of 105–6
    Ghana 85 *see related* parallel imports
inclusion/exclusion, processes of 24, 25, 39, 82, 116, 126 128, 135
indeterminacy
    concept of 12–14, 21, 22
    and law 67
intellectual property
    and AIDS 39, 70, 164–5
    blackboxing of 29, 72
    breach of 130, 137, 139
    complexity of 43, 45
    counterfeit drugs 139, 147
    in Djibouti
        history of 5, 34, 46–9, 65, 91
        lack of institutional framework 65
    expertise 50, 55–60, 64, 67, 68, 80
    framing of 37, 43
    in Ghana 177, 182
        history of 52–5, 63
    as imperialism 31
    knowledge of 156
    legal prescriptions, as set of 65, 72
    lobbying 34
    meaning of 178
    mobilization 68, 70
    rise of 1, 10
    transformation of 177
    translation of 45, 67–8
    travel of 42–4, 79–80
    see also AIDS; actor-network theory; entanglement; expertise
    see related Intellectual Property Committee; Trade Related Aspects of Intellectual Property Rights; World Intellectual Property Organization
Intellectual Property Committee 35

International Federation of Pharmaceutical Manufacturers and Associations 155
international organizations
    in Djibouti 75–8
    in Ghana 155
    pressure on 153
    see also World Health Organization; World Intellectual Property Organization; World Trade Organization

knowledge
    in ANT 15, 23–8, 55
    regulation of 52
    scientific (nature of) 19, 62, 163
    systems 23, 27, 28, 121–4, 163
    traditional medicine 121–4
    transfer 78
    transformation of 62
    valorization of 62
    see also expertise

laboratories, in ANT 12, 13, 15, 18
Latour, Bruno
    ANT general 12, 16, 18
    acting at a distance 15
    actor-networks 14
    cosmopolitics 24
    ethnography 8
    intermediaries and mediators 76
    irreduction 15
    knowledge 55–6
    legal objects 114
    materiality 13, 21
    modernity 25, 26, 124
    ordering 91
    postcoloniality 23
    relationality 13
    technology 45
    TRIPS 38
law
    in ANT 20–2, 43, 67–8, 136, 181
    in action 67, 89, 99
    perceptions of 67, 96
    see also boundaries; ordering; pharmaceutical patents
Law, John 11, 12, 13, 17
least-developed countries 4, 5, 40, 41, 49, 51, 59, 69, 92, 106
local need 42, 46, 54, 76

local(ized) practices 3, 4, 7, 8, 45, 117, 180
lobbying 34, 47, 154 *see related* access to medicines campaign

malaria
  in Djibouti 92
  in Ghana
    counterfeit medicines 141, 144, 158
    generic medicines 148
    health budget 141
    pharmaceutical patents 109
    Roll Back Malaria initiative 156
    treatment of 117, 118, 119
  pre-qualified medicine 175 *see related* World Health Organization
  see also affordable medicines
marketing 41, 69, 79, 80, 88, 96, 10, 107, 114, 123, 151
Médecins sans Frontières (MSF) 38, 56
mobilization
  influence of pharmaceutical industry on 147
  intellectual property and 56, 67, 70, 71
  pharmaceutical patents and 70, 89,
  TRIPS and 31, 50, 69, 71, 151, 153, 180
modernity, in ANT 23, 25–7
modes of action
  introduction 12
  pharmaceutical patents 91, 99, 114
Mol, Anne-Marie 13, 14, 19, 26
monopoly
  pharmaceutical patents 32, 44, 179, 181
  private pharmacists in Djibouti 104

normalization
  of generic medicines 155
  process of 24

ordering
  in ANT 2, 8, 17, 28, 40, 91
  law/legal tools and 22, 65, 67, 177–8, 181
  official and non-official methods of 3
  pharmaceutical patents and 44, 65, 91, 92, 96, 99, 103–10
  TRIPS and 160
Organisation Africaine de la Proprieté Intellectuelle 48

out-of-patent medicines 70, 98, 103, 108, 109, 116, 118
Oxfam International 98, 147

parallel imports 41, 95, 113 *see also* Doha Declaration
patent office 51, 58
performativity 42
pharmaceutical patents
  in Djibouti
    absence from written law 96, 98, 113–14
    creation of 49–52
    and exclusion of generic medicines 92, 103–10
    history of (pre-TRIPS) 34, 46, 47
    patent office 51–2, 57–8
  flexibilities (for developing countries) 52, 53, 54, 57
  framing of 32–3
  in Ghana
    disconnected networks 87–8
    enrolling 78–9
    post-market surveillance 83, 86–7
    registration 79–83, 85–8
    TRIPS in 53–5
  out-of-patent medication 70, 98, 103, 108, 109, 116, 118, 137
  as regulatory tools and materials 65–9, 89, 91, 92, 95–100
  travel of 30, 42–3, 78–80, 88, 99
  TRIPS and 4–9, 30, 34–9, 53, 55
  see also actor-network theory; affordable medicines; Bolar exemption; compulsory licences; Doha Declaration; embeddedness; entanglement; generic medicines; modes of action; ordering
pharmacists
  in Djibouti 95–7, 100–7, 109, 110, 112, 114
  in Ghana 118–20
postcolonial
  ANT and 22, 24–8
  in STS 23
  see also AIDS
Pottage, Alain 12, 21, 29
power, in ANT 15, 16, 20, 22, 23, 26–8
prescription, in ANT 45 *see also* intellectual property; Trade Related Aspects of Intellectual Property Rights
Pretoria trial 39, 61, 164

punctualization
  of government 71–2, 74, 89
  process of 87

regulation 8, 9, 91, 174, 178–9
relationality, in ANT 13
research and innovation
  link to patents 32–3
  and the South 109
Riles, Annelise 21

Sanofi 104
self-medication 123
semiotics 11, 13, 17, 27
South Africa 3
  AIDS controversies 162, 163, 165
  intellectual property and health debate 3, 4, 71
  see also Pretoria trial
stabilisation, in ANT 14, 24
Strathern, Marilyn 26, 29
symmetry, in ANT 13, 28

technology
  in ANT 45
  fluidity of 26, 27
  transfer 59
  see also actor-network theory
Trade Related Aspects of Intellectual Property Rights (TRIPS)
  and AIDS 165, 166, 170, 176
  and access to medicines campaign 152, 153
  as global public health actor 37, 38, 40, 43
  as set of prescriptions 66, 71, 72, 74, 75, 77
  expertise 30, 36, 42, 46, 68
  history of 31–42
  impacts of 6–7, 160, 176, 178, 182
    in developing countries 49, 53, 55, 61, 71, 166
  implementation of 3, 6, 9, 42, 43, 45, 65, 89, 152
  in Djibouti
    formal compliance 50
    institutional framework 51
    mobilization 70–1, 74
    resources 47, 48
    translating in 49–52
  in Ghana
    institutional framework 69
    national laws 69
    resources and expertise 55
    translating in 55
    opposition to 2–3, 36, 38, 62, 153, 154, 160 *see related* access to medicines campaign
  reordering of health networks 153–60
  see also access to medicines campaign; acting at a distance; actor-network theory; affordable medicines; assemblage; blackboxing; Bolar exemption; boundaries; compulsory licences; dislocation; Doha Declaration; embeddedness; entanglement; intellectual property; pharmaceutical patents; travel
trademarks 60, 62, 63
traditional healing 123
traditional medicine
  in Djibouti 95
  in Ghana 118, 122–4
  as medical knowledge system 121–4
  see also boundaries
transformation, process of 165
translation 9, 14, 29, 45, 46, 50, 63, 177–8 *see also* actor-network theory
Transparency International 155
travel
  of pharmaceutical patents 31, 42, 65, 66–7
  of TRIPS 30, 42–5, 65
TRIPS-plus 53, 55
tuberculosis
  affordable medicines 156
  Global Drug Facility 156–7
  in Djibouti 92, 94, 157
  in Ghana 117, 118, 156–7, 159, 160
  Stop TB Partnership 159–60, 168
  pre-qualified medicine 175 *see also* World Health Organization

UK Department for International Development 155

Watson, Matthew 24
World Bank
  AIDS 166–8
  in Djibouti 92, 110, 111, 154, 166–9
  in Ghana 155
  generic medicines 110, 111, 154, 155
  malaria 92

World Health Organization (WHO)
  antiretrovirals 171, 174
  capacity-building 70
  counterfeit medicines 137, 147
  in Djibouti 7, 70, 75–7
    fieldwork 73
    statistics 94–5, 137
  essential medicines list 38, 108–9
    see also enlisting; entanglement
  in Ghana 155, 171, 174
  generics 155
  intellectual property and health 38
  pre-qualification process 174–6
  and TRIPS 42, 71, 75–7
World Intellectual Property Organization (WIPO)
  capacity-building 58, 70
  in Djibouti 48–50, 70, 75, 77
  expertise 58
  in Ghana 58–9
  national laws 59
  pharmaceutical patents 50
  and TRIPS 42, 75
World Trade Organization (WTO)
  and Djibouti 77
  and TRIPS 1, 9, 50, 71, 75, 77
  capacity-building 70
  circulation of patents 49
  Uruguay Round 35
  see related Trade Related Aspects of Intellectual Property Rights

Printed and bound in Great Britain by
TJ International Ltd, Padstow, Cornwall